THE SOCRATIC METHOD

A Practitioner's Handbook

THE
SOCRATIC
METHOD

A Practitioner's
Handbook

WARD FARNSWORTH

GODINE

BOSTON · MASSACHUSETTS

MM·XXI

PUBLISHED IN 2021 BY

GODINE

BOSTON, MASSACHUSETTS

COPYRIGHT © 2021 BY WARD FARNSWORTH

ALL RIGHTS RESERVED

*Library of Congress Cataloging-in-Publication Data
is found on the last printed page of this book*

FOURTH PRINTING, 2023

PRINTED IN THE UNITED STATES OF
AMERICA

* *
*

Contents

Preface

THE Socratic method is a style of thought. It is a help toward intelligence and an antidote to stupidity. This has to be said right away because many people consider the Socratic method, if they consider it at all, to be a technique for teaching. It is that; but the reason the Socratic method is useful in the classroom is that it's a style of thought better than the one we tend to apply naturally to important things. Socrates didn't question people in order to teach us how to question people. He did it to teach us how to think. That is what makes his method a matter of general interest, not a device for specialists or special occasions. This is a practitioner's handbook, and the first lesson is that everyone is a practitioner, or can be, on any given day.

This book explains what the Socratic method is and how to use it—the original method, that is, as practiced by Socrates in the dialogues of Plato. It is a book about the operation of the mind. It is also a practical introduction to the philosophy of Socrates more generally. Socratic philosophy is still startling after all these years because it doesn't definitively answer hard questions. It is an approach to *asking* hard questions and chasing after them. Socratic thought is a route to wisdom but not wisdom in a box; it denies that wisdom can be fit in a box. It is helpful for thinking about every kind of problem, large or small—how we should live and who should walk the dog.

This book also tells the origin story of Stoicism, an ancient family of ideas that many people still find compelling. The Stoic teachings that have had staying power descend from the teachings of Socrates; anyone interested in what the Stoics said should understand how it relates to what Socrates said. And anyone interested in Socrates can in turn find, in the Stoics, examples of how Socratic thinking can be put to work in ordinary life.

The teachings of Socrates can also improve conversations about all sorts of hard subjects. The Socratic method means, among other things, asking and receiving questions fearlessly; it means saying what you think, and not getting hot when others say what they think; it means loving the truth and staying humble about whether you know it. In other words, it's about all the good things that have been vanishing from our culture of discourse.

* * *

That is a short account of this book's purpose. Here is a more complete one.

➤ 1. About 2,500 years ago, Plato wrote a set of dialogues about ethical and other questions. Most of the dialogues, especially those now said to be the early ones, follow the same pattern. Plato doesn't appear. The dialogues depict Socrates having conversations with others. Usually he asks questions to which his discussion partners think they know the answers. Socrates tests what they say, takes apart their claims, and shows that they don't understand the topic as well as they had imagined. Readers tend to come away with the same impression about themselves. This sounds straightforward, but the way Socrates does it, and the reasons why, amount to a good way of thinking about many things. This we will call the Socratic method.

The Socratic method is often described as one of the foremost productions of the classical mind. Gregory Vlastos, the 20th century's most distinguished scholar of our subject, described the method as "among the greatest achievements of humanity" because it

> makes moral inquiry a common human enterprise, open to every man. Its practice calls for no adherence to a philosophical system, or mastery of a specialized technique, or acquisition of a technical vocabulary. It calls for common sense and common speech.[1]

The value of the method extends to law, politics, and all other matters that call for reasoned judgment. John Stuart Mill regarded the Socratic method as a profound influence on his thinking and a mighty asset, causing him to reflect, in an essay on Plato, "on the debt mankind owe to him for this, incomparably his greatest gift."[2]

---

1. Vlastos, "The Paradox of Socrates," 20.
2. Robson, *Collected Works of John Stuart Mill*, 11:46.

So the method is the most valuable legacy of Socrates, and Socrates is perhaps the most illustrious figure in the history of Western thought. We might therefore expect that everyone would be familiar with the principal features of the Socratic method. But most people aren't, and even most intellectual types don't feel any particular sense of profit from the teachings of Socrates, at least not directly. Why, then, is there such a discrepancy between the value of the Socratic method (by reputation, anyway) and popular knowledge of it?

I believe there are three reasons. First, the method is never clearly explained in Plato's dialogues. It runs in the background of discussions that are about other things. The method has to be inferred from the way Socrates talks and acts and from comments he makes about why; the reader who opens a dialogue looking for direct instruction won't find it.

Second, the discussions in the dialogues, and Socrates himself, can be off-putting. The characters often will argue about a question that is of no pressing interest to the reader. They conclude nothing except that they don't have a good answer, and the arguments along the way sometimes seem to be hair-splitting or formalistic. Pushing through those arguments to enjoy the method and learn from it is a kind of work that, for most readers, can charitably be described as an acquired taste.

Third, the Socratic method is never likely to be popular because it doesn't offer what most people think they want. The teachings of Socrates don't propose to make anyone richer or more famous. They don't offer rewards after death. They don't answer the questions that torment us, and they don't confirm that we're right about what we already think. What the teachings do offer is wisdom, but this good thing is always bought at the price of some discomfort. The human appetite for wisdom, and its tolerance for discomfort, has never been great, in ancient times or ours.

These points help explain why the Socratic method isn't known to most people and isn't taught in school. But it should be. The elements of the method are simple and potent, easy to grasp and challenging to master. It can produce results in the hands of those who know nothing else about philosophy. It's helpful for thinking or arguing about things that matter to everyone now, not just things that mattered to Plato. And the method does offer a route to happiness in the ancient sense of that word: a better life, if not a better mood.

Since the dialogues don't set forth the method in an accessible way, that is what this book means to do. It seeks to make the ideas of Socrates, and especially his method, easier to understand.

↦ 2. There are lots of other books about Socrates and Plato, so I should say why another one seemed worth the trouble. Such books are almost all written by scholars in philosophy departments. Their job is to read Plato closely, to debate the fairest way to interpret what he wrote, and to teach students to do the same. I read what those scholars write and admire it. But the question that most interests me is how the Socratic method can be *used*, not just by teachers but by anyone. I mean to approach it as a farm animal rather than a zoo animal. This difference in approach is modest; I'm interested in what Plato meant and will cite a lot of scholarship on that question, too. But I want to focus on applied aspects of the method. The book is for those coming to philosophy the way Socrates did—as the everyday activity of making sense out of life and how to live it—and who want to know what he said about doing that better.

In practice this means the book will spend less time than others on a complete textual analysis of every issue raised. Plato provides endless grist for debate. It takes a lot of time and space to defend any claim you might make about him against every competitor or criticism. But I want this book to be of moderate length, and it's impossible to keep it that way while also chasing down every issue raised by the evidence. The book therefore will treat a lot of hard questions lightly, just showing where they lie and letting the footnotes explain where to read more if you like. The reader who wants a finer-grained exegesis has hundreds of other books to choose from. Many of them are listed in the bibliography, though it is far from being a complete or up-to-date index of the writings on our subject; it mostly just

covers the sources that are cited in the text. But it is enough to give
the interested reader points of entry into the literature.

→→ 3. A few years ago I wrote a book called *The Practicing Stoic*. It
presents ideas from the ancient philosophy of Stoicism that are still
of modern interest. This book is, in effect, a prequel to that one. It
explains where Stoicism came from. The Stoics regarded themselves
as descendants and followers of Socrates, and his influence on them
was immense; the ethical teachings of Stoicism can, indeed, be viewed
mostly as an elaboration and extension of what Socrates taught. This
book shows why. No knowledge of Stoicism is needed to enjoy what
follows, but those who are interested in that subject should also be
interested in this one. Many readers like Stoicism because, more than
some other philosophies, it has constant practical application to their
daily lives. The teachings of Socrates are like that, too. They produce
a mindset that is useful all the time. It is, as we will see, the mindset of
Epictetus; and from that way of thinking, many more specific Stoic
teachings followed naturally as details.

Much the same might be said of Skepticism, another philosophical
tradition with many modern adherents (whether they are conscious of
it or not). The ancient Skeptics were students of Socrates and rivals
of the Stoics. We will spend time on their views as well.

→→ 4. The book will also offer some ideas about how Socratic teachings relate to our current cultural and political difficulties. Let us
backtrack a moment. The ancient Romans built elaborate networks
of pipes to deliver water where they wanted it to go. The networks
were a marvel. But many of the pipes were made of lead, and the water
carried the lead along with it. One school of thought regards this as
part of the reason for the decline and fall of Rome: lead poisoning
gradually took its toll, impairing the thought and judgment of many
Romans, especially at the top. The theory is much disputed; perhaps
it contains no truth. But as a metaphor it is irresistible. We have built
networks for the delivery of information—the internet, and especially
social media. These networks, too, are a marvel. But they also carry
a kind of poison with them. The mind fed from those sources learns

to subsist happily on quick reactions, easy certainties, one-liners, and rage. It craves confirmation and resents contradiction. Attention spans collapse; imbecility propagates, then seems normal, then is celebrated. The capacity for rational discourse between people who disagree gradually rots. I have a good deal more confidence in the lead-pipe theory of the internet, and its effect on our culture, than in the lead-pipe theory of the fall of Rome.

The Socratic method is a corrective. Before viewing it as a technique, consider it an ethic of patience, inquiry, humility, and doubt—in other words, of every good attitude discouraged by social media and disappearing from our political and cultural life. It means asking hard questions without fear and receiving them without offense; indeed, it means treating challenge and refutation as acts of friendship. Socrates, as we shall see, sometimes likes to define an elusive concept by asking for the name of its opposite. That approach can help us here, too. If I were pressed for a one-word opposite of the Socratic method, a strong candidate would be Twitter.

The threat that such technologies pose to the quality of our discourse, and the damage they have already done, are both obvious to all. But the battle is fought between forces that have not been defined as crisply as might be useful. Fanatical partisanship, wishful thinking in place of truth, the shaming of dissenters, the censorship or self-censorship of disapproved views, the inability of people who disagree to talk, let alone cooperate—everyone sees all this on the rise, and most thinking people fear and loathe all that it involves and portends. Those tendencies have not been unified under any coherent heading, though, except insofar as people on one political side say those problems (or the worst of them) mostly belong to the people on the other. And an alternative to all of them at once hasn't been expressed in a programmatic way. Nobody likes what is happening, but the resistance has not had a shape, a plan, or a hero.

This book nominates Socrates as that hero, and the Socratic method as his plan. It is the natural corrective to the entire family of vices named a moment ago. Distinguish between the vices and distribute them between the political extremes as you like; the Socratic mindset is, regardless, the best corrective for them. It is also a worthy muster point: an apparatus of thought that comes with a powerful rationale, a useful set of tools, and a venerable pedigree. Those who mean to push back against the corrosion of our thought and discourse on every front and without partisanship can helpfully say, before they identify by party, that they are Socratics; before they take up arms, they can subscribe to Socratic rules of engagement. This book explains what that commitment might mean.

As an inhabitant of a university, I especially mean this book to broadly suggest the ethic by which such institutions function best. Their health requires Socratic commitments: to reason, to refutation, and to not flinching when hard questions are put on the table. A university should be a Socratic gymnasium.

➤ 5. This book covers a lot of ground related to the Socratic method, and some readers will be interested more in certain parts than in others. Here is a brief roadmap of what the chapters cover and where.

Chapters 1 and 2 provide background. Chapter 1 talks about who Socrates was (or might have been), and the relationship between the historical Socrates and the literary one. Chapter 2 explains the distinction between the substance of Plato's ideas and the methods of the Socrates that he gives us in his dialogues.

Chapters 3–12 show how the Socratic method works. The elements of it are summarized in Chapter 3, then explained in detail in the chapters that follow. Chapter 4 talks about the use of the method in one's own thinking rather than in conversation. Chapter 5 discusses the question-and-answer approach to inquiry. Chapters 6 and 7 explain the elenchus—the type of argument Socrates likes best—and the importance of consistency in Socratic thought. Chapter 8 explains the Socratic approach to drawing and erasing distinctions; Chapter 9 discusses the method's use of analogies. Chapter 10 goes over some ground rules for Socratic dialogue. Chapter 11 is about ignorance and, in particular, double ignorance—that is, ignorance of one's own ignorance: the problem at the heart of the Socratic project. Chapter

12 is about aporia—the impasse to which Socratic dialogue often leads, and the states of mind that can result from it.

Chapter 13 lays out the Socratic case for caring about the benefits that the method provides. Chapters 14–16 show examples of where the method can lead. Chapter 14 summarizes the conclusions that Socrates reached about the meaning of happiness and how to achieve it. Chapter 15 shows how the methods of Socrates were used, and his conclusions extended, by the Stoics. Chapter 16 does the same for followers of Skepticism.

Chapters 17 and 18 show some simple ways to create Socratic questions of your own. The Epilogue turns the Socratic method, and the ethic behind it, into rules of engagement for conversations that take different forms. It also talks about the importance of the Socratic ethic in the life of a school.

➤➤ 6. This book uses footnotes. Sometimes they offer a brief comment from scholarship that is relevant to the main text. Sometimes they just show where an interested reader can find more discussion of a point. I prefer footnotes to endnotes because they don't require flipping to the back of the book. If you don't like footnotes, though, just ignore them here; they are never essential for understanding anything.

Notes on the translations appear at the end of the book. The citations to Plato as we go along will use the Stephanus numbering system. Those numbers make it easy to find the same passage in any edition of Plato's dialogues. They refer to pages in a beautiful edition of Plato's works published by Henri Estienne, a 16th-century French printer (his Latinized name was Stephanus). He published the dialogues in three volumes. Each of the volumes has page numbers that start near 1 and then run into the hundreds. Then he divided each page into parts with the letters *a* through *e*. It is conventional to use the pages and letters in those editions to refer to passages in Plato's works. (Similar numbering is used to cite the works of Plutarch, as we also will see at a couple of points.)

The result is very convenient. Suppose you see a quotation from Socrates here and it's cited as "*Symposium* 221d." If you go get a copy of Plato's *Symposium*—translated by anyone and published by anyone—you can probably find "221d" in the margins, and you will see the same passage there. Technically speaking, "221d" means the quote appeared in section d of page 221 of the volume in which Stephanus put Plato's *Symposium* (which happens to have been volume 3). But the practical point is simple: the number lets you quickly find a line from Plato in any book that contains it.

Acknowledgments. For discussion and for comments on drafts of this book, I thank Henry Abelove, Philip Bobbitt, Robert Chesney, John Deigh, Alexandra Delp, Victor Ferreres Comella, Stanley Fish, Michael Gagarin, Rebecca Goldstein, David Greenwald, Mark Helprin, Anthony Kennedy, Andrew Kull, Saul Levmore, Anthony Long, Susan Morse, Brian Perez-Daple, Reid Powers, William Powers, David Rabban, Christopher Roberts, Fred Schauer, Nicholas Smith, Geoffrey Stone, Eugene Volokh, and Paul Woodruff. I am also grateful to the staff at the Tarlton Law Library at the University of Texas for their generous and skillful assistance.

THE SOCRATIC METHOD
A Practitioner's Handbook

1

The Socratic Problem

WHEN we study the method and thought of Socrates, are we talking about the real person or a literary character? The short answer is that nobody knows. In many ways it doesn't matter, though it's occasionally relevant to how we think about one issue or another in the dialogues. But the arguments about the question are interesting, so the rest of this chapter will spin them out at more length (though still scratching the surface of the literature on the point, which is endless). The reader who doesn't care, or who already knows the arguments, or who just wants to get on with the method without a lot of background, can skip this with no harm done.

Let me start by assuming no knowledge of our topic and briefly introducing Socrates and those who have told us about him.

Socrates. Socrates lived from about 470 BC to 399 BC. We know little about his life. Ancient biographers say that his father was a mason and that the young Socrates may have practiced the craft as well. Socrates served in the Athenian army in the Peloponnesian War against Sparta. He was then in his forties. He had a wife, Xanthippe; legend regards her as a shrew who dumped a chamber pot on him when they fought.[1] He had three sons. His physical appearance evidently was remarkable and is always described as ugly. He was said to have a potbelly, an odd nose (perhaps snubbed), and eyes with a bulging quality.[2] There are jokes about him seeing to the sides like a crab.[3]

Socrates was widely credited with turning philosophy from the study of nature to hard questions in ordinary life—to have made it,

---

1. See Seneca, *On the Constancy of the Wise Man* 18.6.

2. See, e.g., *Theaetetus* 143e: where Theodorus says to Socrates: "he isn't good looking, but he looks like you! He's snub-nosed and his eyes bulge, though not as much as yours"; and see the passage from the *Meno* at the start of chapter 12.

3. Xenophon, *Symposium* ch. 5. For a more extended treatment of what we know of the life of Socrates, see Guthrie, *History of Greek Philosophy*, Vol. 3, ch. 8.

in other words, a fit subject of anyone's personal interest.[4] He wrote nothing of his own but was a familiar and controversial figure in Athens, loved by his students, parodied on the stage, and associated with some famous political villains (we will see more on these points below). At the age of about seventy he was put on trial for impiety and for corrupting the youth of Athens. The jury in the case probably consisted of five hundred male citizens over the age of thirty who were selected by lottery (out of about 20,000 free Athenian men of eligible age). Speeches were made on both sides, and the outcome was determined by a majority vote. Socrates was found guilty and put to death.

Plato. Plato lived from around 427 BC to 347 BC (eighty years). He was born to a prominent Athenian family and had two brothers and a sister. Ancient biographers said that his name at birth was Aristocles, and that "Plato" was a nickname taken from the word *platon*; it meant "broad" and might have referred to some feature of his body or face. But all this is uncertain. We know almost nothing about Plato personally.

The most elaborate source of information about Plato's life is a letter he may have written in old age—the so-called Seventh Letter, the authenticity of which is disputed. The letter is addressed to followers of Dion, a former student of Plato's who became a politician in Syracuse and had recently been assassinated. The letter talks about Plato's interest in politics as a young man and his travels later in life. It also offers some ideas we will discuss in chapter 12. A generation ago, one scholar conducted a tally of others in the field ("purely for amusement") and found that thirty-six accepted the Seventh Letter as genuine and fourteen rejected it.[5] Some are agnostic. The letter

---

4. See Guthrie, Vol. 3, ch. 14; Annas, "Classical Greek Philosophy," 281–83.

5. Guthrie, *History of Greek Philosophy*, Vol. 5, 401. More recently, Kahn writes that "I have no doubt that the letter was written by Plato" (Kahn, *Plato and the Socratic Dialogue*, 48). Annas, to the contrary, holds that the Seventh Letter is "such an unconvincing production that its acceptance by many scholars is best seen as indicating the strength of their desire to find, behind the detachment of the dialogues, something, no matter what, to which Plato is straightforwardly committed" (Annas, *Classical Greek Philosophy*, 285).

largely consists, at any rate, of narration and discussion of events. It tells us little of Plato himself. On our lack of information about him, Emerson offers this comment:

> Great geniuses have the shortest biographies. Their cousins can tell you nothing about them. They lived in their writings, and so their house and street life was trivial and commonplace. If you would know their tastes and complexions, the most admiring of their readers most resembles them. Plato, especially, has no external biography. If he had lover, wife, or children, we hear nothing of them. He ground them all into paint. As a good chimney burns its smoke, so a philosopher converts the value of all his fortunes into his intellectual performances.[6]

Plato was probably in his teens when he began to associate with Socrates as a student. (His uncle was also part of Socrates' circle.) He was in his late twenties when Socrates died. Plato went to Sicily and maybe elsewhere for a number of years before coming back to Athens and founding his school, the Academy. His main writings—perhaps his only ones—were his dialogues. He wrote about thirty. He never figures directly in them, though in the *Apology* he is identified by Socrates as present at his trial. Scholars often suppose that Plato's earlier dialogues were written before the travels noted above, which they suggest produced a turn in his thinking.[7] They wonder whether Plato wrote any of his Socratic dialogues before Socrates died.

Socrates is said to have had an even closer student than Plato: Antisthenes, who reportedly produced more than sixty writings of various lengths, including Socratic dialogues of his own; dialogues of that kind became a little literary genre. None of those writings has survived. We just have testimony from others about what Antisthenes said, and it doesn't help us much in understanding the historical Socrates. But the ancient historian Diogenes Laertius tells us that

---

6. Emerson, *Representative Men*, 48.

7. See, e.g., Guthrie, *History of Greek Philosophy*, Vol. 4, 17–19; Vlastos, *Socrates, Ironist and Moral Philosopher*, 128–30.

Antisthenes and Plato didn't get along, and their feud provides a rare if uncharitable glance at Plato as a character of his own.

> Antisthenes, being about to recite something that he had written, invited [Plato] to be present; and [Plato] having asked what he was going to recite, he said it was an essay on the impropriety of contradicting. "How then," said Plato, "can you write on this subject?" and then he showed him that he was arguing in a circle. But Antisthenes was annoyed, and composed a dialogue against Plato, which he entitled Sathon; after which they were always enemies to one another.[8]

"Sathon" rhymed with a longer form of Plato's name (Platon). It meant "big prick."[9]

Xenophon (about 431–354 BC) was an Athenian general, another student of Socrates, and a contemporary of Plato. He wrote long recollections of Socrates, most prominently his *Memorabilia*. Those recollections are often dialogues between Socrates and others. The Socrates shown by Xenophon is a more earnest and less dazzling moralist than the Socrates of Plato. A quick example:

> In answer to the question: what is envy? [Socrates] discovered it to be a certain kind of pain; not certainly the sorrow felt at the misfortunes of a friend or the good fortune of an enemy—that is not envy; but, as he said, "envy is felt by those alone who are annoyed at the successes of their friends." And when someone or other expressed astonishment that any one friendly to another should be pained at his well-doing, he reminded him of a common tendency in people: when any one is faring ill their sympathies are touched, they rush to the aid of the unfortunate; but when fortune smiles on others, they are somehow pained. "I do not say," he added, "this could happen to a thoughtful person; but it is no uncommon condition of a silly mind."[10]

---

8. *The Lives and Opinions of Eminent Philosophers* 3.35, trans. Yonge.

9. The word can also be translated in other, similar ways; see Kahn, *Plato and the Socratic Dialogue*, 6.

10. Dakyns, *Works of Xenophon*, 3:111 (slightly modified by Michael Gagarin).

Xenophon left Athens shortly before Socrates went on trial. He wrote his memoirs of Socrates later—possibly decades later. His memoirs seem to rely in some places on Plato's dialogues, and at other points they obviously fictionalize. Relying on Xenophon's recollections of Socrates, like relying on Plato, therefore is risky.[11] Whether one of them is more reliable than the other will be considered below.

Aristophanes (about 446–386 BC) wrote comedies (especially *The Clouds*) in which Socrates is mentioned or appears as a character and is ridiculed. This evidence of the historical Socrates is especially tantalizing because it was written while Socrates was alive, and indeed almost twenty-five years before his death. It's clear that he was well known in Athens, and in these portrayals we see some of the traits found in the Socrates of Plato. But in other ways the Socrates of the *Clouds* is different from the one we find anywhere else. He is depicted as teaching science and oratory and expecting to be paid for it. Some think that Aristophanes just used Socrates to generally represent sophists (traveling teachers of rhetoric and virtue);[12] others think Aristophanes was making a more pointed attack on Socrates' ideas about moral education.[13] These theories are all interesting to students of the Socratic problem, but it's impossible to know whether the Socrates in the plays reflects his public image or something more. Aristophanes does not help us much in knowing where the historical Socrates ends and the literary creation starts.[14]

The writings of *Aristotle* (384–322 BC) contain some remarks about Socrates. Aristotle was born about fifteen years after Socrates died. But Aristotle was Plato's most famous student, so it's natural to imagine that Aristotle heard much about Socrates from his teacher as well as from other sources. We can also be sure that Aristotle read

---

11. See Kahn, *Plato and the Socratic Dialogue*, 75–79, 393–401.

12. For good discussion of the sophists, see Woodruff, "Socrates Among the Sophists," and Guthrie, *History of Greek Philosophy*, Vol. 3, ch. 3 and 448–49.

13. See Nussbaum, "Aristotle and Socrates."

14. Some leading analyses of Aristophanes's portrayal can be found in Dover, "Socrates in the Clouds"; Lacey, "Our Knowledge of Socrates"; and Nussbaum, "Aristotle and Socrates."

Plato's dialogues, since he sometimes relies on them unmistakably.
But at other points he says things about Socrates that he *couldn't* have
learned from the dialogues. Unfortunately we don't know when
he's relying on the dialogues and when he isn't, so using Aristotle to
corroborate the dialogues is dangerous.[15] His historical accounts of
other philosophers have also been found less than reliable, so that's
another reason to worry.[16] But his comments sometimes provide light
support for historical reconstructions of Socrates.[17]

We can now consider briefly and directly whether the "Socrates"
shown in the dialogues is the historical Socrates or a creation of Plato's. Here are sketches of three simple ways to answer that question.[18]

⤞ 1. *It's all Socrates.* Maybe all of Plato's dialogues are efforts to
show what Socrates really thought and said. Nobody thinks that the
dialogues are verbatim transcripts; they at least are fictionalized and
elaborated. But still (the theory goes), they all pretty closely show the
real Socrates in action. Those who like this theory argue that many
in Plato's audience would have remembered Socrates and what he
said, and that they would have complained if Plato changed it. And
sometimes Plato uses someone *other* than Socrates as his protagonist.
This shows that Plato used judgment about which words to put into
Socrates' mouth. He probably confined himself to the kinds of things
that Socrates actually said.

    This position has few adherents.[19] Critics of it point out that Soc-
rates takes conflicting positions at different points in the dialogues.[20]
In the *Apology*, for example, he disclaims interest in aspects of phi-

---

15. See Kahn, *Plato and the Socratic Dialogue*, 85–87; Nehamas, "Voices of Silence," 170.

16. See Kahn, *Plato and the Socratic Dialogue*, 79–86.

17. See Lacey, "Our Knowledge of Socrates."

18. Nails, in *Agora, Academy, and the Conduct of Philosophy*, 8–31, provides an excellent overview of modern positions with references to additional sources. See also Waterfield, "Quest for the Historical Socrates"; Dorion, "Rise and Fall of the Socratic Problem"; Brickhouse and Smith, *Socratic Moral Psychology*; Nehamas, "Voices of Silence," 160–65.

19. It is known as the Burnet/Taylor view. See Burnet, *Greek Philosophy*; A. E. Taylor, *Socrates*, 162.

20. See Ross, *Plato's Theory of Ideas*; Popper, *Open Society and Its Enemies*, n. 56.

losophy that he pursues in the *Republic* and *Phaedo*. And Aristotle describes the Theory of Forms as not belonging to Socrates, but Plato shows Socrates talking all about it. So most scholars nowadays feel sure that at least *some* of the dialogues show the thinking of Plato put into the mouth of his Socrates.

➻ *2. It's all Plato.* It could be the other way around: *everything* Socrates says in the dialogues is what Plato thinks, or anyway is invented by Plato. Socrates was cast as the hero of the dialogues as a tribute by Plato to his teacher. There no doubt is some overlap between the literary Socrates and the real one, in the same way that any character in fiction might be loosely based on a real one. But Plato was trying to write philosophy, not history. And he wrote half a million words of it over the course of fifty years, full of brilliance from start to finish. He was probably the source of the genius found in his characters. Socrates inspired him and likely gave him some of his ideas, but the dialogues mostly show the mind of Plato at work. They owe little to Socrates, and we'll never know what.

All this is entirely possible. Plato never says that the Socrates in his dialogues is based on the real one. He just writes stories in which a character named Socrates appears; every claim that the character resembles the historical person is mere inference. And meanwhile we have the writings of another student of Socrates—Xenophon— who doesn't leave it to inference. He tells us that he's talking about the historical Socrates, and his Socrates is unlike the one in Plato's dialogues. Not *radically* different: both characters ask some of the same questions. But the Socrates of Xenophon and of Plato are different in style, sophistication, and in some of their substance where it overlaps. If Xenophon is accurate, Plato embellished immensely, and whatever factual truth his Socrates contains is too scattered and unpredictable to worry about. The dialogues of Plato, on this view, should be read the same way you might watch an inaccurate biopic: enjoy the movie, but don't imagine that it's history.

➻ *3. It changes from Socrates to Plato.* The most common view now isn't either of those extreme ones. It is that Plato started out writing dialogues that showed Socrates more or less as he was.[21] Some think Plato described what Socrates said without adding much, others that Plato speculates about what the real Socrates would have said—but only so long as Plato also believed it.[22] Then there are transitional dialogues where Plato's own ideas start to appear, and late ones that owe nothing to the historical Socrates.

Those who take this view sometimes attack Xenophon. They say that his Socrates can't be the real one (so Plato's early Socrates *can* be the real one). Xenophon's Socrates can't be real because he's too boring: his Socrates wouldn't have attracted the devoted followers and enemies that the real Socrates evidently did.[23] The root of the problem (some suppose) is that Xenophon himself is boring. He didn't have the gifts needed to appreciate the subtlety of Socrates. Since he didn't comprehend the hard parts of what Socrates said, he didn't record them—but those are the parts that mattered most. Bertrand Russell summed up this position memorably.

> A stupid man's report of what a clever man says is never accurate, because he unconsciously translates what he hears into something that he can understand. I would rather be reported by my bitterest enemy among philosophers than by a friend innocent of philosophy. We cannot therefore accept what Xenophon says if it either involves any difficult point in philosophy or is part of an argument to prove that Socrates was unjustly condemned.[24]

Russell's general point seems strong, but he's too hard on Xeno-

---

21. For a survey of this view with supporting evidence, see Graham, "Socrates and Plato"; Vlastos, *Socrates, Ironist and Moral Philosopher*, ch. 2.

22. See, e.g., Guthrie, *History of Greek Philosophy*, Vol. 4, 67: in the early dialogues Plato is "imaginatively recalling, in form and substance, the conversations of his master"; compare Vlastos, *Socrates, Ironist and Moral Philosopher*, 50, 117.

23. See Vlastos, "Paradox of Socrates," 2–3: "Xenophon's Socrates, pious reciter of moral commonplaces, would have elicited nothing but a sneer from Critias and a yawn from Alcibiades, while Plato's Socrates is just the man who could have gotten under their skin"; Burnet, *Greek Philosophy*, 149: "Xenophon's defense of Socrates is too successful. He would never have been put to death if he had been like that."

24. Russell, *History of Western Philosophy*, 82.

phon.[25] Xenophon's memoirs of Socrates are open to readings that suggest they are smart in their own way, either as defenses of Socrates or as efforts to capture sides of him that Plato didn't.[26] But it's true that Xenophon was a military man and not a philosopher, and that he comes off to most of us now as a bit of a bore. And yet this might be a virtue. If we want to see Socrates as he was—if we want a *report*—we might do well to ask someone known to be sturdy and dull. The doings of Sherlock Holmes are better recorded by a Watson than by another Holmes.

Meanwhile even those who think that Plato's dialogues are faithful to the historical Socrates recognize from the way they are written that Plato had great talent. They regard this as a help, but it might make us nervous for the same reason just noted: a genius makes a dangerous reporter.[27] Plato was talented enough to invent a Socrates, and maybe he did.[28]

The trial of Socrates. Now a few other issues on the fringe of the Socratic problem. We saw that those who think Plato shows the real Socrates will sometimes use this argument: many in Plato's audience would have known Socrates and so would have kept Plato honest. The scholar Gregory Vlastos considered that claim especially strong with respect to the *Apology*, which presents Socrates speaking in his own defense at trial. Hundreds of Athenians saw that trial. Plato had to present a character they would recognize as accurate. "And if this is conceded," Vlastos writes, "the problem of our sources is solved in principle. For we may then use the *Apology* as a touchstone of the

25. See Howland, "Xenophon's Philosophic Odyssey"; Vlastos, *Socrates, Ironist and Moral Philosopher*, 99–100; Morrison, "On Professor Vlastos's Xenophon."

26. See Cooper, *Reason and Emotion: Essays in Ancient Moral Philosophy and Ethical Theory*; Morrison, "On Professor Vlastos's Xenophon," 19: "It is a tribute to Xenophon's greatness as a writer that he fooled Professor Vlastos into thinking that his Socrates was too conventionally pious to have been indicted."

27. See Morrison, "On Professor Vlastos's Xenophon," 18: "The doctrine of friendship presented by Xenophon's Socrates is not too dull to have attracted interest; to the contrary, it was new and exciting and wise. It would have been characteristic of Plato's genius and character to have taken that doctrine and made it even more radical, even more exciting—and unrealistic, overblown, and wrong."

28. Russell, *History of Western Philosophy*, 83.

like veracity of the thought and character of Socrates as depicted in Plato's other early dialogues."[29] But this is too quick. The *Apology* is unlike the other dialogues; for the most part it *isn't* a dialogue. It's largely a speech. It isn't hard to imagine Plato writing up that episode more or less faithfully but then sending his literary Socrates off on other adventures that had no comparable basis in fact.

And Plato writing a fictionalized *Apology* might not be surprising either. Xenophon wrote his own account of part of the trial, and it differs from what Plato described. Both of them might have taken liberties for the sake of defending their teacher's reputation. We should consider why. Some students of the trial conclude that it was largely political in character.[30] After losing a war against the Spartans in 404 BC, Athens came under the rule of the "Thirty Tyrants"—a group of oligarchs favorably disposed to Sparta. Their reign was less than a year but was murderous while it lasted. Supporters of democracy were exiled or executed. Socrates stayed and lived.[31] The leader of the Thirty Tyrants was Critias. Critias had been a student of Socrates, and Socrates had relationships with others among the Thirty as well. Critias was killed in the revolt that overthrew his regime. The trial of Socrates occurred four years later. An amnesty had been decreed that would have kept Socrates from being prosecuted for any role in the terrors, but records of other trials suggest that political grievances found their way into prosecutions for "impiety" easily enough.[32] This explains a famous oratorical remark fifty years later from Aeschines: "Athenians, you had the sophist Socrates put to death because he seemed to have been the teacher of Critias, one of the Thirty who destroyed the democracy."[33]

---

29. Vlastos, "Paradox of Socrates," 4.

30. See Waterfield, "Xenophon on Socrates' Trial and Death"; Shorey, *What Plato Said*, 33; compare Grote, *Plato and the Other Companions of Sokrates*, 1:281; Brickhouse and Smith, *Socrates on Trial*, 2–10.

31. In the *Apology*, Socrates refers to a pro-democracy character, Chaerephon, as a friend from childhood, and notes that Chaerephon was involved with others in "your recent expulsion and restoration."

32. Waterfield, "Xenophon on Socrates' Trial and Death," 282–83.

33. Aeschines, 1.173 (*Against Timarchus*).

The reason for the trial and execution of Socrates is a rich question, and I've only noted one side of it. Some scholars disfavor political explanations of the trial and prefer to credit the account in Plato's *Apology*.[34] We have little direct evidence to settle this, so either view can be held responsibly. Maybe the real Socrates was a wise and noble philosopher, too honest for his times; maybe he was closer to a cult leader who taught contempt for democracy and equipped his followers to become tyrants. But the political interpretation should at least make us alert to the risk that the students of Socrates sanitized and mythologized him.

Sequence. Everyone agrees that the dialogues differ from each other in significant ways, and most agree about which of them show the process known as the Socratic method. The true Socratic dialogues are said to be the early ones. But which dialogues are early, and how do we know?

None of the dialogues are dated. Efforts to put them in order have been the subject of hundreds of inquiries; one book on the subject counts 132 alternative sequences that have been proposed.[35] Many studies have made been using stylometry—the examination of little stylistic changes in the dialogues—to show which of them must have been written near to each other in time. But these efforts become unstable if Plato (as many think) went back and revised the dialogues throughout his life, or if he made stylistic changes that were deliberate rather than unconscious. Stylometry also requires some initial decisions, usually on thematic grounds, about which dialogues to treat as a starting point. The debate about which dialogues came before which is striking for the labors that have been spent on it over the centuries and the lack of consensus they've produced on anything but a couple of broad groupings. But then that result is faithful to the Socratic spirit. The process of inquiry can be edifying even if it doesn't give us many answers.

As for those broad groupings, the classification of some dialogues

---

34. See Irwin, "Review: Socrates and Athenian Democracy."
35. Thesleff, *Studies in Platonic Chronology.*

as early and late is treated as a working assumption now by most scholars.[36] The "early" dialogues are usually said to be these, in alphabetical order: *Apology, Charmides, Crito, Euthydemus, Euthyphro, Gorgias, Hippias Major, Hippias Minor, Ion, Laches, Lysis*, and *Protagoras*. Many would add Book I of the *Republic*, which is thought to have been written earlier than the rest of it, and perhaps also the *Menexenus*. This book will draw most heavily from dialogues in that set, but sometimes later ones will be consulted when they shed light on our questions—especially the *Theaetetus*, but also others; a majority of the dialogues will make an appearance at one time or another. I regard Plato as likely having created much of the Socratic method, so comments from throughout his oeuvre can help us understand it.

Unity vs. development. The arguments above overlap with another debate about how to read Plato. Some take a so-called unitarian view: in effect we should read the dialogues as if they were all chapters of a book finished at one time.[37] If there are differences between them, we shouldn't assume Plato changed. We should assume that they reflect his literary judgment, either because that's probably true or because it's the most constructive assumption we can make. These readers might think that Plato formed his philosophy early and then spent his life explicating it.[38] On the other side is the so-called developmental view of the dialogues: that Plato did change his mind over the course of his life and that his writings show this. The developmental view goes along naturally (but not inevitably) with the idea that the early dialogues show us the historical Socrates and the later ones don't.

---

36. For discussion of grounds for uncertainty, see Annas, "What Are Plato's 'Middle' Dialogues in the Middle Of?"; Kahn, *Plato and the Socratic Dialogue*.

37. The unitarian view is originally associated with Friedrich Schleiermacher, a German philosopher who published influential scholarship on Plato in the early 19th century. Examples of more-or-less unitarian positions taken in the 20th century include Kahn, *Plato and the Socratic Dialogue*, 38–40; Friedlander, *Plato*, 162; and Shorey, *Unity of Plato's Thought*, 88 (on which see Sprague, "Platonic Unitarianism, or What Shorey Said").

38. See Shorey, 88: "Plato on the whole belongs rather to the type of thinkers whose philosophy is fixed in early maturity."

Working assumptions. This book will largely go along with the assumptions that have become most common among scholars. First, the Socratic method is best shown by a set of dialogues that likely came early in Plato's career. Second, those "early" dialogues show us roughly how the real Socrates acted; I will speak of Socrates saying and doing this and that. Even if the Socrates in the early dialogues is mostly a character developed by Plato, his approach and ideas differ from those in the dialogues that came later. It's convenient to have a way to distinguish between them. Talking as though the earlier dialogues show what "Socrates" said, as distinct from Plato, is helpful even if our confidence in the claim can't be too strong.

My own view—worth little, but it might as well be said so you can discount for it—is that the Socrates we know from the early dialogues is a composite of Plato's imagination and memory, and probably more the former than the latter. But regardless of what solution to the Socratic problem seems best, remember the uncertainty that surrounds it. Any position has a substantial chance of being wrong. This book will nevertheless make the assumptions just noted so that we can get on with the work of learning. If the assumptions are wrong (as they might be), most of the discussion that follows would still be about the same.

2

Method vs. Doctrine

THIS chapter explains the difference between the Socratic *method* and the substance of the ideas that Plato wrote about. We will learn about this in part through the words of John Stuart Mill, the eminent British philosopher who was one of the Socratic method's foremost champions. There are many ways to look at Socrates and learn from him. This book generally tries to approach him in the spirit that Mill suggests.

Text and footnotes. Plato's stature among academic students of philosophy needs no comment. For people outside that circle who have philosophical interests, though, respect for Plato without much interest or affection is a common attitude. They know his significance and give all credit where it's due. They've probably heard Whitehead's suggestion that the European philosophical tradition consists of "footnotes to Plato." [1] But in truth they prefer the footnotes. They don't think of themselves as Platonists, don't like to read Plato, and don't associate him with any particular ideas that they value. If they remember Plato for anything, it is for the Theory of Forms, or for the idea that all learning is recollection of knowledge, or for the concept of philosopher-kings, and they don't believe in any of that. This all makes it common for many readers to react to Plato as Thomas Jefferson did in a letter he wrote to John Adams after reading the *Republic*:

> While wading thro' the whimsies, the puerilities, and unintelligible jargon of this work, I laid it down often to ask myself how it could have been that the world should have so long consented to give reputation to such nonsense as this? ... With the Moderns, I think, it is rather a matter of fashion and authority. Education is chiefly in the hands of persons who, from their profession,

---

1. Whitehead, *Process and Reality*, 2.1.1.

have an interest in the reputation and the dreams of Plato. They give the tone while at school, and few, in their after-years, have occasion to revise their college opinions.[2]

I don't display this harsh verdict to endorse it. I like Plato. I just mean to show how he is sometimes viewed even by educated readers who enjoy classical learning. (Jefferson was philosophically curious, was well versed in Greek, and loved Epictetus, Epicurus, and other philosophers of antiquity.)[3]

Socrates, as distinct from Plato, means little more to most lay readers. They associate him with the saying that the unexamined life is not worth living (though what he said might be closer to "the unexamined life is not to be lived" or "is not livable").[4] And they know that his rationality and brave example influenced others. But his own ideas don't contribute to theirs. They admire him by reputation, but that really is all. Often they never recovered from an initial impression that Socrates went around annoying other people in ways that didn't seem productive.

Substance vs. method. To take back the legacy of Socrates it helps to consult Mill, the most distinguished British philosopher of the 19th century. Mill's thinking was notably farsighted. *On Liberty* is a classic of political thought that continues to persuade and inspire many. (Chapter 2 of that essay amounts, in many respects, to an eloquent modern defense of the Socratic stance.) *The Subjection of Women* was a book well ahead of its time in which Mill anticipated arguments for women's rights that would prevail years after he died. He also wrote influentially about logic, economics, and history. His

---

2. Jefferson, letter to John Adams (July 5, 1814) in Ford, *Writings of Thomas Jefferson*, vol. 9, 463.

3. See Jefferson's letter to William Short (1819) in Ford, *Writings of Thomas Jefferson*, vol. 10, 144: "I have sometimes thought of translating Epictetus (for he has never been tolerable translated into English) by adding the genuine doctrines of Epicurus from the Syntagma of Gassendi, and an abstract from the Evangelists of whatever has the stamp of the eloquence and fine imagination of Jesus."

4. *Apology* 38a; Kraut, "Examined Life," 230–31, argues for the first alternative translation.

collected writings run to 33 volumes. (He also found time to serve
as a member of Parliament.)

I recite this background because Mill will have some importance for
the rest of the book. He isn't liked by everyone (who is?), but his credentials as a reasoner are sterling, so his own teachers are a matter of
some interest. Mill was, like Jefferson, a lover of philosophy. Unlike
Jefferson, he also was a lover of Plato. Mill was educated energetically
by his father and was an intellectual prodigy. He was reading Plato
in Greek by the time he was seven. In his twenties he translated nine
of Plato's dialogues into English and wrote commentaries on some
of them. Mill's written appreciations of Plato and Socrates have not
been bettered. He held that the Socratic method "is unsurpassed as
a discipline for abstract thought on the most difficult subjects. Nothing in modern life and education in the smallest degree supplies its
place."[5] He went on to say that the method

> became part of my own mind; and I have ever felt myself, beyond
> any modern that I know of except my father and perhaps beyond
> even him, a pupil of Plato, and cast in the mold of his dialectics.[6]

We should try to understand why.

Mill saw Plato as having two sorts of lessons to teach. There were
his philosophical ideas—his dogmatic side, as Mill described it. By
"dogmatic" Mill didn't mean, as we might, an unquestioning adher-
ence to claims that haven't been proven. He meant the side of Plato's
writings that reaches conclusions and takes positions. The other side
was Plato's style of thought—that is, the *method* used by Socrates
in the dialogues. Mill's view was that the method shown in Plato's
writings is the best part of them.

> There are thus, independently of minor discrepancies, two com-
> plete Platos in Plato—the Socratist and the Dogmatist—of whom
> the former is by far the more valuable to mankind, but the latter
> has obtained from them much the greater honor. And no won-
> der; for the one was capable of being a useful prop to many a

---

5. Mill, "Early Draft of John Stuart Mill's Autobiography," 24.   6. Ibid.

man's moral and religious dogmas, while the other could only clear and invigorate the human understanding.[7]

Elsewhere Mill made the point more strongly:

> I have felt ever since [childhood] that the title of Platonist belongs by far better right to those who have been nourished in and have endeavored to practice Plato's mode of investigation, than to those who are distinguished only by the adoption of certain dogmatical conclusions, drawn mostly from the least intelligible of his works, and which the character of his mind and writings makes it uncertain whether he himself regarded as anything more than poetic fancies, or philosophic conjectures.[8]

It is too late for the word "Platonist" to be used as Mill suggests. The word is accepted by all as referring to those who believe in the substance of what Plato seems to have thought. Those devoted to the methods of Socrates are better described as Socratics. Explaining what it might mean to be a Socratic is, in effect, the topic of this book.

The ailment. What is the purpose of the Socratic method? To put the question in a more Socratic way: we wear glasses because we don't see the external world clearly without them; we take x-rays to see inside the physical self. What is the Socratic method for? It lets us see something else more clearly: the workings and failings of the mind and its productions. How Mill put it:

> The Socratic method, of which the Platonic dialogues are the chief example, is unsurpassed as a discipline for correcting the errors, and clearing up the confusions incident to the *intellectus sibi permissus*, the understanding which has made up all its bundles of associations under the guidance of popular phraseology.[9]

Intellectus sibi permissus means "the mind left to itself." It is an expression that had been used a lot by Francis Bacon, and it is a good way to explain why the Socratic method is helpful. The mind left to itself

---

7. Robson, *Collected Works of John Stuart Mill*, 11:415.
8. Ibid., 1:25.   9. Ibid.

tends toward irrationality and idiocy. The Socratic method improves its performance. Mill had a good friend and political ally, George Grote, who was the author of one of the finest treatises ever written on Plato. Grote saw the problem addressed by the Socratic method in much the way Mill did—as an inveterate flaw in the workings of our natures. As Grote said:

> In the natural process of growth in the human mind, belief does not follow proof, but springs up apart from and independent of it; an immature intelligence believes first, and proves (if indeed it ever seeks proof) afterwards.[10]

Mill also offered this different but compatible idea of the mistake that the Socratic method corrects:

> The enemy against whom Plato really fought, and the warfare against whom was the incessant occupation of the greater part of his life and writings, was not Sophistry, either in the ancient or the modern sense of the term, but Commonplace. It was the acceptance of traditional opinions and current sentiments as an ultimate fact; and bandying of the abstract terms which express approbation and disapprobation, desire and aversion, admiration and disgust, as if they had a meaning thoroughly understood and universally assented to.[11]

This way of understanding Plato clarifies his influence on Mill and Mill's devotion to him in return; for Mill was a forceful questioner of the commonplace in his own culture. He continues:

> The men of his day (like those of ours) thought that they knew what Good and Evil, Just and Unjust, Honorable and Shameful, were, because they could use the words glibly, and affirm them of this and of that, in agreement with existing custom. But what the property was, which these several instances possessed in common, justifying the application of the term, nobody had

---

10. Grote, *Plato and the Other Companions of Sokrates*, 1:258.
11. Robson, *Collected Works of John Stuart Mill*, 11:403.

considered.... The grand business of human intellect ought to consist in subjecting these general terms to the most rigorous scrutiny, and bringing to light the ideas that lie at the bottom of them. Even if this cannot be done, and real knowledge be attained, it is already no small benefit to expel the false opinion of knowledge; to make men conscious of their ignorance of the things most needful to be known....

This is Plato's notion of the condition of the human mind in his time, and of what philosophy could do to help it; and anyone who does not think the description applicable, with slight modifications, to the majority even of educated minds in our own and in all times known to us, certainly has not brought either the teachers or the practical men of any time to the Platonic test.[12]

Mill's comments assign the Socratic method a purpose that has, from a certain point of view, as much to do with cognitive psychology as with philosophy. Our minds stumble and exaggerate and lie; they fool us and are fooled. We think and talk in certainties that feel solid but have nothing much behind them. The Socratic method is a corrective. It exposes this state of affairs and helps us build something humbler and stronger.

Mill's interpretation of Plato is powerful and appealing. It treats the Socratic method as useful for everyone. Mill translated the dialogues because he thought the methods they taught should be common property. The scholar Gregory Vlastos thought so, too: "Where in the annals of Western philosophy could we find a sharper antithesis to [the] restriction of ethical inquiry to a carefully selected, rigorously trained elite than in the Socrates of Plato's earlier dialogues?"[13] That's the right way to think about Socrates; for apart from whatever specific teachings may be attributed to him, he himself was an egalitarian character—poor, ugly, and happy to talk about the most important questions with anyone at all.

---

12. Ibid., 11:404.

13. Vlastos, *Socrates, Ironist and Moral Philosopher*, 110.

3

Elements of the Method

THIS chapter explains the elements of the Socratic method: the features that the dialogues have in common and that might be considered essential to the style of inquiry favored by Socrates.

A skeletal example. What *is* the Socratic method? The term is a modern invention; Plato never referred to a method, and Socrates never sets forth his procedures in a systematic manner. He shows rather than tells. I don't quite propose to define the method, either. It will be more productive to identify some recurring elements that are found in the way Socrates carries out his part in the dialogues.

We should start by looking at an example. It isn't feasible to reprint an entire dialogue here, but we can walk through an outline of one—the *Laches* (pronounced *lay*-keez), in which Socrates and some companions talk about the meaning of courage. Later in the book we will see many actual quotations from this and other dialogues. The skeleton that follows is a paraphrase meant to show the overall shape that a typical dialogue might have. We aren't concerned now with whether the arguments are persuasive. We're simply interested in the style of reasoning the dialogue shows—in other words, the method.

The dialogue begins with a pair of fathers asking two generals whether the sons of the fathers should be trained to fight in armor. They turn to Socrates for his views. After some conversation about the benefits of such training, they conclude that the purpose of it is to develop courage. Socrates then turns the discussion to the *meaning* of courage. Here is how it runs.

> SOCRATES. What is courage?
>
> LACHES. It's what soldiers have when they hold their ground instead of running away from the enemy.
>
> SOCRATES. But that can't quite be right, can it? Some people

show courage *while* running away from an enemy. You need a definition that covers them, too. Also, someone can be courageous in other situations—in politics or in poverty or in dealing with desires, for example. A definition of courage would need to cover what courage in a soldier has in common with courage in all those other ways. Do you see what I mean?

LACHES. No.

SOCRATES. It's like defining speed. Speed can be shown in lots of settings—when someone is speaking or running or making music on a lyre. So we might say that speed *generally* means the ability to get a lot done in a short time. Courage is a quality, like speed. Can you describe it in a general way that is comparable?

LACHES. How about: at the most general level, courage means persistence of mind. [Or perseverance of spirit.]

SOCRATES. Okay, but I'm not sure you mean that, either. You think courage is admirable, right?

LACHES. Yes.

SOCRATES. And sometimes persistence can be foolish rather than wise, yes?

LACHES. True.

SOCRATES. And foolishness isn't admirable, is it?

LACHES. No.

SOCRATES. But you said that courage *is* admirable. So our definition seems wrong: it makes courage sometimes sound bad, but it's good.

LACHES. Yes, there's something wrong with the definition.

SOCRATES. Perhaps you meant that courage is *wise* or *intelligent* persistence of mind?

LACHES. That's better.

SOCRATES. Yet it still creates problems. First, some cases of intelligent persistence have nothing to do with courage, as when someone persistently invests money because it will produce a good return. That sort of person wouldn't be called courageous, right?

LACHES. Right. Not courageous.

SOCRATES. So the definition covers some cases that you think it shouldn't. But the definition also doesn't cover some cases that you probably think it should. Imagine a soldier who is persistent because he knows that help is on the way; compare him to one who is persistent but doesn't know that help is coming. Which is more courageous?

LACHES. The second one seems more courageous—the one who doesn't know that help is coming.

SOCRATES. Yet the persistence of the second one might seem *less* informed and *less* intelligent. In fact, it's starting to seem that courage might really be *unintelligent* persistence!

LACHES. Well, I'm sure that's wrong. I don't mean to produce that result.

SOCRATES. All right, but let's not give up. Let's show our own persistence, and try something different.

NICIAS. Maybe this captures the idea: courage really amounts to a kind of wisdom or knowledge.

SOCRATES. You can't mean just any sort of knowledge. Which kind?

NICIAS. A courageous person is one who understands what is worth fearing and what isn't.

LACHES. But doctors know what is worth fearing by their patients, yet we wouldn't necessarily describe doctors as courageous, would we?

NICIAS. Not on that account, no. But doctors just know what the physical effects of various things might be. They aren't experts on what is ultimately worth fearing and avoiding.

SOCRATES. So you must think that animals can't be courageous. They never have the kind of knowledge you describe, do they?

NICIAS. That's right. There's a difference between being fearless and courageous. I'd say some animals are fearless, but I wouldn't give them credit for courage.

SOCRATES. But still, there's another problem. Courage is just one kind of virtue—as opposed to, say, showing self-control or being just, right?

NICIAS. Yes.

SOCRATES. Good; I'll come back to that point. Now when we talk about knowledge of what's worth fearing, what does that really mean? It seems that something worth fearing can be described more generally and simply as a bad thing to come—an evil in the future, as opposed to something good in the future. Agreed?

NICIAS. Yes, fair enough.

SOCRATES. Courage, then, is the same as an understanding of what's truly good and truly evil in our possible futures—is that what you'd say?

NICIAS. Yes, that sounds right.

SOCRATES. But if you understand whether something to come is worth fearing—in other words, whether it's an evil—then you also must know whether it was good or evil if it happened in the past. Judgments about what is genuinely bad, and what merely *seems* bad, shouldn't depend on whether it's coming or already happened, should they?

NICIAS. True enough.

SOCRATES. So then courage isn't just knowledge of whether things *to come* are worth fearing—that is, good or evil. It amounts to an understanding of what's good and what's evil, period—yes?

NICIAS. That does follow.

SOCRATES. But people who have *that* knowledge would have more than courage. Since they understand the true nature of what is good and what is evil, they would also be just and pious; indeed, it's hard to think of a virtue they *wouldn't* have, isn't it?

NICIAS. So it would seem.

SOCRATES. Yet we said that courage was just one kind of virtue. Now we've defined it in a way that covers too much. We've turned courage into a form of knowledge that doesn't make it distinctive from other virtues. So I'm worried that we still haven't figured out exactly what courage is.

NICIAS. No, it seems we haven't.

Elements. That sketch is abbreviated and leaves out many details. And you probably would have offered a different definition and made different objections. But leave those points to one side. Let's consider the style of reasoning the dialogue displays, which is typical of the Socratic method generally.

First, it proceeds by question and answer. Some of the questions are open-ended, as when Socrates asks Laches to propose a definition. At other points Socrates asks whether his partners agree with what he has said. Regardless, the result isn't a lecture and isn't quite an argument, either. Socrates gets his partners to consent to every step he takes. (This book will generally refer to the person being questioned as a "partner" of whoever is asking the questions, because that is the best spirit in which to approach Socratic dialogue. The parties are doing something together.)

Second, Socrates is always focused on the consistency of his partners. He probes it with a device known as the elenchus. His partners make claims. Then Socrates gets them to agree to other things that turn out to be inconsistent with what they've just said. Now they feel compelled to refine their claims or abandon them. Notice that he doesn't say his partners are wrong. He says, "can we agree that the following idea is true?"—and then his partners conclude for themselves (with his prompting) that something they said earlier wasn't quite right.

Third, his questions identify the principle behind what his partners are saying. Then he shows that the principle doesn't cover things that it should, or that it does cover things that it shouldn't. For example, Laches offers a definition of courage: standing firm. But Socrates gets Laches to agree that the definition leaves out some cases that ought to be included, such as courage shown in retreat. Or Laches defines courage as persistence of mind, but that can't be right, either, because it goes too far. Sometimes persistence is stupid, and Laches agrees that courage isn't courage if it's stupid.

Fourth, Socrates uses concrete examples to drive his reasoning:

soldiers running away, someone playing a lyre, doctors and their patients. The examples often involve everyday people and situations. Sometimes the everyday examples illustrate big conceptual points. Sometimes he uses them to build analogies between things that are familiar and things that aren't. One way or another, he tries to make headway on large issues by talking about specific cases that are easy to imagine.

Fifth, Socrates doesn't claim expertise. He confesses his own ignorance, and that is where the dialogue ends: at an impasse, and without an answer.

The Socratic method, broadly speaking, amounts to the skillful use of the elements just described. Each of those elements, as well as a few others that are less prominent, will be discussed and illustrated in the chapters to come, and chapters 17 and 18 will talk about how to devise those kinds of questions in familiar settings.

In a nutshell. Now I want to restate the usual workings of the Socratic method in more colloquial terms—that is, to suggest how the elements just recounted can be treated as a process that is practical and not in the least esoteric. I'll oversimplify a bit here, and then the rest of the book will offer as much detail as the reader may choose to tolerate.

Let's say, then, that you just want to get going. Here is the Socratic method in crude form: When someone makes a claim about right and wrong or good and bad, question it. Ask what the claim means, and about other things its holder believes, and look for tension between those points; show with your questions that the claim must in some way be unsatisfactory to the person who made it. In effect you deny what your discussion partners say, but the denial is artful. If you do this right, it won't even sound like an argument. They will refine their claims, and now you do it again.

On a Socratic view, denying what someone says is the act of a friend; you should want friends who deny what *you* say. Such denials produce good things. If someone has a talent for denying your claims (hopefully with some indirection and tact), you might change your mind for the better. If not, you're at least likely to end up with a better sense of why you think what you do. You will more clearly

see the details and qualifications that go with it. You might become
less sure what you think altogether. That will feel like a loss, but
you will be closer to the truth, even if it's a truth that, in some cases,
you may never finally reach. In that event you still hold beliefs, but
you hold them a little differently. You're more humble, more aware
of your ignorance, less likely to be sure when you shouldn't be, and
more understanding of others. Socrates regarded these as great gains
in wisdom.

All this is what Socratic partners try to do for each other. They
are good-natured and subtle contrarians. In practice this might nevertheless sound like a set of instructions for becoming unpopular or
getting yourself killed. That's what it was for Socrates. Take heart,
though: describing the method as something practiced by one person
on another is mostly a convenience to illustrate how it works. In real
life—and when reading Plato, too—Socratic questioning is better
viewed mostly as a way to think about hard questions on your own.
You challenge yourself and harass yourself and test what you think
and deny what you say, all as a Socrates would. That might sound
easier than doing it to others. In fact it's considerably harder. But it's
also more rewarding and less dangerous.

Consistency. We have seen that the Socratic method involves the use
of questions to test one's consistency. We will talk more about this
point in Chapters 6 and 7, but a further word about it is in order now
because consistency can sound at first like a boring aim of modest
importance. To Socrates it is everything. Not that he is against people
changing their minds; quite the contrary. The consistency he wants is
between the different things you claim to think at any given time. To
put it more practically, Socrates starts with whatever you say—call it
X. Then he gets you to admit that you also believe Y. Then he causes
you to see for yourself that X and Y are inconsistent. Neither has
been proven wrong, but at least *one* of them must be. Since you can't
believe both, you're forced to change one or the other. So Socrates
isn't your antagonist; he's the one who shows you that you are your
own antagonist.

That sketch makes the Socratic method sound like something that anyone can use, because it is. But using it *well* is an art. Asking good Socratic questions takes ingenuity, especially when it comes to spotting Y—the thing you believe, perhaps deep down, that is inconsistent with whatever you've just said. Sometimes Y has to be drawn out with hypothetical questions that you hadn't thought about before. It also takes stamina to keep answering such questions when they get uneasy. All this is why it's easier to put Socratic questions to someone else than to do it in your own thinking, which is always hard and sometimes seems impossible. So we don't need to worry about thinking Socratically all the time. Nobody does, or ever did. The question is whether we do it any of the time, and how we might do it better and more often.

The Socratic style of reasoning is potent. If you want to get closer to the truth, working out inconsistencies in your own thinking is a powerful way to do it; the task may sound unassuming, but it can turn one's approach to life upside down. If you want to refute the claims of others, showing inconsistencies in their thinking is a powerful way to do it; it can leave an argument, or the maker of it, in tatters. And a failure to think Socratically, in the sense just described, is at the root of most of what's foolish and infuriating in our ethical and political culture. People routinely say things that they don't really believe, or wouldn't believe if they thought longer about it. By "wouldn't believe," I mean that what they say isn't consistent with other things they believe more deeply. Or they wouldn't say it if the facts were changed in ways that they think should be irrelevant.

All this usually seems obvious when listening to others with whom we disagree. When it comes to ourselves, it's not obvious; it's invisible, though just as likely to be the case. A large share of the Socratic struggle, whether in philosophy or politics and law, is to separate claims from rooting interests, so that when you praise or condemn something, you mean you would praise or condemn it with the same force no matter who did it. Or, if not, that you can explain why not. You stay ruthlessly consistent. This is all difficult to do, and won't get you a job writing op-ed pieces. But it helps prevent more additions to the riot of arrogance and hypocrisy that is modern political discourse.

Indirection. The elements we've considered might make the Socratic method seem to be purely a matter of technique—a set of steps that push understanding forward. It can be just that. But the method also has indirect aims. Socrates often tries to persuade his partners of one claim or another. But he accomplishes more by his efforts than persuasion, and also less: the persuasion might not happen, but other things do. The same can happen when you read a dialogue. You aren't quite convinced by the arguments, so the dialogue seems to fail on its stated terms. But it succeeds on other terms, which are probably its real terms. It affects us. We will see other examples of such indirection as we go along—Socrates saying something other than exactly what he means, or Plato doing the same through Socrates. Indirection is, we might say, an additional feature of the Socratic method, but one that is better left off the list of formal elements and appreciated indirectly.

Some examples of such indirect benefits are discussed by Mill. He thought many of the arguments made by Socrates were bad. His leading example is the *Gorgias*, a dialogue in which Socrates talks with three others about the relationship between justice and happiness, the pleasant and the good, and various other ideas. It is one of Plato's most celebrated works. Yet there is widespread modern agreement that at least some of the arguments Socrates makes are defective,[1] and Mill said that "they are nearly all of them fallacies."[2] This might seem to call the value of the dialogue into question, since the arguments look like the whole point of it. But Mill thought otherwise.

> It is not by its logic, but by its ἦθος [ethos], that [the dialogue] produces its effects; not by instructing the understanding, but by working on the feelings and imagination. Nor is this strange; for the disinterested love of virtue is an affair of feeling. It is

---

1. Santas, *Socrates*, 260–303, is a comprehensive and rigorous analysis, and it contains references to other sources as well.
2. Mill, "Grote's Plato," 11:415.

impossible to prove to any one Plato's thesis, that justice is supreme happiness, unless he can be made to feel it as such....
The Socrates of the dialogue makes us feel all other evils to be
more tolerable than injustice in the soul, not by proving it, but
by the sympathy he calls forth with his own intense feeling of it.[3]

Mill's claim can seem to be a paradox. The Socratic method looks
at first like the ultimate rational enterprise. Socrates—the hero—uses
logic to fight illusion and falsehood and vice until at last he is over-
taken by the enemy and nobly elects not to capitulate but to die for
his devotion to the truth. Beginners view the heart of the story as
the logic. Later, maybe after discovering that the logic is not always
very compelling, we understand the heart of the story to be the fight,
the nobility, and the devotion. And yet those good things are, on
the Socratic model, best obtained not by dwelling on them but by
dwelling on what inspires them: the truth, and its passionate pursuit
by rational means.

The most important feature of a dialogue, when seen in this way,
isn't whether its arguments are finally persuasive. The most important
feature is the effect that the dialogue has on the reader. Sometimes
arguments that fail, or that refute one another, help an audience toward a certain understanding or frame of mind. That frame of mind
may be more valuable than being persuaded of this proposition or
that one. The frame of mind may be a new perspective from which
it is apparent that *all* the propositions in the dialogue are inadequate.
It may be a perspective from which the chase after the truth is seen
to be the highest human pursuit even if (or perhaps *because*) the
complete capture of that truth is not possible. A reader sometimes is
brought to such a perspective more effectively by taking part in an
exhausting and failed chase rather than by being told to adopt the
perspective directly.[4]

---

3. Mill, 11:416. For extended discussion of how the Socratic legacy played out in Mill's
life and work, see the essays collected in Demetriou and Antis, *John Stuart Mill: A British
Socrates*.

4. For more discussion of this way of looking at the dialogues, see Fish, *Self-Consuming
Artifacts: The Experience of Seventeenth-Century Literature*.

This pattern repeats in other ways in the study of Socrates. Side effects turn out to be more valuable than primary ones. At first, for example, Ben Franklin regarded the Socratic method as a bag of tricks for winning arguments.

> I found this method the safest for myself and very embarrassing to those against whom I used it; therefore, I took delight in it, practiced it continually, and grew very artful and expert in drawing people, even of superior knowledge, into concessions the consequences of which they did not foresee, entangling them in difficulties out of which they could not extricate themselves, and so obtaining victory that neither myself nor my causes always deserved.[5]

The dialogues warn about this pattern.[6] Eventually Franklin grew in wisdom and abandoned it. But he kept some indirect benefits of his Socratic studies. They were milder in character than the ones described by Mill but evidently served him well.

> I continued this method some few years, but gradually left it, retaining only the habit of expressing myself in terms of modest diffidence.... This habit, I believe, has been of great advantage to me when I have had occasion to inculcate my opinions and persuade men into measures that I have been from time to time engaged in promoting; and, as the chief ends of conversion are to inform or to be informed, to please or to persuade, I wish well-meaning, sensible men would not lessen their power of doing good by a positive, assuming manner, that seldom fails to disgust, tends to create opposition, and to defeat every one of those purposes for which speech was given to us, to wit, giving or receiving information or pleasure.[7]

Franklin's remarks about persuasion have much merit. We will come back to those points in chapter 18. I show these comments from Mill

---

5. Cairns, *Benjamin Franklin's Autobiography*, 17.
6. See Book VII of the *Republic*, especially 539b.
7. Cairns, *Benjamin Franklin's Autobiography*, 17.

and Franklin here, however, to support a general approach to our subject. The time anyone spends in Socratic dialogue with others or oneself is always going to be rewarding but, in the end, is never going to be long. But the Socratic method also means to change one's way of thinking when it isn't directly in use. It produces a mindset that is useful hourly. It's like studying a martial art for a lifetime but never using it in a fight. The benefits can still be felt all the time if it makes the student a different sort of person.

The Socratic ethic. That is how this book means to present the Socratic method. Plato's dialogues show how the elements of the method can work in a specific and pure context: a long one-on-one conversation about a hard ethical question. But you can have a Socratic dialogue that doesn't include all the elements of the method; and more to the point, you can use the elements when you aren't having a dialogue. The search for consistency, for example, is presented in the dialogues as a formal way to structure a conversation. But once that point is understood, the value of consistency seems greater all the way around. You think more about it whether you're asking Socratic questions or not. And indeed, after seeing lots of Socratic questions, and lots of inflated claims punctured by them, you may not need to see every new claim punctured to get the point. You *know* how easily fat claims can be punctured, and many slender ones, too. You think and live accordingly.

The same might be said for drawing careful distinctions, for the value of speaking the truth, or any of the other customs and by-products associated with the method. They produce a Socratic ethic that can become pervasive: a way of being, more than a technique. You don't wait around to be Socratic until you find someone who wants to be grilled or to perform a Socratic grilling. (It might be a long wait.) You're being Socratic when you press skeptically against easy answers, go many questions deep, and are mindful of your ignorance. These aren't modest aims; they change the way one responds to everything. Seeing them acted out in dialogues is a good way to learn about their value, but that value isn't found principally in dialogues that we rarely conduct. It is found in the way we think about problems every day.

The Socratic ethic can also help explain a certain kind of life story. Some people spend years struggling with hard questions and never quite find peace about them. They sometimes look with envy at others who seem to have found satisfactory answers early. Not having found answers of their own feels like unfinished work, a road half traveled, a test not completed. But the Socratic view is the other way around. Dissatisfaction with the answers you give yourself is a symptom of good health. Coming to rest means surrender to a kind of comfort that is always deceptive, no matter how tempting it looks or how deserved it feels. The Socratic way seeks a different kind of comfort—with uncertainty, with fallibility, and with beliefs that are never more than provisional. On this view the good life isn't a result reached by winning the struggle. The struggle is the good life.

4

The Socratic Function

THIS chapter looks at the Socratic method as a way of thinking to yourself rather than as a way to talk with others. It is an important perspective to have in mind from the outset because it makes the method usable by everyone rather than being a tool for specialists. This also seems to have been how Plato thought about the method.

Self-examination. It is a commonplace that Socrates meant to teach us how to think. Yet some people still find it surprising to regard the Socratic method as an activity for one, and most definitions describe it as an activity for two. Socrates tells us, though, that the "philosophical life" consists of "examining myself and others." [1] So self-examination is part of his mission, and the dialogues openly compare what happens in the mind to what happens in a conversation. They are two versions of the same thing.

> SOCRATES. Do you describe thinking as I do?
> THEAETETUS. How is that?
> SOCRATES. As a discussion which the mind has with itself about whatever it is investigating. Now, I'm not making this assertion as an expert: it's just that the image I get of thinking is that the mind is simply carrying on a conversation: it asks itself questions and answers them, saying yes or no. And when it reaches a conclusion (which may take quite a long time or may involve a sudden leap), stops being divided and starts to affirm something consistently, we call this its belief. So I call a belief a statement, but one which is not made aloud to someone else, but in silence to oneself.

Theaetetus 189e–90a

Compare this similar idea Plato offers in the *Sophist* (a dialogue in which Socrates barely appears):

---

1. *Apology* 28e.

STRANGER. Thinking and discourse are the same thing, except that what we call thinking is, precisely, the inward dialogue carried on by the mind with itself without spoken sound.

The process of questioning yourself is illustrated in the *Hippias Major*.[2] There Socrates tells Hippias that he—Socrates—needs help in responding to interrogation by an unnamed questioner. It gradually becomes clear (to the reader, but not to Hippias) that the unnamed questioner is an alter ego within Socrates: a part that questions himself. The internalized questioner is a rough customer, full of ridicule and disrespect.[3] Hippias is surprised and wonders who could be treating Socrates so mercilessly.

HIPPIAS. Who is the man, Socrates? What a boor he is to dare in an august proceeding to speak such vulgar speech that way! SOCRATES. He's like that, Hippias. Not refined. Garbage, really. He cares about nothing but the truth. Still the man must have an answer....
HIPPIAS. Won't you tell me who he is?
SOCRATES. You wouldn't know if I told you his name.
HIPPIAS. I know this, at least: he's an ignoramus.
SOCRATES. Oh, Hippias, he's a real pain.

Socrates goes on to recount his questioner's tactics: if I say this, he'll say that; if I say something else, he'll laugh at me. "He stops at nothing, and he never accepts anything easily" (289e). The types of arguments the questioner uses against Socrates are the same kind that Socrates uses against others. They're just a little more brutal.

To be sure, conversation with others has its great advantages. We will consider some of them below. The point for now is that the dialogues themselves recognize the close similarity between talking to others and thinking about things for yourself. The first can be practice for the second.[4]

---

2. A dialogue that most scholars regard as genuine, though there are occasional dissenters. See, e.g., Kahn, "Beautiful and the Genuine."

3. For discussion, see Woodruff, "Self-Ridicule: Socratic Wisdom."

4. See Nettleship, *Philosophical Lectures and Remains*, 9: "Though philosophy need not

Thinking out loud. As a witness in favor of the Socratic method practiced solo, we might call Plato himself. Why did he write dialogues
instead of just explaining what he thought? We don't know, but there
are many theories. The dialogue might have been meant mostly as
a dramatic device, or as a way for Plato to distance himself from the
claims made by his characters.[5] I'd emphasize a different answer:
dialogues were a way for Plato to talk to himself.[6] He wrote them to
work through his own competing lines of thought by assigning them
to his characters. That is what Mill imagined:

> As regards Plato himself, the probability is that there was a
> period in his life when he was, on merely speculative points, a
> real Seeker, testing every opinion, and bringing prominently
> forward the difficulties which adhere to them all; and that during
> this period many of his principal dialogues were written, from
> points of view extremely various, embodying in each the latest
> trains of thought which had passed through his mind on the
> particular subject.[7]

Treating the characters as sides of Plato's own mind is a helpful
way to think about the value of the dialogues now. It lets them serve
as a model for the same in anyone else: a way to think about things
on your own. Granted, any philosopher's writings—in a treatise or
essay, say—might be viewed as a thought process that the reader is
invited to internalize. But a dialogue is distinctly well suited for the

---

proceed by discussion between two people, its method must always be in principle the same;
a person who really thinks elicits ideas from himself by questioning himself, and tests those
ideas by questioning; he does, in fact, the same sort of thing with himself that Socrates did
with other people." See also Seeskin, *Dialogue and Discovery: A Study in Socratic Method*,
23: "Even when one is engaged in silent reflection, the model Plato looks to is that in which
two people secure agreement before moving ahead."

5. For good discussion of various theories, see Gill, "Dialectic and the Dialogue Form";
Kraut, *Cambridge Companion to Plato*, 26ff; Griswold, *Platonic Writings/Platonic Readings*;
Seeskin, *Dialogue and Discovery: A Study in Socratic Method*.

6. As Sedley put it, the dialogues "can legitimately be read by us as *Plato thinking
aloud.*... They are an externalization of his own thought process." Sedley, *Plato's Cratylus*,
1 (emphasis in original).

7. Mill, "Grote's Plato," 431.

purpose. Questions and answers are the sound of thought happening. An essay or lecture is usually the sound of thought *having* happened, then polished up so the result is clear and the process of getting there is no longer visible. Ordinarily that's good. If you know what you think and want someone else to know it, explaining it straight out makes sense. But if you want to provide a model for getting there—for what to do before you know what you think—a dialogue is ideal because it illustrates the process of figuring that out. In Plato's case the dialogues are studies in how to think about hard things. They show him doing it.[8] And writing out your own little dialogues is, in fact, a good way to sort out your thinking and to develop ability with the Socratic method.

Viewing the dialogues this way can also make the reader less anxious about some moments in them that are hard to reconcile with each other. In one dialogue Socrates seems to argue that the good and the bad amount to pleasure and pain; elsewhere he argues the contrary.[9] He defends a definition of courage in one dialogue that he attacks in another.[10] Some of these conflicts might be ironed out through long analysis, but in other cases they may better be understood to show arguments Plato was having with himself.[11] Socrates in such a case isn't quite a mouthpiece for Plato, who would then be caught in an inconsistency. Socrates is just a personification of the fearless reasoner. He dissects whatever you put in front of him, even if it's what he said yesterday.

---

8. Thus Paul Woodruff's suggestion: "Socrates's mission is to set an example of self-questioning that ordinary Athenians can apply to themselves." Woodruff, "Socrates's Mission," 187. And to Woodruff's way of looking at Socrates, compare Sedley's way of looking at Plato: "When we think, what we are doing is precisely to ask and answer questions internally, and our judgements are the outcome of that same process. Hence it seems that what Plato dramatizes as external conversations can be internalized by us, the readers, as setting the model for our own processes of philosophical reasoning.... [T]he inter-personal discussion portrayed in the dialogues is not the only mode in which such discussion can occur: internal discussion is another, and perhaps even the more fundamental mode." Sedley, *Plato's* Cratylus, 1–2.

9. Compare *Protagoras* 351b–358d and *Gorgias* 492d–500d.

10. Compare *Protagoras* 360cd and the discussion starting at *Laches* 194d.

11. For discussion of this general idea, see Bett, "Socratic Ignorance," 229.

Roles. The "thinking aloud" way of looking at Plato's dialogues has another implication. The characters in the dialogue are all saying things that the author is thinking, if only for the sake of satisfying himself that they're wrong. A dialogue might therefore be regarded like a dream in which every character is an aspect of the self.[12] This perspective gives us a new way to think about whether Socrates is a good example to follow. Some readers are repelled by him. One scholar describes him as sometimes having a "gratuitously hostile edge." [13] Others convict him of "frigidity," of a lack of capacity for love, or of related forms of inhumanity.[14] Who would want to resemble such a person? But that's the wrong question on the view we're considering here, in which the characters in a dialogue are aspects of the self. You wouldn't want to *be* the Socrates we find in Plato's dialogues. But you should want to *have* such a Socrates.

Another way to look at it: psychologists speak of the executive function—the cognitive ability to make plans, pursue goals, and show self-control. Plato teaches the value of a well-developed *Socratic* function: a capacity to engage in skeptical questioning of yourself. That function is underdeveloped in most of us. Maybe it can also be overdeveloped, but it isn't the voice of a debilitating skepticism; it's a healthy variety. It helps with the resistance of foolishness, cowardice, partisanship, hypocrisy, rage, vanity, and other demons. From a Socratic standpoint those are varieties of ignorance and weakness of understanding (as we will see in chapter 14). The internalized Socrates tames them.[15]

---

12. Paul Friedlander said: "As Goethe is in Tasso and Antonio, so Plato is not only in Socrates—or in the disciples Charmides, Theaetetus, Alcibiades—but also, to a certain degree and manner, in the opponents of Socrates.... If there had not been something of Callicles—the 'Strong Man'—in himself, he would hardly have been able to portray the former with such overwhelming power." Friedlander, *Plato*, 1:167.

13. Brennan, "Socrates and Epictetus," 295.

14. Vlastos, *Philosophy of Socrates*, 16–17; Nussbaum, "Chill of Virtue," 39; Nehamas, "What Did Socrates Teach," 281; Brennan, "Socrates and Epictetus," 292–93.

15. Again Friedlander put it well: "Plato, endowed with overabundant powers, probably had more to conquer within his nature than is generally assumed. But he also had Socrates within him, and the decisive struggles and victories that he made public were within himself." Friedlander, *Plato*, 168.

In keeping with the criticisms of Socrates noted a moment ago, however, the Socratic function does have a more vicious side. It can be disagreeable in the ways sometimes shown by the literary Socrates: relentless, taunting, sarcastic. Those traits are insufferable to other people. There is just one party at whom they can be directed with impunity and in good conscience: oneself. Or more precisely they can be used on the pompous and ethically weak parts of the self that deserve the full measure of Socratic invective and may not respond to anything less. That is why the most abrasive questioner shown in the dialogues is the alter ego that Socrates unleashes on himself in the *Hippias Major*.

The way of the gadfly. The Socratic function has a rightful role in the mind that might look like the role of Plato's Socrates in Athens: a truth-teller, a questioner of convention, an irritant. Meanwhile there were things Socrates could not do and roles he wasn't able to play, and he knew it. Athens would not have survived if everyone were like Socrates, and the self can't survive on those terms, either. But a city needs someone like him even if it also needs other types. The place of the Socratic function in the self is comparably uneasy. It is a friend and it is disruptive. It exposes the truth and creates discomfort. In many personalities it ends up being served the hemlock.

Seeing Socrates this way—as an aspect of the mind, or self—provides a way to think about some passages where he describes his place in the world. The relationship between Socrates and the state can sometimes be viewed as similar to (or a stand-in for) the relationship between the Socratic function and the self.

Apology
30e–31a

If you kill me you will not easily find a successor to me, who, if I may use such a ludicrous figure of speech, am a sort of gadfly, given to the state by God; and the state is a great and noble steed who is tardy in his motions owing to his very size, and requires to be stirred into life. I am that gadfly which God has attached to the state, and all day long and in all places am always fastening upon you, arousing and persuading and reproaching you....

I am certain, O men of Athens, that if I had engaged in politics, *Apology*
31de
I should have perished long ago, and done no good either to
you or to myself. And do not be offended at my telling you the
truth: for the truth is, that no man who goes to war with you or
any other multitude, honestly striving against the many lawless
and unrighteous deeds which are done in a state, will save his
life; he who will fight for the right, if he would live even for a
brief space, must have a private station and not a public one.

Interpreting those passages as describing an internal situation might
seem extravagant if Plato were not also the author, in the *Republic*, of
such a long and famous comparison of the city and the soul.[16] Treating
the outer state as a metaphor for the inner one isn't a strange possibility for him or his readers. I think the resonance of the metaphor,
even if half-conscious, helps explain why the story of Socrates has
captured the imagination of so many for so long. The mind loves a
metaphor for itself. (We may be excused for sometimes suspecting
that it loves *only* this.) The story of Socrates is the story of anyone's
own conflicted relationship with rationality and with higher and
lower inclinations. We all know what it is to live among Athenians,
what it's like to be shocked by their ignorance and presumption, and
what it is to be resented for exposing these things to them. We know
it without talking to anyone else.

Primary vs. secondary. Earlier we saw Socrates say that he was engaged
in "examining myself and others." Is one of those activities primary
and the other second best? We've seen examples of Socrates treating self-examination as natural. But another tradition of scholarship
holds that conversation with others is the more primary philosophical
activity. The dialogues leave enough evidence each way to make
either reading reasonable.[17]

---

16. For the principal exposition of the comparison, see *Republic* 368c–369a, 425c–442c,
543c–578b. For discussion, see Blössner, "City-Soul Analogy."

17. See, e.g., *Protagoras* 347e–348a; Robinson, *Plato's Earlier Dialectic*, 77; Fink, *Development of Dialectic from Plato to Aristotle*, 2. For those interested in chasing down the
textual evidence both ways, A. G. Long, *Conversation and Self-Sufficiency in Plato*, is a fine
book devoted entirely to this issue.

So instead of parsing the interpretive problem any further, look at it from the standpoint of utility. To persuade anyone of anything by boxing them in with questions is very rare. Indeed, chances to engage in live Socratic dialogue at all are rare. One reason is that Socrates so often has compliant partners. They have an exaggerated willingness to go along with his arguments.[18] It's like watching a magician do miracles with stooges planted in the audience. You can't be surprised when real life is less cooperative. Most ordinary people don't like Socratic questioning; challenging your partners to constantly define their terms will leave you without partners soon enough. In the end, real life didn't cooperate with Socrates, either, inasmuch as he got himself killed.

But chances to internalize the Socratic method, and to engage in Socratic examination of your own thinking, are routine and safer. It becomes something you do all the time in interpreting the world and forming your reactions to it. Using the Socratic method yourself isn't *easier* than using it in conversation. In fact it's a good deal harder. The defects in someone else's views are no trouble to spot. Seeing them in your own is a much tougher challenge. It is like exercise. It's easier with a trainer, but possible to do well without one. And Socratic questioning is like physical exercise in an additional sense: it's good for you, but doesn't feel good when you're doing it; in fact it's often good for you just to the extent that it's uncomfortable. That is why nothing is more common than intellectual obesity.

---

18. "Tutors who have attempted to follow Socratic method will have been made aware of the importance of the fact that Plato was able to script the answers as well as the questions." Flew, *Dictionary of Philosophy*, s.v. "Socratic method."

5

Question and Answer

A PHILOSOPHY is often thought to mean a system of ideas that provides answers to fundamental questions. Socratic philosophy is different. It is a commitment to a process rather than to a result. Socrates does reach some conclusions, but they're all provisional (see chapter 14). Mostly he goes back and forth in dialogues that make progress but never come to rest on answers. The *question* is the unit of Socratic practice, and the currency of it; that is the first point to grasp about our subject. The Socratic method departs from other styles of teaching and thought, first, in this simple way: the practitioner does not lecture, does not explain, does not scold, and does not tell. The practitioner asks. Much of this book talks about what the questions do, how they are formed, and where they leave you. But first this chapter considers questions as such.

Questions vs. answers. We've seen some possible reasons why Plato wrote dialogues. We can also ask why he ended them without answers. He could, after the more modern fashion, have written something like a preface in which he explained this. The preface would have eliminated the need for thousands of pages of scholarship speculating about why he did what he did. This confirms his wisdom in *not* writing a preface, and also provides a clue to his method in general. Plato and his Socrates like questions and the state of mind they produce.

The posture of Plato as an author is of a piece with the posture of Socrates as a character. Plato never comes out and says what he thinks. He hides behind his characters and lets the reader wonder. He creates a hero who likewise states no answers but provokes people to think harder and reconsider what they believe and how they live. The implied point: we're at our keenest when we work on a question, not after it's answered. On every level the dialogues help us into that state and hold us there. Assimilating the lessons that the dialogues teach means keeping ourselves in that state when we aren't reading them. The practitioner of the Socratic method thinks in questions, is at home with uncertainty, and knows how to value a search that doesn't end.

Chapters 2 and 4 suggested that the Socratic method corrects bad habits of the mind left to itself. The emphasis on questions can be considered an example. In this case the bad habit is the love of holding opinions. It feels good to know what you think. When people turn to philosophy they usually want more of that pleasure—if not more of what they already think, then something else to be sure about. Socrates won't cooperate, which seems frustrating. Where's *his* philosophy? But in his view our most urgent problem is that we're certain when we shouldn't be and think we know what we don't. That is why the philosophy of Socrates mostly isn't a set of beliefs. It's an activity. The Socratic method doesn't replace your current opinions with better ones. It changes your relationship to your opinions. It replaces the love of holding them with the love of testing them.

Style of thought. Let's consider a few ways to think about what a question *is*—how it works, that is, as an instrument of thought. A question, when passed from one person to another, is generally a request that something be said or done. Sometimes questions are easy and the demands they make are mild. But Socratic questions aren't like that. They push. Asking and answering them is like operating a pump. They take work. They can reveal latent beliefs that are surprising to their holders. They can enlarge understanding far beyond the point where it started. A steady drip of questions can fill a glass or carve out a canyon; it's possible to see almost any edifice of thought as the result of many such questions asked and answered, and as a monument to the gradual power of that process, often within one person. The process of asking and answering can be a creative force as well as a force for refutation and refinement.

Questions, in short, are *productive* in ways that declarations aren't. But most thinking consists of opinions and reactions, worries and hopes, satisfactions and regrets, all expressed half-verbally but more or less declaratively. The Socratic approach means fewer declarations and more questions, and especially questions about things presupposed in those other kinds of thoughts. When you think and talk in declarations, you aren't learning anything. When you think and talk in questions, you might be. Someone says something you hate; instead of saying you hate it, you ask questions. What does it mean? Is it consistent? What's a good comparison? You say something *they* hate. Instead of defending it, you ask questions. (What did *you* mean by it?) You give up some of the pleasures of holding strong opinions, and in return the ones you do hold are better founded.

A question puts pressure on whoever receives it. If you ask questions of yourself, you are the recipient of the pressure. That's good. Stating an opinion is roughly the opposite. It releases pressure. Pressure is uncomfortable, so most people think and talk in opinions. But the unpressured mind tends toward laxity and corruption. A true Socratic dialogue is an exercise in which the pressure is intense: a full-court press. But the pressure can be kept healthier, even if less intense, anytime. Some people have dangerously low blood pressure; in others the Socratic pressure is too low. It can be raised to a better level by thinking more in questions.

Every time you ask and answer good questions, your understanding gets a bit deeper. You better understand the other side and the weaknesses on your side. You see more complexity. To the extent that you're Socratic in outlook, you like all this. And conversely you aren't very interested in hearing quick reactions from others—reactions, at least, to anything that matters—because those opinions are worth so little. They are one ply deep. You would rather read a decent debate or wait to hear from someone whose words reflect a debate-like process of thought. This can be a hard taste to satisfy. It makes most public commentators insufferable. They operate under no Socratic pressure, internal or external. It's like driving on an interstate highway and wanting anything other than fast food. You have to hold out a long time, or go off the beaten path, or make it yourself.

Looking at the Socratic method in these ways helps to keep it simple and unexotic. Whatever else the method means, it boils down to asking more questions and improving their quality.[1]

Pacing. The Socratic method is unhurried. The questions make progress by small degrees. Each question takes a small bite out of an issue. The reader might wonder whether attention spans have changed, or whether Plato knew how annoying a string of small questions can seem. But we know that he knew it, because he worked that complaint into the dialogues.

Gorgias
497bc

CALLICLES. All these futile little questions are typical of the way Socrates tries to prove people wrong, Gorgias.

GORGIAS. Why should that matter to you? In any case, it's not up to you to assess their value like that, Callicles. Just let Socrates test your views any way he wants.

CALLICLES. Go on, then. If that's what Gorgias wants, ask your lowly little questions.

So the small questions are deliberate. They tell us how Socrates thinks the truth is best approached. You do best with careful steps. Perhaps the reader wants to hurry up and get to the point. That's natural once the point is known to be coming on the next page. But that isn't how actual thought works. You aren't sure where it's going. You climb the face of the mountain with your fingers a few inches at a time. That is how Socrates does it. He takes a single point, often a mundane example, and understands it completely. Then another. There is a healthy contrast between the high stakes of a dialogue and the small questions used to carry it out.

Small questions have other advantages. They make Socratic dialogues easier to follow and build. This especially helps because the method is challenging in some other ways that can't be made easy. Asking questions takes creativity; you have to be able to think of hypothetical cases that will put pressure on what someone else has said, or on what you've said. If you're a reader or listener, this takes concentration. Sometimes it's hard to tell if a piece of logic is sound

---

1. For further discussion of Plato's attachment to the question-and-answer format, see Robinson, *Plato's Earlier Dialectic*, 65–67.

the first time you see it. And the topic of a dialogue may be large and complex. But at least the questions used to carry out the dialogue aren't large and complex. They break the reasoning down into clear steps. If something goes wrong, this makes it easier to figure out where. And from all this we can draw a more general lesson about how to discuss difficult things. If you're going to make conceptual demands, try not to also make rhetorical demands. The harder the question, the more important it is to be clear and deliberate when you're talking about it.

Small questions also are good because they slow everything down. This matters in part just because the truth tends to be complicated. Complexity can't be seen in a hurry. Really understanding an argument—why someone would think this or that, and whether it holds up—is like taking apart a machine and putting it back together. You have to keep track of all the little screws. And the Socratic method also takes intellectual empathy. You have to look at a problem the way someone else does. You might think you "get it" right away, or that there's nothing much to get. But that's probably wrong; it takes a while to actually understand what someone else means. Asking a lot of small questions is a useful habit, or discipline, for that purpose. You ask and then listen, without being in a rush to get to the bottom line.

The same principle applies when you aren't listening to someone else but are just learning about an idea—an idea from Socrates or from anywhere else. It might only take a short time to understand it well enough to repeat it back. But slowing down in the Socratic way means having a certain sense of what it is to actually comprehend something. Some people (perhaps all of us sometimes) approach ideas like tourists in a museum who think they have seen all the art it contains because they have laid eyes on all the paintings. But you have to visit with a good painting at length, and more than once, and above all without hurrying, to really see what it is and what it means. Socrates looks at an idea in the way that a connoisseur looks at paintings, and he asks the listener or reader to do the same.

The slow pacing of Socratic questions has a further attraction. Socrates tells us that he's interested in the care of the psyche—his own, and that of his partner in dialogue, and (inevitably, though it is not said) the reader's. The care might mean operating the mind at a certain speed. The pacing of the dialogues is an implied argument about this—that is, about the optimal pace of speech and thought. A different kind of pace creates a different kind of person. Socrates displays a sense of equanimity on all occasions, and the slow rhythm of his approach is part of that. He's never in a rush.

Cross-examination. There is another moving part when you ask Socratic questions: how open-ended they are. Sometimes Socrates asks questions that might be answered in a hundred ways. He wants to know what his partner thinks, so their exchange starts out easy. Then his partner settles on a claim, its edges get clarified, and Socrates bears down on it. The questions are no longer open-ended. They are often of the yes-or-no variety: Would you admit X? Can we agree on Y? The dialogue becomes, in effect, a cross-examination. The legal scholar John Wigmore called cross-examination "the greatest legal engine ever invented for the discovery of truth." [2] Socrates evidently thought the same was true in philosophy. Why?

Consider the rules under which a cross-examination is done. The rules in court and in a Socratic dialogue are similar in many ways. First, all questions have to be answered as long as they aren't out of order. You can't say "I'd rather not say." Second, the witness in court is supposed to tell the truth, and that is a rule in Socratic inquiry, too: say what you think. (See chapter 10.) Third, the interrogator can ask leading questions—in other words, questions that imply their answers: "Isn't it true that … ? Wouldn't you agree that … ?" Leading questions leave no room for answers that evade. They force the witness to confront the point. Cross-examination thus allows witnesses to be probed, their weaknesses shown, their secrets found out. These properties make it a superb device for testing the truth and beliefs of a witness or of anyone else.

Leading questions have their downside. The asker does all the thinking; the witness just confirms or denies. Sometimes that isn't

---

2. Wigmore, *Evidence in Trials at Common Law,* § 1367.

what you want. You want to find out what the witness thinks. In that case you use direct examination rather than cross-examination. No leading questions are allowed; you have to let the witness talk freely and answer the question in whatever way seems best. Cross-examination has its place *after* those answers are on the table. That's how Socrates does it: he takes his time and asks easy questions until he understands exactly what is being said. Then comes the cross.

Leading questions, when used in a conversation, can have the additional problem of putting your partner on the defensive. Most people don't enjoy getting cross-examined. Being pushed to say X makes anyone not want to say X or to otherwise cooperate with whoever is doing the pushing. So leading questions have to be couched in a great deal of good nature on both sides to be tolerable. Or they have to be phrased in a manner skillful and gentle enough to hide their character—a manner that bears no resemblance to the courtroom. Sometimes Socrates takes that sort of trouble and sometimes he doesn't. The importance of it depends on whether you're using the method to move someone else or to challenge yourself.

The adversarial system. Here's another way to look at the point just made. Cross-examination in court generally happens when questioning a witness called by the other side. The lawyer and the witness have an adversarial relationship. Adversarial behavior is nothing unusual and doesn't require a literary role model. And it typically isn't constructive when you're working with a partner. But adversarial *thinking*—that is, an adversarial approach within your *own* thinking—isn't usual at all and is very constructive. Most of us interpret the world to confirm what we already think about it and what we wish were true. Cognition probably evolved to convince ourselves, and others, that whatever helps us is for the best. Or maybe there are other reasons for motivated reasoning, confirmation bias, and our countless other forms of chronic misjudgment; in any event, searching them out is not a favorite activity of the mind left to itself.

Socratic questioning is a remedy. It's needed for the sake of good government. There has to be an opposition party within the self—

something that argues against what you feel that you know. The internalized Socrates amounts to an honorable adversary. That much is a reiteration of chapter 4. The point for *this* chapter is the method by which that adversary proceeds. It isn't by sabotage or self-loathing. It is by inquiry, however rough. In the self as in a parliament, there has to be question time.

Socrates particularly likes to question beliefs that his discussion partners take for granted. This shows another good reason to want an adversary within your thinking. It breaks your sense of identification with the views you hold. We all have false beliefs about the world or ourselves—views that wouldn't withstand Socratic scrutiny and don't usually get it. They're half-conscious ideas that we take for granted and that are kept out of view. Socratic questioning takes off the camouflage. A belief that had seemed too obvious or sacred to get grilled is put on the stand. For as long as the questioning lasts, the belief isn't so much a part of you. It had been talking through you; now you are talking to it. Adversarial thinking separates us from our prejudices and expectations.

Plato's later dialectic. Plato's early dialogues use the Socratic method but don't discuss it. His later ones use it less but discuss it more. By then Plato's other ideas seem to have changed, so it's hard to know whether all of his late comments about method apply to what Socrates was doing in the dialogues earlier. But we should at least glimpse what Plato said about the method in his later work, because it shows the place of honor he always gave to the process of question and answer.

Plato treats "dialectic" as having different meanings at different moments in his writings.[3] Most generally, though, it means pursuing the truth by question and answer. Plato's later Socrates describes it as the road to knowledge and to discovery.

Cratylus   SOCRATES. And who will be best able to direct the legislator in
390be   his work, and will know whether the work is well done, in this
    or any other country? Will not the user be the man?

---

3. See Robinson, *Plato's Earlier Dialectic*, ch. 6, and especially 69–70; Kahn, *Plato and the Socratic Dialogue*, ch. 10.

HERMOGENES. Yes.

SOCRATES. And this is he who knows how to ask questions?

HERMOGENES. Yes.

SOCRATES. And how to answer them?

HERMOGENES. Yes.

SOCRATES And him who knows how to ask and answer you would call a dialectician?

HERMOGENES. Yes; that would be his name.

In the *Republic*, Socrates describes an ideal and just society ruled by philosophers. Their most important quality would be a talent for asking and answering questions. That art is said to be the way to the truth not only about moral philosophy but all else of importance. Here Socrates questions Glaucon:

> Surely you would not have the children of your ideal State, whom you are nurturing and educating—if the ideal ever becomes a reality—you would not allow the future rulers to be like posts, having no reason in them, and yet to be set in authority over the highest matters?
>
> *Republic*
> 534de
>
> Certainly not.
>
> Then you will make a law that they shall have such an education as will enable them to attain the greatest skill in asking and answering questions?
>
> Yes, he said, you and I together will make it.
>
> Dialectic, then, as you will agree, is the coping-stone of the sciences, and is set over them; no other science can be placed higher—the nature of knowledge can no further go?
>
> I agree, he said.

Plato treats dialectic not just as a method but as a system of philosophy in which the essences of things are found through investigation by question and answer.[4] We aren't talking in this book about philosopher-kings, the truths they perceive, or other late innovations

---

4. See discussion in Janssens, "Concept of Dialectic in the Ancient World," 175–76; Robinson, *Plato's Earlier Dialectic*, 71–75.

of Plato. But those discussions still show us what a lifelong source of fascination the process of question and answer was for Plato. He probably interpreted its use differently as he got older, but it was central to his vision at all times.

Side effects. Socratic questioning gives you a more intelligent understanding of a subject. It makes you reach conclusions more slowly and puts a brake on many kinds of foolishness. But in return you give up the satisfaction of easily knowing what you think and usually feeling certain that you are right. This is the Socratic trade, and it involves a risk. Instead of being sure of too much, you might be sure of too little. In deciding which error is better to risk, you might reflect on which erroneous parties tend to cause more harm or do more good: those who claim to have all the answers or those who don't make that claim. Perhaps you can think of examples either way. Historically speaking, however, I will venture that the more skeptical ones tend to come off well in that accounting.

The Socratic trade seems most worrisome when it's not made symmetrically by both sides to a dispute. We all wish the trade were made more often—by our adversaries. But people naturally fear that if they ask hard questions and their enemies don't, the enemies will always win. It looks like unilateral disarmament. Thoughtful Socratic types will be overrun by Nazi types who show no doubts and have hordes of followers. We will have Yeats's result: "the best lack all conviction, while the worst/Are full of passionate intensity." If you aren't absolutely sure about things, what are you fighting for when your enemies come along?

You're probably fighting for whatever you've always fought for. But you're doing it with more knowledge of the complexity of the issue and a better understanding of the other side. The Socratic sort is not disabled by that knowledge, and is embarrassed to suppose that the will to fight depends on stupidity, on oversimplifying things, and on black hats for the villains. In fact you are always in combat against exactly those tendencies, in addition to whatever other stakes may lie in the foreground. You are fighting for love of the truth, even if you can't claim a monopoly on it. If these causes sound too bloodless—as if they were things no one would go to war or die for—we can be glad that we don't have just the words of Socrates. We have his example.

6

The Elenchus

THE *elenchus* is the name of a procedure that Socrates uses often. (It's pronounced eh-*lenk*-us; the adjective is *elenctic*.) Socrates doesn't use the term "elenchus" to describe his approach, but he sometimes uses variants on the word. Its primary meaning is "search," and its etymology also includes notions of testing, of refutation, and of shaming and ridicule. The word is sometimes used by others to refer to refutation in general, with the *Socratic* elenchus being one variety. Others have supposed that the use of the elenchus *is* the Socratic method. I think that's a mistake, but it suggests how central the elenchus is in the dialogues.

The elenchus, despite its unfamiliar name, isn't an arcane idea. It's a useful, familiar, but underused technique for arguing about hard topics. This chapter explains how it works in the dialogues. Chapters 17 and 18 show how to create an elenchus practically.

Examples. The Socratic elenchus can be defined in various ways, and some scholars think the device takes too many forms to be defined at all. But here's what the term is most commonly said to mean: You make a claim. Socrates gets you to agree to some other proposition. Then he shows, sometimes surprisingly, that the new point to which you've agreed is inconsistent with what you said before. In short, he causes you to contradict yourself.

The elenchus is often a subtle device—or rather its distinctiveness is subtle. You can easily read an elenchus without realizing it. Here is a simple case drawn from the dialogue we saw in skeletal form in chapter 3. Socrates, you will recall, has asked Laches what courage is.

Laches
192bd

LACHES. I think courage is a sort of mental persistence. That's what I'd say, if I had to identify the nature of courage in all situations.

SOCRATES. Well, that's exactly what we have to do, if we're to

answer the question we asked ourselves. Now, I'll tell you what
I think: I don't think you take every instance of persistence to
be courage. My reason for saying this is that I'm almost sure,
Laches, that you count courage as something rather admirable.

LACHES. Yes....

SOCRATES But what about unintelligent persistence? Isn't that,
on the contrary, dangerous and harmful?

LACHES. Yes.

SOCRATES. Well, if anything is harmful and dangerous, is it
admirable, would you say?

LACHES. No, that wouldn't be a defensible position, Socrates.

SOCRATES. So you wouldn't agree that *this* kind of persistence
was courage, since it isn't admirable, but courage is an admirable
thing.

LACHES. That's right.

Trace the elenchus. Laches says that courage is persistence. (That's
claim 1.) Then Socrates gets him to agree to something else (claim
2): courage is admirable, right? Once Laches agrees to that, his
definition is sunk; claim 1 and claim 2 are inconsistent, though it
will take a moment for him to realize it. Socrates gets him to agree
that persistence is sometimes foolish, which means it isn't admirable,
which means it isn't courage. Notice that Socrates uses questions to
get the agreement of his partner at every step. Didn't you say this,
and don't you also think that—and don't they conflict? This matters
because it means, when the final result arrives, that Laches has contradicted himself rather than being contradicted by Socrates. He has
full ownership of the problem.

When Socrates finds an inconsistency, it means that at least one
thing you've said has to go or be modified. But it might not be clear
which one. In the example above, Laches *could* say "hmm—maybe
courage isn't always admirable after all." But that happens rarely.[1]
This can be a fair source of frustration with the dialogues. Somebody
makes claim X, then Socrates shows it isn't consistent with concession

---

1. See, e.g., *Charmides* 164c; *Gorgias* 482de.

Y that was made afterwards. His partner usually abandons the claim rather than reconsidering the concession. Maybe it should more often be the other way around. There is no reason in principle why it can't be. But Socrates tries to make concession Y a more firmly felt point than the claim in the foreground.

Socrates uses the elenchus in all the earlier dialogues. In the *Gorgias*, for example, Callicles says that the good life is the one with the most pleasure in it. Socrates doesn't make a frontal attack on the claim. He asks Callicles if a catamite lives a good life if his appetites are satisfied.[2] (By a "catamite" he probably means a submissive homosexual man or a male prostitute—someone very shameful in Greek culture.)[3] Callicles can't bring himself to say yes, but he also doesn't say no. He tries to change the subject. So then Socrates guides Callicles into another contradiction that is less loaded. He asks whether cowards and fools are bad sorts of people. Callicles says yes. Now Socrates has the admission that he wants, so he completes the elenchus: do cowards and fools have as much pleasure as people who are brave and wise? (Yes.) Aha: so bad people have as much good associated with them (because they have as much pleasure) as good people do. This shows that the good and pleasurable aren't the same. Callicles has to let go of that position in favor of a modified one: the pleasurable is the good, but some pleasures are better than others. And so it goes from there.

Shame. Whether that last argument from Socrates is logically sound has been much debated.[4] Regardless, notice that those arguments Socrates made wouldn't necessarily prove anything to someone other than Callicles. Callicles *could* have said that he has no problem with catamites or with cowards. But those options weren't available to him; he was trapped either by his beliefs or by fear of shame. The proof

---

2. *Gorgias* 494e.

3. For exploration see Kahn, "Drama and Dialectic in Plato's *Gorgias*," 3:80.

4. The argument contains a difficulty that Callicles does not notice: Socrates slides between using "good" to describe people and experiences. The difficulty may or may not have been surmountable. For discussion, see Kahn, "Drama and Dialectic in Plato's Gorgias," 3:82; Santas, *Socrates*, 270–78.

Socrates uses to defeat Callicles is only as strong as those constraints. If Socrates were working with a Callicles in a different time and place, he might have needed different examples to make the elenchus work.

Notice that shame can figure into Socratic questioning in two ways.[5] Sometimes it forces one of Socrates' partners into a concession that would be too embarrassing to deny.[6] The embarrassment might arise from opinions of others. Occasions for that kind of shame vary with the time and place, and whether shame of this sort is rational depends on whether the community is rational.[7] This is a point to remember when challenging your own consistency or anyone else's. Fear of what other people will say and think, as such, has no rightful place in moral reasoning so far as Socrates is concerned. To the contrary, it is a threat to the project of honest inquiry and has to be firmly kept away from the process. But if you think those other people are *right*, that's different. Then your real shame is in front of yourself. The views of others just remind you of it.

Shame can also enter Socratic questioning as a reaction to your own inconsistency.[8] This kind of shame doesn't depend on time and place or whether the community is rational. It's the discomfort of realizing that you don't know what you're talking about or that you were sure when you shouldn't have been. It's a homemade form of shame, strictly between you and yourself, so it can be felt identically by people thousands of years apart in radically different situations. It's a sign that you are making progress.

Different purposes. An elenchus can have different consequences for those questioned in a dialogue. First, it may show that they don't believe what they say they believe; it may show that they don't know what they think they know. Their claims don't hold up. These varieties of elenchus have been called "purgative" because they purge

---

5. On the role of shame in elenctic argument, see Woodruff, "Socrates and the Irrational," 132–35 and 143–46; Kahn, *Plato and the Socratic Dialogue*, 134ff.

6. See Kahn, "Vlastos's Socrates," 1:173.

7. See Woodruff, "Socrates and the Irrational," 133, for development of this point.

8. Woodruff, 144–45.

conceits of knowledge from their holders. Those conceits are replaced with more accurate feelings of ignorance.[9]

Skeptics like the purgative elenchus because they don't want to prove anything. They want to get rid of people's false feelings of certainty. (More on this in chapter 16.) That sometimes looks like what Socrates is doing, too, and it describes his effect on some readers. But his aim can also be viewed a bit differently. He isn't just trying to leave his partners feeling uncertain. He wants them to feel refuted, which isn't exactly the same. He may also want to suggest the truth of other claims by implication.[10]

That last point leads to a second use of the elenchus: to fend off *challenges* to a claim of truth. Socrates says that he thinks X is true, and then shows that anyone who denies X ends up contradicting himself. This has been called a "defensive" elenchus because it's used to support a claim by showing how hard it is to refute, not to prove someone else's ignorance.[11] Put more plainly, an elenchus can support a claim by showing how hard it is to say otherwise. Again the *Gorgias* provides an example. Socrates uses an elenchus to show that doing wrong is worse than suffering it. He doesn't quite claim to *know* that this is true, but he says that nobody has managed to argue otherwise with success.

Gorgias
509a

All I'm saying is what I always say: I myself don't know the facts of these matters, but I've never met anyone, including the people here today, who could disagree with what I'm saying and still avoid making himself ridiculous.

So the Socratic method isn't just a way to show that big claims made by others (or yourself) always tend to fall apart in the end, though that is one tendency of it. The method can be a way to defend an idea. Or the elenchus can be used to test an interpretation of something—the words of an oracle then, or a text now. Deny it and watch what happens.

---

9. Woodruff, "Skeptical Side of Plato's Method," 26–28.
10. See Woodruff, "Expert Knowledge in the *Apology* and *Laches*," 107.
11. Woodruff, "Skeptical Side of Plato's Method," 26, 28–29.

Consistency and truth. The elenchus is mostly a device for refuting claims. At first this might sound unexciting. Who wants to spend all their time falsifying things? Isn't it better to build than to tear down? But on a Socratic view those are two sides of the same coin. Mill said it best:

> It is the fashion of the present time to disparage negative logic—that which points out weaknesses in theory or errors in practice, without establishing positive truths. Such negative criticism would indeed be poor enough as an ultimate result; but as a means to attaining any positive knowledge or conviction worthy the name, it cannot be valued too highly; and until people are again systematically trained to it, there will be few great thinkers, and a low general average of intellect, in any but the mathematical and physical departments of speculation. On any other subject no one's opinions deserve the name of knowledge, except so far as he has either had forced upon him by others, or gone through of himself, the same mental process which would have been required of him in carrying on an active controversy with opponents.[12]

That is a strong and venerable view of the Socratic method. It is the art of falsification. Without mastery of this, you can't expect to get close to the truth.

At the same time, however, Socrates does seem to hold some positive beliefs of his own. Chapter 14 will discuss them. There is a lively debate about where those beliefs come from, and about whether his use of the elenchus might produce them. Some readers say no: any affirmative beliefs have to come from somewhere else, because all an elenchus ever shows is that his partners are being inconsistent.[13] This might prove that they don't know or believe what they thought they did, but it doesn't show which of their beliefs is right (they might both be wrong). In short, all Socrates does is refute others, and from this he (and we) can conclude nothing affirmative. But others—most

---

12. *On Liberty*, in Robson, *Collected Works of John Stuart Mill*, 18:252.
13. See Grote, *Plato and the Other Companions of Sokrates*, 292.

prominently Vlastos—have a different idea. They think that Socrates gathers knowledge *from* his use of the elenchus.[14] How?

First, it's true that Socrates sometimes talks as though the elenchus proves the truth of the belief that is left standing after a contradiction is shown and resolved. Return to his claim noted a moment ago—that doing wrong to someone else (and getting away with it) is worse than having a wrong done to yourself. His partner, Polus, disagrees with this, but Polus's positions are shown to be undercut by other admissions he makes—a classic elenchus. Then we have this exchange:

Gorgias
479e

> SOCRATES. I was claiming that Archelaus or anyone else who does wrong without paying the penalty is likely to be far worse off than others; that doing wrong always makes people more miserable than suffering wrong does; and that evading punishment always makes people more miserable than paying the penalty does. Wasn't that what I was saying?
>
> POLUS. Yes.
>
> SOCRATES. And have I been proved right?
>
> POLUS. Apparently.

This should be startling if you understand what an elenchus does and doesn't do. Socrates has shown that when Polus pushes back, he contradicts himself. But how does this show that Socrates is right? First of all, he's only shown that Polus believes two things that conflict; he hasn't shown which one has to yield. But assume Polus agrees that his original view has to go. This still doesn't seem to establish anything. If your argument against my view is shown to be wrong, my view isn't thereby proven. Or so it would seem.

Some scholars treat that claim from the *Gorgias* as an anomaly.[15] Usually Socrates refutes what others say and doesn't claim to have proven anything. But suppose we insist on accounting for that passage. Here is the solution from Vlastos: on a Socratic view every-

---

14. Vlastos, *Socratic Studies*, 17–29. For a review of the many responses to Vlastos's theory, see Wolfsdorf, "Socratic Philosophizing."

15. See, e.g., Kraut, "Comments on Gregory Vlastos, 'The Socratic Elenchus,'" and Benson, *Socratic Wisdom*, 57–95, which reviews a great many examples of the elenchus and rarely, if ever, finds a clear claim by Socrates that it has led him to an affirmative conclusion.

one has *some* true beliefs. This might be because we are born with them (as Socrates suggests in the *Meno*). Or maybe everyone has a conscience with at least moments of accuracy.[16] In any event, false beliefs you hold, if traced out far enough, will come into conflict with some of those true ones. If you find a belief that doesn't conflict with any others you hold, the lack of conflict—that consistency—is some evidence that the belief is true. It's a survivor.

Socrates' personal project, on this theory, is to accumulate truths. His collection slowly grows as he finds more ideas that are all consistent. As his mass of consistent claims becomes larger, it gets easier for him to detect falsehoods and expel them. Then someone like Polus comes along and takes a contrary position, and it's shown to fail because it is inconsistent with other things that Polus thinks and that Socrates probably thinks. Another challenger to Socrates' set of beliefs has failed to lay a glove on them. Their probability of being right has gone up a little more. As a proposition holds up under different conditions, confidence in it rises. The elenchus thus becomes a device for finding truth, not just refuting what others say. It can produce cumulative consistency.

Cumulative consistency is more than reassuring. It leads to enlargement of your knowledge and confidence in it; it snowballs. In this way the elenchus helps along the formation of the self. It causes you to figure out what your moral conscience is made of. There is a conflict in your views; you have to decide which to keep and which to drop. It is like an inner tournament with winning and losing ideas. You understand yourself better after many rounds of it.[17] The Socratic method thus helps toward fulfillment of the instruction inscribed over the entrance to the Temple of Apollo at Delphi: know thyself.[18]

This theory also explains how Socrates can claim that he doesn't know anything and yet still have beliefs about hard questions—that doing wrong is worse than suffering it, or whatever else. Those beliefs aren't quite things he *knows*. They just seem true to him because

---

16. The suggestion of Woodruff, "Socrates and the Irrational," 145–46.

17. See Brickhouse and Smith, "Socrates' Elenctic Mission," 126–27.

18. On which see Brickhouse and Smith, *Plato's Socrates*, 101–2.

they've survived all testing so far. An argument, or an adversary, might still appear and be sharp enough to show that the claims Socrates makes don't hold together in some way. So if consistency is the test of truth, it never settles a question once and for all. It forces you to hold views provisionally, and to always be in a state of search for more confirmation or refutation.

Consistently wrong. But how reliable *is* consistency as a test for truth? Again, the Socratic assumption, as Vlastos has it, is that everyone holds at least *some* true beliefs—some bedrock moral intuitions that are reliable. False beliefs will always run afoul of them eventually, or they would if you were examined by Socrates. This assumption is highly productive in many settings. That does not necessarily mean it is true in all settings. It is interesting to think about whether, in fact, a repellent set of ideas can be internally consistent, not just from side to side but from top to bottom, and so fend off even the most determined efforts to show a contradiction in its holder.[19] Plato has Socrates flag this general problem.

Cratylus
436ce

CRATYLUS. You have a clear proof that he has not missed the truth, and the proof is—that he is perfectly consistent. Did you ever observe in speaking that all the words which you utter have a common character and purpose?
SOCRATES. But that, friend Cratylus, is no answer. For if he did begin in error, he may have forced the remainder into agreement with the original error and with himself; there would be nothing strange in this, any more than in geometrical diagrams, which have often a slight and invisible flaw in the first part of the process, and are consistently mistaken in the long deductions which follow. And this is the reason why every man should expend his chief thought and attention on the consideration of his first

---

19. Rorty, *Philosophy as Cultural Politics*, 67–68, makes a similar suggestion: "Nobody would want to break bread with Eichmann or Suslov, but we can easily imagine that the stories those men told themselves about who they were and what they were doing had the same coherence as those that Orwell and Trilling told themselves about their lives, and as the ones we tell ourselves about ours."

principles:—are they or are they not rightly laid down? and when he has duly sifted them, all the rest will follow.

You may recall arguing with people whose beliefs seemed terrible but consistent. The question is whether that was really true or only seemed that way because you lacked the talent of a Socrates for finding inconsistencies within them. The question was hard in old Athens and is hard now. We live in polarized times. That is so because different people have different bedrock intuitions about the world. The Socratic question isn't just whether their views in the foreground are consistent with those deeper ones. It is whether their deepest beliefs are consistent with each other. But the closer you get to those deep beliefs and their consistency, the more emotionally they are defended. That is why it is so rare—unheard of—for sudden political conversions to be produced by Socratic questioning. Slow ones, maybe.

You might think this account explains a lot about your adversaries. What they claim to think is inconsistent with what they really know deep down, but it's hard to get them to see this. Socrates would say that you're probably right. But then he would also say the same about whatever apparently seamless beliefs *you* hold. For it is a common trap to suppose that Socratic questioning, if only it were good enough, would eventually bring everyone else around to your own opinions or politics. An important early aim of Socratic practice is to get rid of fantasies like those. The rightful first subject of skepticism isn't others. It's ourselves.

To view the point more broadly: if everyone became much more Socratic in orientation than they are now, you might imagine that they would all come to gradual agreement as they work their way toward consistency with the same master truths. Or rather you might imagine this if you were a Martian. Here on earth it's unlikely. But a world in which the Socratic method were fashionable—as unthinkable as that is, too—would still be a big improvement. People would reckon their chances of being wrong, or deficient in understanding, much higher than they do now. This would make them more tolerable to each other and more likely to make progress when they talk. Overbearing certitude would be regarded with distaste and embarrassment by adults, and sneered at by the young as Socratically incorrect. These would be small gains when compared to the dream of perfect Socratic harmony, but tremendous when compared to our current state. And even if we can't have that world, a few such outposts in this one shouldn't be so much to ask.

Self-examination. Speaking of self-skepticism, though, how can you use the elenchus on yourself? In some ways it's impossible, or nearly so; in some ways it's merely difficult. To begin with the first: between partners, the elenchus functions like a trap. Socrates gets his partner to agree to a proposition that doesn't look like a problem, and then works backward to show that it conflicts with whatever claim the partner made earlier. But you can only set that kind of trap if you see the conflict coming when you ask the questions. Socrates asks for his partner's assent to a damaging proposition because Socrates knows where it leads and his partner doesn't. That works fine when you can see ahead better than your partner does, but you can't quite do it alone. It's like sneaking up on yourself.

But even if you can't apply the form of the elenchus to your own thinking, you can produce the substance of it. Elenctic thinking amounts to a search for contradictions between what you're saying now and other things you believe. That is an inquiry that can be made anytime. You take your own beliefs and follow their implications as far as you can, and keep going after you flinch. You test them with extreme cases; you look at them from different perspectives; you imagine what you would think about your view if the winners and losers produced by it were reversed; and so on, with other kinds of questions we will see in chapter 18 and elsewhere.

Asking these questions of yourself is hard to do effectively. We all have blind spots and are good at persuading ourselves that we don't; our inconsistencies are glaring to others but not to us. People who are clever imagine that they are better than others at avoiding this hazard, but they probably have the worst of it. Their ingenuity allows them to find easy ways to make their views look harmonious to themselves. That may be why the cleverest are not famous for also being the most moral and admirable.

The response to these problems was discussed in chapter 4 and is a general theme of this book: developing a Socratic function in the mind that is skeptical and is tough about it. What does an understanding of the elenchus add to that point? Just a better sense of how much work the Socratic function takes to develop. An internalized Socrates has to carry out a job that two people can do far more easily and also more gently. When one person uses the elenchus on another, it can make the exposure of inconsistency less painful. It brings your conflicts to light by a circuitous route in which you've agreed to every step on the way. A gracious partner drives the process forward while creating the sense that you are puzzling over a problem together. If you don't have a partner, there is nobody to push or soften the process in those ways. The elenchus may need to be replaced by brute force.

So a Socratic posture toward one's own thinking is a heroic state of mind. Chapter 4 compared the solo version of the Socratic method to exercise done without the help of a trainer. Now we see that it may be more like performing surgery on yourself: far more challenging than having it done by someone else, both practically and because anesthesia is out of the question. There is no partner to complete the incision when your courage runs out. The simile is severe because the process is severe if taken seriously. The best compensation—that is, the best way to make Socratic scrutiny of the self endurable—is an attitude of acceptance and good humor toward your own constant state of error. The previous section of this chapter suggested that such an attitude makes it easier for others to put up with us. But it also makes finding the truth easier because you aren't so desperately attached to your own views. You get used to the idea not only of being wrong a lot but of being wrong more often than you think (that's something else that you're wrong about). This makes it a little less agonizing to dig out the next example.

7

Consistency

WE'VE seen how the elenchus works. It refutes what you say by showing that it's inconsistent with something else you think. This chapter dwells further and more generally on consistency because it is so central to the Socratic method. We will consider why Socrates regards consistency as important, how consistency relates to the truth, and why inconsistency sometimes seems less a pressing problem to us than it does to him (and whether it should).

Internal critique. It is natural to imagine that a philosopher—a Socrates—would try to talk you into accepting his beliefs as your own. But that isn't the Socratic method. Or if Socrates wants to show that you're wrong, you might expect that he would attack what you've said as inconsistent with the facts or as morally repellent. That isn't quite the Socratic method, either. The Socratic method, in its classic form, consists of internal critique. It tests whether you're being consistent with yourself and believe all that you think you do. Socrates doesn't tell you that you're wrong; he shows you that *you* think you're wrong. This explains the value of the frequent stops Socrates makes to get his partner to say, "Agreed." Those pauses might seem pointless, but they aren't, because his eventual goal is to show that his partner doesn't agree with himself.

That last point is the core of an elenchus: using the views of the people being questioned as the main resource in arguing with them. At one point a bystander asks Socrates to say what's wrong with a theory Theaetetus has offered. Socrates says that isn't how he operates.

Theaetetus
161ab

SOCRATES. I like the way you see me as a sort of repository of ideas, so that I can pick one out, just like that, to claim that the theory's wrong. You're overlooking what's been happening: none of the ideas have come from me, but always from whoever is talking with me. My knowledge is limited to a reasonable understanding of ideas which I get from others, the clever ones. So, in this instance too, I won't try to say anything for myself, but I will try to get Theaetetus's viewpoint.

Socrates overstates his passivity. True, he refutes what others say by working with their own admissions. But he is the one who proposes what they admit, and coming up with those proposals can take imagination. Still, he does *start* with his partner's beliefs, and then he stays within them as he pushes the dialogue forward. If you tell him that you don't buy what he's saying, he finds something else that you do buy and that he can use as a way to reason with you.[1] Once his partners find themselves stuck, they're stuck between things they believe or thought they did—even if they hadn't realized that they held such beliefs until they were asked. Socrates has hogtied them with cords fashioned by their own consent even if not of their own making.

Versatility. The use of internal critique in the Socratic method helps explain why the method has lasted. First, it puts power in the hands of anyone. It requires no big theory and little philosophical or factual knowledge to use. It does take imagination and skill; you need to know how to listen and how to think of good questions. And you have to be able to see where a principle leads and where it will run into problems. But the materials for carrying out the method are all in your partner or within yourself, as the case may be. It's like a martial art that you can master even if you're small because it uses the weight of your opponents against them. Their claims fail because they have implications that are too much to bear.

Second, internal critique is a method for all times and places. It doesn't depend on any particular circumstances or beliefs to work. Socrates seeks a showdown between aspects of the self, and that contest is always possible to arrange. It's like tuning an instrument not with a tuning fork but by testing whether it's in tune with *itself.* A talent for that sort of tuning is versatile. Anyone can use it on themselves or on anyone else, in 400 BC or today.

---

1. As Richard Robinson said it, "The art of elenchus is to find premises believed by the answerer and yet entailing the contrary of his thesis." Robinson, *Plato's Earlier Dialectic,* 15.

Inconsistency and truth. Now let's consider why Socrates thinks inconsistency is such a serious problem. For openers, being inconsistent means being wrong. You find yourself holding two beliefs that are (let us assume) in undeniable conflict; they can't both be right. That means you evidently believe something that is false, or your claim to believe them both is false. In this sense internal inconsistency isn't a special problem. It's just a style of proof, but a strong one. Refuting a claim generally means showing that it's inconsistent with something—with the facts, or with logical rules, or with other things you say. This last type of inconsistency is the one Socrates most likes to use, and it's distinctly convincing. If someone shows that your views are in conflict with new information, you might doubt the data. When your beliefs are in conflict with each other, it's uncomfortable in a more direct way. You can't attack the author of the study.

The test of consistency puts a helpful brake on the fear that true and false are up for grabs. That fear can sometimes arise after long exposure to Socratic questioning. The search for truth, Socratically pursued, is bedeviling. Socrates is a master of refutation, so it becomes hard to be certain about anything important. Conclusions that stand unrefuted are provisional; they may *yet* be refuted. But at least the search for what is false is decisive. If you've said two things that can't both be right, you're wrong. For the Socratic practitioner, this sure sense of error can be reassuring and even welcome. You take your certainties where you can find them.

But now we should qualify the claim that inconsistency amounts to sure error. First, it's a claim about propositions that are inconsistent. Sometimes inconsistencies of other kinds can survive without trouble, which is usually to say that they might not really be inconsistencies after all. It's entirely possible, for example, for two *policies* to seem inconsistent but be rationally favored by the same person. Together the policies might represent a reasoned compromise between different interests. Second, consistent claims (or any other claims) may not be necessary to support a given view. Sometimes—maybe often—we might hold moral beliefs on grounds that owe nothing to reason at all. Socrates naturally would have questions about those beliefs and whether you are sure that they're on strong enough footing, but at times he himself claims to take guidance from god and from some sort of divine voice within.[2] That isn't the problem we're talking about now, either.

The problem of consistency arises for Socratic purposes, rather, when you articulate two beliefs that can't both be right. You're *trying* to reason about a question. You want to say true things about it, but it's hard to get them aligned. It's like a balance sheet where the numbers come out wrong. Something is amiss. If you don't care, that's your business—but if you don't care, why are you using a balance sheet? Once you do care about reason, a contradiction creates felt discomfort—embarrassment, even. If it doesn't, Socrates probably needs to go back to work.

The focus on consistency is rooted in the value at the center of the Socratic project. An ethical system can be built around any number of such values—equality, utility, liberty, and so forth. Socrates starts with the *truth*: the search for it, the love of it, and the saying of it, no matter how dangerous it might be.

> SOCRATES. Renouncing the honors at which the world aims, I desire only to know the truth, and to live as well as I can, and, when I die, to die as well as I can. And, to the utmost of my power, I exhort all other men to do the same.

Gorgias
526de

Passages like these show that Socrates believed there are truths to be found about ethical questions, not just opinions or points of view. You can use the Socratic method effectively without holding that position, but serious study of the method at least provokes confrontation with it. Socrates has a rare combination of beliefs: confidence that truth exists, but humility about whether he knows it. (Think of how strangely common the reverse has become.) That is part of why inconsistency matters so much. It doesn't just show that you are wrong. It shows that it's possible to *be* wrong. And perhaps ethical questions with wrong answers can also have right ones or at least

---

2. See, e.g., *Apology* 23ab, 31cd; and for discussion, see Woodruff, "Socrates and the Irrational."

better ones. If we can get farther from them with bad reasoning that is inconsistent, we should be able to get closer with good reasoning that is consistent.

Care of the psyche. We have seen how inconsistencies show that something is wrong with the reasoning that produces them. But inconsistency signals more than that to Socrates. It also suggests something amiss in the *self*, like a blob on an x-ray. Indeed, Socrates views internal contradiction as a kind of moral sickness. The discussion a moment ago suggested that Socratic inquiry is like tuning an instrument to itself. That comparison—the instrument out of tune—belongs to Socrates. Callicles says it's good if you manage to do a wrong without getting caught. Socrates gets him to agree to some other points that end up conflicting with that one, then gives this warning if Callicles can't find a way out of the argument put in front of him:

Gorgias
482bc

SOCRATES. If you leave it unrefuted, then I swear to you by the divine dog of the Egyptians that it'll cause friction between you and Callicles, Callicles; there'll be discord within you your whole life. And yet, my friend, in my opinion it's preferable for me to be a musician with an out-of-tune lyre or a choir leader with a cacophonous choir, and it's preferable for almost everyone in the world to find my beliefs misguided and wrong, rather than for just one person—me—to contradict and clash with myself.

This is stronger language than most of us would now use to talk about being inconsistent. It follows from the distinct way that Socrates thinks about living well. When people believe two things that can't both be right, they're half-asleep or half-mad. They don't actually think anything in particular. They just imagine that they do. They lack knowledge of who they are, and so are ridiculous without realizing it.

Philebus
48cd

SOCRATES. The ridiculous is in short the specific name which is used to describe the vicious form of a certain habit; and of vice in general it is that kind which is most at variance with the inscription at Delphi.

PROTARCHUS. You mean, Socrates, "Know thyself."

SOCRATES. I do; and the opposite would be, "Know not thyself."

People at odds with themselves in this way, on a Socratic view, also have practical problems. Their internal conflicts may disable them from acting decisively in the world, or can make them dangerous if they do. Thus the remark of Socrates about the effect of injustice within the self:

> Is not injustice equally fatal when existing in a single person; in *Republic*
> the first place rendering him incapable of action because he is 352a
> not at unity with himself, and in the second place making him
> an enemy to himself and the just?

The Socratic method thus means thinking more about consistency than usual, and caring more about it than usual.

The threat posed to the self by inconsistency should not be viewed as an obscure philosophical problem. For many people it is immediate and pressing. They live their lives in ways that are inconsistent—out of harmony, as it were—with their deeper beliefs, whatever those might be. They come to feel lost, stuck, or otherwise miserable. They wonder why. Socrates would regard those results as natural and easy to understand. But it is also true that Socrates sees a problem in such a case even if it isn't felt in full by the person who has it. In some ways the problem then is worse. It is a horrifying state that resembles dementia. We will spend more time on this point in chapter 14. Either way, though, make no mistake: taking consistency more seriously—not just in theory but actually doing it—can be very affecting: constructive and revelatory, disruptive and painful. The engine of Socratic inquiry, once fully engaged, does not leave things where it finds them.

Resistance. An inconsistency doesn't always appall us in the way that Socrates says it should. Someone points out that you're inconsistent and perhaps you shrug it off. That reaction can be interpreted a few ways. The first is that the claim of inconsistency doesn't feel convincing. The proof seems flawed in some respect that you can sense but not yet explain. Sometimes that feeling is accurate: your intuition rightly detects that the logic looks good but isn't. A possible example appears early in the *Phaedo* when Socrates and Cebes are talking about suicide. Socrates accepts that suicide is wrong, but he has also said that there are times and places when death is preferable to life. Cebes notes the strangeness of this, and Socrates replies:

Phaedo
62bc

I admit the appearance of inconsistency in what I am saying; but there may not be any real inconsistency after all. There is a doctrine whispered in secret that man is a prisoner who has no right to open the door and run away; this is a great mystery which I do not quite understand. Yet I too believe that the gods are our guardians, and that we are a possession of theirs. Do you not agree?

Yes, I quite agree, said Cebes.

And if one of your own possessions, an ox or an ass, for example, took the liberty of putting himself out of the way when you had given no intimation of your wish that he should die, would you not be angry with him, and would you not punish him if you could?

Certainly, replied Cebes.

Then, if we look at the matter thus, there may be reason in saying that a man should wait, and not take his own life until God summons him, as he is now summoning me.

That argument might not seem impressive now, but it displays one type of response to an inconsistency: it may be explained on terms not yet fully worked out. This prospect can sometimes make it rational to persist for a while in holding two beliefs that seem to conflict, especially when the belief under challenge has the sanction of long and seemingly successful usage. How Mill put it:

The majority of mankind would need to be much better cultivated than has ever yet been the case, before they can be asked to place such reliance in their own power of estimating arguments, as to give up practical principles in which they have been born and bred and which are the basis of much of the existing order of the world, at the first argumentative attack which they are not capable of logically resisting.[3]

Mill was arguing that women should have the same legal rights that men do. He knew that his arguments were a hard sell to his audience. He was accepting that they *should* be a hard sell. People shouldn't be too quick to give up their way of life just because someone has made an argument they don't know how to answer. Maybe their old custom has more sense in it than the new argument does, and they aren't good at arguing.

But of course the opposite is also a possibility. There is a real problem—a true inconsistency in your views. You resist seeing it because your views are comfortable. You're accustomed to thinking what you think, and it hasn't caused you any trouble until now, so you distrust an argument that calls it into doubt. This time reason is wiser than feeling; feeling has to catch up. (That is what Mill thought was really going on when he made the remarks shown above.) But it can take time and repetition for logic to penetrate the fortifications of belief, if it ever happens at all. Socrates recognized this situation, too.

> CALLICLES. I can't explain it, Socrates, but I do think you're *Gorgias* making your points well. All the same, I'm feeling what people 513c invariably feel with you: I'm not entirely convinced.
> SOCRATES. It's the demotic love residing in your heart which is resisting me, Callicles. If we argued the issues through over and over again, you'd be won over.

It can be hard to tell these two situations apart. You see a nagging conflict in what you think about something but don't yet *feel* it as a problem. You aren't sure whether the logic is bad or you're just being stubborn. The Socratic response is to press on the reasoning until the defect in it is shown or until its implications sink in. This becomes a matter more of stamina than of logical ability. The dialogues are studies in that kind of stamina and nerve. Most people give up and wave away the problem. Socrates won't.

---

3. Mill, *Subjection of Women*, in Robson, *Collected Works of John Stuart Mill*, 21: 262–53.

Indifference to consistency. From time to time you will find people whose view goes beyond the resistance just shown. They claim outright not to care about consistency. Those with this view may quote or misquote Ralph Waldo Emerson or Lewis Carroll in support of their indifference, or they might say it has something to do with quantum mechanics, or that it follows from philosophical arguments about the unavailability of objective truth.

Such people are best approached in the good Socratic spirit—with congratulations on having reached peace with problems that have been troublesome to so many for so long. You can ask whether they would be game to answer some questions, and then inquire about whatever sorts of inconsistencies trouble you. A true indifference to consistency amounts to an indifference to reason, which some might say is their position but which ends up being hard to sustain. Those who take such a view will usually walk away from questioning after a while, just as characters sometimes do at the end of Plato's dialogues.

When people claim to deny any interest in consistency, it usually turns out that something else is going on. They may be talking at a level of metaphysical abstraction that is gaseous and doesn't matter much to anyone. Or they are defining consistency in an unexpected way. Or they think the same claim can be both true and false because it can be true in one sense and false in another. But then there's no actual inconsistency; the original claim just wasn't precise. Whatever the rationale for the claimed indifference may be, the procedure in response to such claimants is the same: Socrates explores whether they really mean it. The person who will have none of this—one who rejects consistency and won't pursue the point—is entitled to that view, and perhaps to compassion.

Applicability. The remarkable point about consistency is the *power* of it as a value or goal. When that value is hooked up to the mechanism of Socratic questioning, it doesn't just annihilate. It can also be productive. It destroys a bad idea but can help confirm a sound one. It can tear down a way of life and then generate one that is better. And it is relevant to every little choice we make, not just to the big ones.

The search for consistency thus makes the Socratic method useful in all sorts of situations, not just the kind we usually associate with moral philosophy. Plutarch said that

> For Socrates to play the philosopher there was no arranging of forms, seating himself in a chair, or observing a fixed time—arranged with his associates—for a discussion or discourse. He played the philosopher while joking with you, perhaps, or drinking with you, or possibly campaigning with you, or at market with you, and finally when he was in prison and drinking the poison. He was thus the first to show that life affords scope for philosophy at every moment, in every detail, in every feeling and circumstance whatsoever.

Plutarch, *On Old Men in Public Life* 796d

At first this description might seem pleasing but puzzling. Most of us deal with most questions without paying any attention to philosophy, at least consciously, and we don't feel its absence. That is because it is so easy to think of philosophical questions as the kind most people can do without in their ordinary lives. A lot of academic work now described as philosophy does fit that description. But on a Socratic view, philosophy is relevant to just about everything, high and low. It isn't a set of problems that some care about and some don't. Philosophy means thinking carefully about whether you believe all that you say and whether it's true. It is the effort to stay awake.

8

Systole and Diastole

A DIALOGUE looks different if you see it less as about a given topic and more as a model of how to think generally—as if you replaced the subject of the dialogue with an X, so it turns into an example of how to analyze anything. You might consider the topic a MacGuffin, as Alfred Hitchcock would say: necessary to the plot and a source of motivation to the characters, but not significant in itself. The *Laches* is about the meaning of courage, but you aren't likely to read it now primarily to learn about courage. You read it to learn about patterns of reasoning.

This chapter is about one such pattern of reasoning that Socrates uses constantly. You offer a view. Socrates asks you to state the principle behind it—the premise that leads to your result. Then he asks questions that show your principle is too narrow; it leaves out things that it needs to cover. Or your principle is too broad; it includes things that it shouldn't. You keep refining what you say to bring it nearer to the truth. You may never get there, but you're closer at the end than you were at the start. This simple process is a great share of better thinking in a nutshell. It is easy to understand but rarely carried out. Socrates carries it out in every dialogue.

Systole and diastole. The Socratic method makes constant use of two operations of the mind. The first is seeing similarities between things that look different. The second is seeing differences between things that look similar. Socrates very often says either "you're drawing too many distinctions" or "you aren't drawing enough." In the first category would be moments like these:

➻ His partner gives examples of courage or some other concept. Socrates says that he doesn't want examples. He wants a single definition that covers what all the examples have in common.
➻ His partner gives a definition of something. Socrates points

out a case that the definition doesn't cover but probably should. So the definition has to be made broader.

➤ His partner talks about two things as if they're different. Socrates says they really are the same thing if you understand them rightly.

Notice what those moments have in common. In each case Socrates wants fewer distinctions to be drawn. He asks for things that are being treated as separate to be treated as the same. He wants their commonalities seen.

In the second category would be moments like these:

➤ His partner gives a definition of something. Socrates points out a case that the definition covers but probably shouldn't. The definition has to be made narrower.

➤ His partner gives a definition of something. Socrates says that the key word in the definition can mean more than one thing. He asks his partner to say which he means.

➤ His partner says that two concepts are the same. Socrates argues that they really are different if you understand them rightly.

Notice what those moments have in common. In each case Socrates wants *more* distinctions drawn. He asks for things that are being treated as the same to be treated as separate; he wants their differences seen.

It would be nice to have a pair of words for those two general operations. I will half-borrow from Greek and call the first kind of thinking *systolic* or just *systole* (*sis*-toe-lee, pronounced like *fiscally*). The second can be called *diastolic* thinking or just *diastole* (pronounced sort of like *hyperbole*). "Systole" has the Greek meaning of "a drawing together." "Diastole" has the Greek meaning of "separation." Their modern biological use in English, in which they refer to the two phases of the cardiac cycle, is not a bad association for us. They are the back-and-forth rhythm of Socratic analysis.

Systole with definitions. To start with systole: When Socrates wants a definition of a word, his partner usually starts by giving examples of what the word means. Socrates always replies that he doesn't want examples. He wants a definition into which the examples can all be fit. Thus in the *Laches* the question is the meaning of courage. Laches says that courage means holding your ground when the enemy is bearing down on you. Socrates isn't sure that is a good example of courage, but anyway it's the wrong kind of answer to his question. He wanted something else.

Laches
191de

SOCRATES. I meant to ask you not just about courage for heavy-armed soldiers, but also about courage for horsemen and every other kind of soldier; and I wanted to find out what constitutes courage not just in warfare, but when facing danger at sea, or when up against illness and poverty, or even in political life; and I wanted to know what constitutes courage not just in the face of pain or fear, but also when people fight heroically against desire or pleasure (whether they do so by remaining at their posts or by turning around). After all, Laches, there are people who are courageous in these situations too.

LACHES. There certainly are, Socrates.

SOCRATES. So all these people are courageous, but some display courage in situations involving pleasure and others in situations involving pain, some in situations involving desire and others in situations involving fear. And presumably cowardice can also be an attribute people display in these situations.

LACHES. Yes, they do.

SOCRATES. So what actually is each of these attributes, courage and cowardice? *That's* what I wanted to find out. Let's take courage first, then, and could you please try again to tell me what it is that's the same in all these situations?

That is a classic example of systolic thinking. Socrates wants to understand a quality, and this means knowing what features are there whenever the quality appears. You can't look at only one case and think about it. You have to look at every case and find words that cover them all. You need fewer distinctions, or a lens with a wider angle. A lot of the dialogues start with an exchange like this.[1] Socrates always tries to move from this or that particular case to a level of principle that accounts for all of them.

Tools for erasing distinctions. Systole happens in many other ways in the dialogues. Someone will say that two things are different. Socrates will say that they're really the same. The *Laches* provides a good example here, too. Nicias says that courage means knowledge of which future events should be feared and which shouldn't. Socrates says that claim can be converted into one that is broader: things that should be feared amount to kinds of evil, and things that shouldn't be feared can be called good. Courage, then, is the knowledge of future *good and evil* (a broader idea than the initial one). But wait: if you understand what good and evil mean in the future, you must know what they mean generally, because their meaning doesn't depend on whether they appear in the future or the past. So courage doesn't mean knowledge of *future* good and evil; it means a knowledge of good and evil, period (again a broader idea). And if that's true, then courage comes to seem the same as wisdom or virtue (broader still). Notice what's going on in this sequence: he's erasing one distinction after another, assimilating smaller categories into larger ones.

And sometimes Socrates carries out systolic arguments through other steps. He argues in the *Protagoras* that wisdom and moderation must be the same. Why? Because different things can't have the same opposite, and the opposite of wisdom and the opposite of moderation are the same: foolishness. (The argument loses something in translation because our words don't perfectly match his.) Later he talks about two other concepts that seem different: knowledge of what is best to do, and weakness when you are tempted to do otherwise. He says again that it only looks like there are two things here—knowledge vs. weakness. In fact there is just one: knowledge or a shortage of it. If you succumb to temptation, it means you don't *really* understand the consequences of what you're doing. (See chapter 14 for discussion.)

---

1. See, e.g., *Theaetetus* 146ce; *Meno* 71c–72c.

These arguments are all different ways of saying similar things: You're thinking too small; you're inventing distinctions that don't matter, or are distracted by false distinctions that others have drawn. Try looking at these many things as one thing. It's all systole.

Diastole. The opposite pattern is diastolic. Two things look the same, and Socrates shows that they aren't. We saw him make a demand of Laches: give me a definition of courage that covers *all* the cases we call courageous. So Laches tries a general definition: courage means persistence of mind. Socrates says this definition is too broad; it covers cases that it shouldn't. Isn't some persistence of mind foolish? That wouldn't be courage, would it? Laches agrees and revises the definition: courage is *intelligent* (or "wise") persistence of mind. The dialogue continues:

Laches
192e–93a

SOCRATES. But let's consider the context in which intelligent persistence occurs. Would you describe it as courage in every situation, big or small? For example, if someone persists in spending money and does so with intelligence, in the sense that he knows that by spending now he'll get more later, would you call him a man of courage?

LACHES. By Zeus, no, I wouldn't.

SOCRATES. What about if a doctor, whose son (or whoever) was suffering from pneumonia and was begging him for something to drink or to eat, were to persist in steadfastly refusing to give him anything?

LACHES. No; that wouldn't be an act of courage either, not in the slightest.

Laches sees that his definition of courage needs to be more exact. It covers cases that don't fit. The process of showing this is simple: here are some cases that your definition covers but that don't seem to show courage. Did you mean to include them? Try again, then. Say something more limited.

In the *Gorgias* we have the same pattern.[2] Socrates asks what rhet-

---

2. 450ac–453b.

oric is, and Gorgias gives him an answer: rhetoric is concerned with discourse. Well, doctors conduct discourse with their patients; is that "rhetoric"? (No—so an act of diastole, or separation, has occurred.) What's the difference? Gorgias says that rhetoric, unlike medicine, involves *only* the spoken word. But Socrates isn't satisfied. Discourse about math might only involve speech. Are you saying that math is rhetoric? (No, it isn't—diastole again.) Gorgias says the difference this time is that rhetoric is discourse about the most important human affairs, and math isn't. Socrates says that still won't do: everyone thinks their own business is the most important. Those claims must be distinguished. (More diastole.) Gorgias says, then, that rhetoric is about using persuasion to influence people who have power. Good enough, says Socrates; now we can discuss what rhetoric persuades people *about*.

Tools for drawing distinctions. Look at the techniques that Socrates uses to produce diastole. His partner tries to say what rhetoric means—"discourse" or "discourse that doesn't depend on material results" or "discourse about the most important things." So as before, Socrates thinks of items that are covered by those words but that don't fit. Sometimes his examples are historical. Sometimes he cites everyday cases from the world. And you can also make diastole happen with a hypothetical case. Elsewhere in the *Gorgias*, Polus argues that power is the ability to do whatever you want to other people. Socrates thinks this is too simple, and shows it with a thought experiment.

SOCRATES. Imagine I'm in the agora when it's chock-full, and I've got a dagger tucked in my armpit. I tell you, "Polus, I've recently gained an incredible amount of power, as much as any dictator. Look at all those people. If I decide one of them has to die, he's dead, just like that; if I decide one of them should have his head split open, it'll be split open on the spot; if I decide someone's cloak needs shredding, shredded it is. So you can see that I have a great deal of power in this community." And suppose you don't believe me, so I show you my dagger. I bet you'd say, "Socrates, in that case everyone has a great deal of

Gorgias 469de

power, since by the same token you could also burn down any houses you decide to burn down—and then there are the Athens' dockyards and warships and the whole merchant fleet in public and private ownership." So the ability to do what you feel like doing isn't a sign of great power.

Socrates shows that the ability to kill, which we all have (anyone can get a knife), isn't much of a power in itself because we aren't better off if we use it; we would be punished. Of course when Polus spoke of the power to do what you want, he meant the ability to do it *without* being punished. But Socrates wanted to get the narrow end of the wedge into Polus's claim: power is only meaningful if using it actually makes you better off. Now Socrates can ask questions about what it means for an act to make you better off, and away we go. The example shows the value of hypothetical cases in Socratic questioning. You can make them extreme in ways that go right to the point and that cause everyone to agree. They may take ingenuity to devise, but they don't have to be realistic. They just need to show that a principle leads someplace where its author might not want to go.

Diastolic arguments use other techniques as well. Socrates will sometimes show logical problems that follow from treating two things as the same when they're different. Callicles argues in the *Gorgias* that the good and the pleasurable are the same (and that evil and painful are the same). Socrates says that can't be right: good and bad are opposites, but pleasure and pain aren't; they're mixed in some cases. That means the good and the pleasurable must be separate ideas. Then Socrates goes on to make the same point using an approach we saw in chapter 6: Fools and cowards are bad people, yes? (Yes.) But they can have as much pleasure in their lives as good people, right? (No doubt.) Again, then, the good and the pleasurable must be distinct.

Here as ever it's best not to focus on whether the arguments Socrates makes are convincing. They have their problems; but notice that he always gets his partner's agreement before going on. If the partner balks, Socrates explains the point more or tries a different one. He would have done the same if he had been arguing with you.

Knowing it when you see it. Systolic and diastolic arguments are ways of closing in on the truth. You make a claim that something is so, or is an example of something else: this is courageous, that is unjust; this is fair, that is unfair. Systole and diastole force you to explain what you mean, and they test whether it holds up. The alternative to such analysis is to say that you don't need to bother because you know it when you see it—whatever "it" might be (courage, injustice, fairness, etc.). That is how most people think most of the time. It is, as Mill would put it, the approach of the *intellectus sibi permissus*—the mind left to itself. It seems convincing but is highly prone to error.

Yet sometimes Socrates does let his partners "know it when they see it." He has to; otherwise it's hard for the job of finding definitions to get off the ground. If you can't point to any examples of courage that you feel sure are good, how do you know what cases a definition should cover? Some say that Socrates did catch himself in paradoxes of that kind.[3] They think he claims that if you can't define a word like "courage" or "virtue," you don't know anything about what courage and virtue are (this idea is known as the priority of definition). And that can't be right. You might be able to identify examples of a concept without being able to define it. Supposing that you need a definition first has been described, fairly or not, as the Socratic fallacy.[4] The original maker of that complaint warned about a Socrates who tells young people that they can't know whether cheating is wrong until they define the word, which they probably can't do—so they end up thinking that cheating is fine, and turn into the Thirty Tyrants who terrorized Athens, some of whom Socrates had tutored.

That is an alarming prospect. But most scholars think it misunderstands why Socrates wanted definitions.[5] He didn't mean that you know nothing about X until you can give a definition of it. He wanted definitions because they let us resolve hard cases. They put us in the position of an expert. Without a definition, we know more

---

3. Geach, "Plato's *Euthyphro*"; Robinson, *Plato's Earlier Dialectic*, 53.

4. Geach, "Plato's *Euthyphro*," 371.

5. See, e.g., Santas, "Socratic Fallacy"; Beversluis, "Does Socrates Commit the Socratic Fallacy?"

than nothing but we lack clarity. We're left with knowing things when we see them, which sometimes produces a true belief and sometimes doesn't and so shouldn't feel reassuring. Most atrocities, large and small, are committed by people who think they know it when they see it. And if we can't come up with an airtight definition of a concept, we still can earn *provisional* knowledge that one thing is an example of another—enough to allow you to say, "I have a working definition that seems right; I'll let it go if there's a good argument against it, but it's been through testing and I haven't heard one yet." The Socratic mindset is also hospitable to generalizations, including defective ones—as long as you know that's what they are and have decided that they are the best you can do for now. What Socrates can't stand is the generalization that its holder believes is right without understanding the ways in which it isn't.[6]

This limited use of "knowing it when you see it" is consistent with how Socrates acts. He's game to trade examples of courage with Laches without having a definition of the word. That is the implied position of Socrates: there are hard questions when it comes to ethics, but also easy ones; and the easy ones can be used to get a toehold when working on those that are harder. Maybe the easy ones can be made harder than they look, too, but part of good Socratic judgment is knowing when it's worth the trouble. Indeed, Socrates is sometimes ready to suggest a "know it on sight" approach when inquiry fails. In the *Charmides*, for example, he and his partners can't come up with a good definition of soundness of mind (or self-control—it's hard to translate).[7] But Socrates still has an idea about how to go forward, which he offers as a suggestion for young Charmides.

---

6. For a Socratic (in spirit) defense of generalizations, see Schauer, *Profiles, Probabilities and Stereotypes*.

7. The transliterated Greek is *sophrosyne*, which has no perfect English equivalent. The word has overtones of good order (it was a favorite of the Spartans); a possible opposite is *mania*. Mill describes it as "one of the most difficult words to translate in the whole Greek language. The common rendering, Temperance, corresponds to a part of the meaning, but is ridiculously inadequate to the whole. Continence, Modesty, Moderation, are all short of the mark. Self-restraint and Self-Control are better, but imply the coercion of the character by the will, while what is required is rather a character not needing coercion. There is also

SOCRATES. Although the inquiry found us to be easy-going and compliant, it still failed to uncover the truth; in fact, it mocked the truth, in that it came to the utterly outrageous conclusion that self-control, as defined by our agreements and constructions, did us no good at all.... I don't really think this is right. I think it's just that I'm a useless investigator. In my opinion, you see, self-control is a very good thing and you're lucky to have it. So why don't you check to see whether you do have it? If you do ... I'd advise you to regard me as a wrongheaded fool, incapable of conducting a reasoned examination of anything, and to think of yourself as happy to exactly the extent that you're self-controlled.

Charmides
175e–76a

Charmides is shown as a youth in the dialogue. The real Charmides had been a student of the real Socrates. He was also an uncle of Plato's. He is said to have later become one of the Thirty Tyrants.

Platonic collection and division. In later dialogues, Socrates uses a way of defining things known as collection and division. This approach is associated more with Plato than with Socrates, but a brief look at it will be worthwhile because it bears on our current topic. Collection and division defines a subject by putting it into one of two categories, then dividing that category into more categories, etc. In the *Sophist* we see a sample of it carried out to define an angler, or fisherman. It goes on for many pages, then is summarized (not by Socrates) this way:

STRANGER. You and I have come to an understanding not only about the name of the angler's art, but about the definition of the thing itself. One half of all art was acquisitive—half of the acquisitive art was conquest or taking by force, half of this was hunting, and half of hunting was hunting animals, half of this was

Sophist
221ac

---

in the Greek word an implied idea of order, of measure, and, as may be seen from this very dialogue, of deliberateness, which are wanting in the nearest English equivalents. Unobtrusiveness, too, is an essential part of the concept; and there is a connotation besides of Judgment or Intelligence (let us say Reasonableness).... Sobriety, a word used several times in this connexion by Mr. Grote, perhaps comes nearest to the Greek word in its variety of applications; but even this hardly admits of being substituted for it in discourse, without a perpetual running comment." Mill, "Grote's Plato," 408.

hunting water animals—of this again, the under half was fishing, half of fishing was striking; a part of striking was fishing with a barb, and one half of this again, being the kind which strikes with a hook and draws the fish from below upwards, is the art which we have been seeking, and which from the nature of the operation is denoted angling or drawing up.

The process is then repeated for the definition of a sophist, and (in the next dialogue) for the definition of a statesman.[8]

Defining a concept by making divisions of this kind became known as *diairesis*. The approach is related to Plato's Theory of Forms. He seems to have thought that items in a category were held together by bonds that existed in nature. Most people now don't believe that, and diairesis is not an approach they would use to define anything. But it's still possible to learn things about a subject by thinking of it that way, because making divisions will force you to compare the subject to other things and see how it's like them and how it's different.

But put aside the metaphysical views of Plato that are outside the scope of our inquiry. We can still see this business of collection and division as yet another kind of systole and diastole. Consider this comment on the method that Socrates offers in the *Phaedrus*.

Phaedrus
266bc

SOCRATES. I am myself a great lover of these processes of division and generalization; they help me to speak and to think. And if I find any man who is able to see "a One and Many" in nature, him I follow, and "walk in his footsteps as if he were a god."[9] And those who have this art, I have been in the habit of calling dialecticians.

That is another way to look at the ideas in this chapter: systole means seeing many things as one, and diastole means seeing one thing as many. We noted in the previous chapter that Plato had a lifelong attachment to the process of question and answer. That pattern can also be seen in his fascination with systole and diastole. He turned them to different purposes as his ideas developed.

---

8. See discussion in Lesley Brown, "Division and Definition in the Sophist."
9. An allusion to Homer's *Odyssey*.

9

Analogies

SOCRATES talks about large and abstract questions: What is a good life? What is knowledge? What is justice? But he avoids talking about them in large and abstract terms. He uses simple examples to show how a claim works or fails. Socrates especially likes to use analogies that compare abstract problems to ordinary ones that seem more familiar. Analogies aren't arguments; they just suggest parallels. But they can make arguments more convincing and make reasoning more clear. This chapter looks at how Socrates creates analogies and what he does with them.

Fill-in-the-blank analogies. Socrates sometimes uses an incomplete analogy to move a conversation forward. He shows the start of the analogy; his partner's job is to finish it. We've seen that in the *Laches* Socrates asks what courage means. His partner gives him an example. Socrates needs to explain that he doesn't want examples; he wants a definition that covers all of them. He uses an analogy.

> SOCRATES. Suppose I'd asked you what speed is. Now, speed is *Laches* something which manifests in a large number of human situations 192ab (such as running, playing music, speaking, and learning) and which is an attribute of almost every activity worth mentioning, whether it involves the use of the hands or the legs or the mouth or the voice or the mind. Don't you agree?
> LACHES. Yes, I do.
> SOCRATES. So if I were asked: "Socrates, what is this property you call 'speed,' wherever it occurs?" I'd reply that I use the term "speed" to refer to the ability to get a lot done in a little time, whether one is speaking or running or whatever.
> LACHES. And you'd be right.
> SOCRATES. So, Laches, please can you do the same for courage? Try to tell us what it is that, as the identical ability in all the

situations we were just mentioning, such as pleasure and pain, comes to be called courage.

Socrates creates an analogy with three out of its four elements filled in. We have (a) examples of speed and (b) a definition of speed; and then we have (c) examples of courage, but still need (d)—a definition of courage. Now Laches can fill in the blank.

The pattern recurs in other dialogues. In the *Theaetetus*, Socrates asks what knowledge means. He's told that it includes sciences such as geometry and crafts such as cobbling. Socrates says this is a bad answer; it's like saying that clay is something used by brickmakers and also by potters. A better answer would be that clay is moistened earth.[1] What would be a comparable definition of knowledge?

These analogies are, among other things, tools for clarification. Socrates uses them to help along his partner's understanding without the need for an abstract explanation. Analogies work in part because we often can see and feel the force of a comparison before we can explain why (or even if we *can't* explain why). They show rather than tell. Instead of saying "be more general," Socrates talks in examples and says "do it like this."

Fill-in-the-blank interrogations. Analogies of the style just shown can be used for a range of purposes. In the previous chapter we saw Socrates talk with Gorgias about the meaning of rhetoric. Now we can go back to that same discussion to see how Socrates used analogies to push it forward. When he's first introduced to Gorgias, they have the following exchange:

Gorgias
447d

SOCRATES. Ask him who he is.

CHAEREPHON. What do you mean?

SOCRATES. I mean such a question as would elicit from him, if he had been a maker of shoes, the answer that he is a cobbler.

Gorgias replies that he's a rhetorician. Socrates renews the analogical pursuit:

---

1. *Theaetetus* 147ac.

Gorgias
449d

SOCRATES. As you profess to be a rhetorician, and a maker of rhetoricians, let me ask you, with what is rhetoric concerned: I might ask with what is weaving concerned, and you would reply (would you not?), with the making of garments?

(Yes.) And musicians create melodies? (Yes.) So what do rhetoricians create? Gorgias says that they create discourse; they use words. Socrates replies that lots of activities use discourse and words. Mathematicians use them to talk about numbers; astronomers use them to talk about the stars.[2] Rhetoricians evidently use discourse and words for something else—but what? Complete the analogy. The answer from Gorgias: the most important things. But as we've seen, Socrates says this cuts no ice because people in all walks of life think that whatever they do is most important. He uses another analogy: the assembly of Athens consults a builder for help with a construction project. They should consult a rhetorician when they want to know or do—what?[3] Complete the analogy.

Notice how the line of questioning draws in the partner. The first analogy isn't too challenging: someone who makes shoes would be called a cobbler; what are *you* called? Gorgias is invited to play a game that looks easy. He starts answering and has the hang of it. Then the analogies get harder and more threatening. We know what good a cobbler or builder does; tell us what comparable good *you* do.

This style of inquiry is a good example of how Socrates reasons about hard and unfamiliar things by starting with easy and familiar ones. Begin with what you know—with distinctions and examples that you're sure about. Then try to map them onto the problems that you aren't so sure about. See where the fit is easy and where it's hard, and ask why. If someone is struggling to give the kind of answer that you're hoping to talk about, show what that kind of answer would look like in a setting where it's easy to understand.

Extended comparisons. The analogies so far have been simple: A is to B as C is to D. But Socrates also likes to create more elaborate

---

2. *Gorgias* 451c.   3. *Gorgias* 455bc.

comparisons. They can clarify an abstract idea by matching it to a concrete one point by point. An instance of this appears in the *Protagoras*, where Socrates compares knowledge to food and follows the comparison through several points of contact.

Protagoras
313ce

SOCRATES. Knowledge is the food of the soul; and we must take care, my friend, that the Sophist does not deceive us when he praises what he sells, like the dealers wholesale or retail who sell the food of the body; for they praise indiscriminately all their goods, without knowing what are really beneficial or hurtful: neither do their customers know, with the exception of any trainer or physician who may happen to buy of them. In like manner those who carry about the wares of knowledge, and make the round of the cities, and sell or retail them to any customer who is in want of them, praise them all alike; though I should not wonder, O my friend, if many of them were really ignorant of their effect upon the soul; and their customers equally ignorant, unless he who buys of them happens to be a physician of the soul.

Socrates maps the similarities between the two subjects one by one, showing their sameness. Notice that an analogy like this doesn't prove anything. The fact that knowledge resembles food in some ways doesn't mean that it resembles it in others. But the claim seems more convincing as the parallels get more numerous and vivid. Vividness isn't an argument, but it functions like one and can feel as persuasive or more. That should make us wary of vividness, but also mindful of its uses.

Socrates keeps talking about the analogy, but now in the opposite way: he describes a respect in which it fails.

Protagoras
313e–14b

SOCRATES. If, therefore, you have understanding of what is good and evil, you may safely buy knowledge of Protagoras or of any one; but if not, then, O my friend, pause, and do not hazard your dearest interests at a game of chance. For there is far greater peril in buying knowledge than in buying meat and drink: the one you purchase of the wholesale or retail dealer, and carry them away in other vessels, and before you receive them into the body as food, you may deposit them at home and call in any experienced friend who knows what is good to be eaten or drunken, and what not, and how much, and when; and then the danger of purchasing them is not so great. But you cannot buy the wares of knowledge and carry them away in another vessel; when you have paid for them you must receive them into the soul and go your way, either greatly harmed or greatly benefited.

This example shows how an analogy, once established, can be turned to make a clinching point. These two things are alike in many ways, yes, but then they differ in this final way. The same claim could have been made without an analogy. Socrates could have said that you should be careful who you listen to because it's hard to unlearn a bad idea once you've taken it in. But the analogy adds force by setting up a contrast. Think of how much *more* danger is found here than in food.

Clarity can also be improved by offering a choice between analogies: is the subject better compared to this or that? If two things are alike (or different), is it in this way or that way? Again the *Protagoras* provides a good example. Socrates starts:

I want you to tell me truly whether virtue is one whole, of which justice and temperance and holiness are parts; or whether all these are only the names of one and the same thing: that is the doubt which still lingers in my mind.

Protagoras
329ce

There is no difficulty, Socrates, in answering that the qualities of which you are speaking are the parts of virtue which is one.

And are they parts, I said, in the same sense in which mouth, nose, and eyes, and ears, are the parts of a face; or are they like the parts of gold, which differ from the whole and from one another only in being larger or smaller?

I should say that they differed, Socrates, in the first way; they are related to one another as the parts of a face are related to the whole face.

The analogy forces a clarification. Socrates asks Protagoras to choose one comparison or another, and the choice makes him explain the relationship between a set of concepts—that is, a series of virtues. The choice is made: they're like the parts of a face. Socrates follows out the analogy.

Protagoras
329e–30b

You would not deny, then, that courage and wisdom are also parts of virtue?

Most undoubtedly they are, he answered; and wisdom is the noblest of the parts.

And they are all different from one another? I said.

Yes.

And has each of them a distinct function like the parts of the face;—the eye, for example, is not like the ear, and has not the same functions; and the other parts are none of them like one another, either in their functions, or in any other way? I want to know whether the comparison holds concerning the parts of virtue. Do they also differ from one another in themselves and in their functions? For that is clearly what the simile would imply.

Yes, Socrates, you are right in supposing that they differ.

Then, I said, no other part of virtue is like knowledge, or like justice, or like courage, or like temperance, or like holiness?

No, he answered.

The parts of virtue are like the parts of a face; but this means the parts of virtue are *unalike* in their functions, in the same way that eyes and ears are unalike. The two cases are similar in their differences.

Argumentative analogies. To repeat, a comparison isn't an argument but can be used to express one. Eventually the other characters in the *Gorgias* ask Socrates what *he* thinks rhetoric is. He says it's a craft rather than an art, and a disreputable one; and he makes the claim by analogy. Cooking, he says, makes foods seem tasty even if they're bad for you; in that way it's a kind of flattery that deceives, as opposed to medicine that actually *is* good for you but doesn't taste that way. Cosmetics or "ornamentation" are an example of the same pattern:

they make people look healthy even if they aren't; they produce fake versions of the results that would be produced for real by exercise. Rhetoric is similar—and now Socrates doesn't ask his partners to fill in the blanks of his analogy. He does it himself.

> SOCRATES. As ornamentation is to exercise, so cookery is to medicine—or rather, as ornamentation is to exercise, so sophistry is to the legislative process, and as cookery is to medicine, so rhetoric is to the administration of justice.

Gorgias 465c

As before, Socrates could have made make his point without an analogy. He could have said that rhetoricians pander. The analogy adds force because the parallel is vivid and ties the abstract claim to things that everyone has experienced with the senses. The analogy operates on the listener's intuitions; that is, it plays to the organs of perception rather than reason. The analogy also lets insults be heaped on the subject indirectly. Socrates uses harsh words when he talks about cosmetics: "knavish, false, ignoble, illiberal." That's safe enough; there are no cosmeticians around to complain. But once the repulsive character of cosmetics is established, those words can be transferred to rhetoric without too much effort. If the relationships are parallel, the ugly implications follow. The passage isn't a forceful piece of logic, but (ironically) it's a good piece of rhetoric.

Resistance. When Socrates tells his partner to complete an analogy, he's implying that the things compared in the analogy are alike. That may not be true. Sometimes the best response to an analogy is to challenge it rather than complete it—to say it's relying on a similarity that isn't there. We see this when Socrates goes back and forth with Critias (in the *Charmides*) about the meaning of self-control. He tries his usual analogical tricks, but Critias will have none of them.

> SOCRATES. If you were to ask me what I'd identify as the product of building, which is knowledge of building houses, I'd reply that its product was houses. And I'd give similar answers to questions about all the other arts and crafts. Since you claim that self-control is knowledge of oneself, you ought to be able

Charmides 165c–66a

to answer the equivalent questions. So suppose you were asked: "Critias, if self-knowledge is knowledge of oneself, what is its product and does its product deserve to be called desirable?" Let's hear what your answer would be.

CRITIAS. Socrates, you're going about the investigation in the wrong way. Self-control differs from other branches of knowledge (which also differ from one another, anyway). But you're conducting the investigation on the basis of an assumption that they're all similar. I mean, tell me: what product is there of arithmetic or geometry which is equivalent to a house in the case of building, or to clothes in the case of weaving, or to the many equivalent products that one could point to in the case of many arts and crafts?

Socrates pursues this a little further, is hit with a similar reply again, and so abandons that line of attack. It is good of Plato to show a case where a Socratic analogy is beaten back in this way. It's a reminder that analogies look like observations but actually make claims. Keeping the claim below the surface can make it more effective because no direct examination of it is invited. The question asks the partner to assume the truth of the parallel and to finish it; asking whether there *is* a parallel would be different and might lead to a different discussion. As the passage from the *Charmides* shows, either side can raise the point.

Why analogies? We've seen that analogies are a routine part of Socratic discourse. Plato was self-conscious about their constant use. He has his other characters talk about it. A critical example:

Gorgias
491a

CALLICLES. You simply never stop going on and on about cobblers and fullers and cooks and doctors, as if they had the slightest relevance to our discussion.

A more sympathetic view:

Symposium
221d–22a

ALCIBIADES. Even his ideas and arguments are just like those hollow statues of Silenus. If you were to listen to his arguments, at first they'd strike you as totally ridiculous; they're clothed in words as coarse as the hides worn by the most vulgar satyrs. He's always going on about pack asses, or blacksmiths, or cobblers, or tanners; he's always making the same tired old points in the same tired old words. If you are foolish, or simply unfamiliar with him, you'd find it impossible not to laugh at his arguments. But if you see them when they open up like the statues, if you go beyond their surface, you'll realize that no other arguments make sense. They're truly worthy of a god, bursting with figures of virtue inside. They're of great—no, of the greatest—importance for anyone who wants to become a truly good man.

Why does Socrates use so many analogies? First, he is trying to get his partners to think hard in unaccustomed ways. Analogies make the process seem more familiar. He draws comparisons to everyday things and activities—to cobblers and clay. These images give relief from abstraction and create some comfort. They also suggest that anyone can do this, not just specialists. Socrates says: talk the way you are used to talking about the things you know, but do it while thinking about things that are larger.

Second, there's a risk that the topics Socrates cares about—justice or virtue, say—might seem to be only words, and to matter less than the tangible things we know from ordinary life. Socrates worries that ideas don't seem real to us. Consider his speculation about death:

> If at the time of its release the soul is tainted and impure, because it has always associated with the body and cared for it and loved it, and has been so beguiled by the body and its passions and pleasures that nothing seems real to it but those physical things which can be touched and seen and eaten and drunk and used for sexual enjoyment, and if it is accustomed to hate and fear and avoid what is invisible and hidden from our eyes, but intelligible and comprehensible by philosophy—if the soul is in this state do you think that it will escape independent and uncontaminated?

Phaedo
81b

(No.) Socrates thinks of ideas as every bit as important—more so, indeed—as what we can see and touch, and he tries to get others to look at them that way, too.[4] He wants people to care for their insides (the psyche, the soul) with the kind of energy and attention they spend on their physical selves and whatever else they see. Think of Socrates as up against a bias: we treat what is available to our senses more seriously than what is only available to our minds. He is at war with that bias. Analogies are a weapon against it.

The epagoge. We've seen that analogies don't prove the comparisons they make but can be convincing when they have intuitive appeal. And then if two things are similar in some ways, perhaps they really *are* similar in others; maybe a common principle is at work in both. When viewed that way, analogies can resemble a form of "epagogic" reasoning, another kind of argument that Socrates uses and that is best discussed here briefly.

An epagoge (*ep*-ah-go-*gay*—sounds like *epic delay*) is an argument in which specific examples lead to a general conclusion. An example from the *Protagoras* (Socrates speaks first):

Protagoras
332c

I said, is there anything beautiful?
Yes.
To which the only opposite is the ugly?
There is no other.
And is there anything good?
There is.
To which the only opposite is the evil?
There is no other.
And there is the acute in sound?
True.
To which the only opposite is the grave?
There is no other, he said, but that.
Then every opposite has one opposite only and no more?
He assented.

An epagoge is usually considered another way to speak of inductive reasoning—that is, arguing from specific examples to general

---

4. See *Phaedo* 83c.

conclusions. Socrates, though, puts that general pattern to uses that sometimes require more interpretation.[5] He does often cite a few cases that work a certain way, then suggest that all cases are like that, as in the passage just shown. But it often isn't clear what relationship he claims between his examples and the conclusions. He might (at least in theory) mean to say: we've looked at all the relevant evidence; now here's the rule that explains it. He might mean: we've looked at some of the evidence; here's a rule that seems probable on account of it. He might mean: we've seen some examples; here's the general point that they all illustrate (but that they don't prove), or here is the universal idea they all represent. That example from the *Protagoras* can be viewed as inferring a rule from a few examples, or as giving some examples of a rule that seems intuitive. There are debates about which of those patterns describes which arguments in the dialogues. We won't trace them here, but the reader should be alert to the possibilities.

The epagoge and the analogy are staples of Socratic argument. They are similar because they both involve working back and forth between particulars that are familiar and concepts that aren't. A lot of the action in Socratic moral reasoning happens in that bottom-up fashion: Is a given case more like this one or that one? What can we gather from the things we know? Socrates seeks agreement to simple claims, then leverages the agreement into big claims.

---

5. See Robinson, *Plato's Earlier Dialectic*, 33–38; Vlastos, *Socrates, Ironist and Moral Philosopher*, 267–60.

10

Socratic Rules for Dialogue

SOCRATES sets out rules for engaging in dialogue. This chapter looks at some of them: trying to find the truth, rather than trying to win; examining people, not just claims; judging arguments on their merits regardless of who makes them; candor, or saying what you think; the one-witness principle—that is, treating the other party to the dialogue as the judge of what it has shown; the principle of charity; and not giving or taking offense. These rules were not discussed as central elements of the Socratic method in chapter 3, because some might fairly be considered details and because some aren't followed as regularly as the other elements. But they are important all the same.

Rules taken lightly. Some of the rules that Socrates offers can be described as "rules" only with unease, because Socrates himself has an uneasy relationship to rules. He makes them and breaks them. He tells his partners not to make long speeches, then he makes a long speech.[1] He uses some bad arguments, giving rise to debate later about whether he did it on purpose.[2] He seems earnest; he seems disingenuous. He brings irony to philosophy and then dies for philosophy. Either Socrates and Plato or both had a taste for fun, for slyness, for the side of the self that isn't all direct and sober in the way that Socrates seems at first. Pascal's comment:

> We can only think of Plato and Aristotle in grand academic robes. They were honest men, like others, laughing with their friends, and when they diverted themselves with writing their *Laws* and the *Politics*, they did it as an amusement. That part of

---

1. See, e.g., *Gorgias* 449bc, 464b–466a.
2. See discussion and references in Vlastos, *Socrates, Ironist and Moral Philosopher*, 132–56; Cohen, "Aporias in Plato's Early Dialogues"; Sprague, *Plato's Use of Fallacy.*

their life was the least philosophic and the least serious; the most philosophic was to live simply and quietly.[3]

Nietzsche:

Socrates excels the founder of Christianity in being able to be serious cheerfully and in possessing that wisdom full of roguishness that constitutes the finest state of the human soul.[4]

This ability to contain opposites is part of the Socratic spirit. Literary, philosophical, and other powers come from movement between polarities, not from either one of them alone. Philosophy in the Socratic style is an example. It is high-stakes and also playful, and therein lies much of its appeal. Emerson's take:

The rare coincidence, in one ugly body, of the droll and the martyr, the keen street and market debater with the sweetest saint known to any history at that time, had forcibly struck the mind of Plato, so capacious of these contrasts.... The strange synthesis in the character of Socrates capped the synthesis in the mind of Plato.[5]

But if some of the rules of Socratic dialogue sometimes seem made to be broken, they're useful anyway. They contain wisdom. They are policies with reasons behind them, and understanding the reasons is a help toward better thinking. You just have to remember that the Socratic method also has another strain that sometimes takes its own rules lightly.

Seeking the truth (dialectic vs. eristic). The Socratic method, as originally understood, is a search for truth, not a debating exercise. The first of those approaches is sometimes described by Socrates as *dialectic*—as opposed to *eristic* argument carried out for sport or for the sake of winning.[6]

---

3. Trotter, *Blaise Pascal: Thoughts*, 116.
4. Levy, *Friedrich Nietzsche: Human, All Too Human*, 242.
5. Emerson, *Representative Men*, 77.
6. For discussion of the meaning of "eristic," see Vlastos, *Socratic Studies*, 136.

Republic
539bd

SOCRATES. Youngsters, as you may have observed, when they first get the taste in their mouths, argue for amusement, and are always contradicting and refuting others in imitation of those who refute them; like puppy-dogs, they rejoice in pulling and tearing at all who come near them.... But when a man begins to get older, he will no longer be guilty of such insanity; he will imitate the dialectician who is seeking for truth, and not the eristic, who is contradicting for the sake of amusement; and the greater moderation of his character will increase instead of diminishing the honor of the pursuit.

As the passage shows, "eristic" can be used to describe an argument or a person who makes such an argument.[7] It seems to have been mostly a term of abuse.[8] Socratic dialogues can themselves seem eristic; readers sometimes come away with the sense that Socrates will make any argument to knock down the other side's claim. Socrates or Plato or both of them were probably criticized for having that tendency, rightly or wrongly, since we see it come up in the texts. Critias makes that kind of charge against Socrates:

Charmides
166c

You are only doing what you denied that you were doing just now, trying to refute me, instead of pursuing the argument.

Gorgias
482e–83a

CALLICLES. You pretend that truth is your goal, Socrates, but in actual fact you steer discussions towards this kind of ethical ideal—ideas which are unsophisticated enough to have popular appeal, and which depend entirely on convention, not on nature.... This in fact is the source of the clever, but unfair, argumentative trick you've devised: if a person is talking from a conventional standpoint, you slip in a question which presupposes a natural point of view, and if he's talking about nature, you substitute convention.

Such criticisms may be why Socrates is sensitive about the point (Plato might have worried that they were right), and why Socrates

---

7. See Nehamas, *Virtues of Authenticity*, 112–13.
8. See Grote, *Plato and the Other Companions of Sokrates*, 1:554 n.

is careful to say that eristic arguments are exactly what he *isn't* making—that he's always trying to get it right, not win.

People, not just claims. The Socratic method, as originally understood, doesn't only test claims. It tests people. It's a personal undertaking.[9] When Socrates describes his activity in the *Apology*, he speaks of "examining myself and others," not examining propositions.[10] And while the dialogues are on topics such as courage or piety, most of them don't have titles like "On Courage" or "On Piety." The dialogues are usually named after *people—Laches, Euthyphro, Charmides*, and the rest. We don't know if those titles were created by Plato himself, but in any event they are apt. Those characters aren't just excuses to talk about philosophy. They are part of the subject matter.

> NICIAS. Anyone who is close to Socrates and enters into conversation with him is liable to be drawn into an argument, and whatever subject he may start, he will be continually carried round and round by him, until at last he finds that he has to give an account both of his present and past life, and when he is once entangled, Socrates will not let him go until he has completely and thoroughly sifted him.

Laches
187e

Modern philosophers usually argue about questions in the abstract and try to settle them for everyone. Socrates is different because he's interested in the general questions *and* in how they play out in the people he examines. His method implies that separating them isn't easy and maybe isn't desirable.[11]

The point can be stated in terms sometimes described as therapeutic.[12] Socrates is out to find the truth and is devoted to the care of the psyche, or soul. He treats these as inseparable parts of philosophical practice.

---

9. See Robinson, *Plato's Earlier Dialectic*, 15–17; Tarrant, "Socratic Method and Socratic Truth," 256–63; Talisse, "Misunderstanding Socrates," 52–53.

10. *Apology* 28e.

11. See Brickhouse and Smith, *Plato's Socrates*, 12–14.

12. See Vlastos, *Socratic Studies*, 10.

Apology
30a

SOCRATES. I go about doing nothing else but urging you, young and old alike, not to care for your bodies or for your money sooner than, or as much as, for your *psyche*, and how to make it as good as you can.

"Psyche" is the original (transliterated) word in Greek. It's sometimes translated as "soul" or (by Mill) as "mental nature." Socrates evidently meant one's true self, or intelligence, between which he did not distinguish.[13]

Some scholars describe Socratic questioning as ad hominem. Nowadays that term usually means attacking an idea by attacking the holder of it. An ad hominem argument in that sense has no place in Socratic discourse, as we will see in a moment. But in Socratic discourse the expression can mean something different. First, it's the idea that Socrates is always testing the holder of a claim as well as the claim itself. He usually finds that the holder is being inconsistent—but this proves that the holder has a problem, not necessarily that the claim does. Second, Socrates argues by using his opponent's own premises. He doesn't say they're valid.[14] He says: assuming you believe X, let's see where it takes you. In practice Socrates usually moves the dialogue along by supplying some additional points, but he gets agreement to them and so is still able to go forward in the ad hominem spirit. An argument of that kind isn't a straight path (it may not be any path) to the truth. It just shows where someone is mixed up. But that matters to Socrates because he doesn't distinguish between his mission as a philosopher and his mission as an investigator of people and their minds.

The personal aspect of Socratic inquiry can also explain the slow rate of progress in moral philosophy. Some of the questions that troubled humanity thousands of years ago trouble us now about as much. This should be unsurprising if we look at philosophy the way

---

13. For discussion of the word's meaning at the time, see Guthrie, *History of Greek Philosophy*, 467–70.

14. See Annas, "Plato the Skeptic," 316–22.

Socrates did. Philosophy of the Socratic kind has to be carried out from scratch in each person who tries it.

The priority of reason. But Socrates treats inquiry as an impersonal affair in other important respects. First, he makes no ad hominem arguments in the sense of the term now most familiar: he never attacks his partners personally. Strictly speaking we might say that Socrates doesn't argue with them at all; he only causes them to argue with themselves. But he does challenge what his partners say. And he sometimes does it with a persistence that irritates them and might irritate the reader. Yet Socrates is also relentlessly courteous, and never uses a hard epithet to describe an argument or the person making it. (An exception occurs in the *Hippias Major*, when he does appear to use strong language—against himself.)

And the impersonal character of reason runs deeper than the avoidance of insult. So far as Socrates is concerned, the value of an argument is independent of the identity of the person making it. That is why he will talk to anyone and listen to anyone. He is ready to refute what is said by the mighty, and he will accept refutation from any source so long as the reasoning is sound.

> I permit rich and poor alike to question me, or if they please, to answer my questions, and to hear what I have to say.

Apology 33b

> POLUS. You are hard of refutation, Socrates, but might not a child refute that statement?
> SOCRATES. Then I shall be very grateful to the child, and equally grateful to you if you will refute me and deliver me from my foolishness.

Gorgias 470c

> Then, I said, be cheerful, sweet sir, and give your opinion in answer to the question which I asked, never minding whether Critias or Socrates is the person refuted; attend only to the argument, and see what will come of the refutation.

Charmides 166e

This principle has implications with two sides. First, Socrates defers to nobody when considering an argument. He considers the most illustrious people fair game for inquiry; the subjects of his questioning include generals and aristocrats. The *Apology* recounts his search for people with wisdom that might entitle them to deference.[15] He finds none. Second, Socrates regards anyone as eligible to refute *him*. The poor aren't disqualified by their status or by any absence of education. The rich aren't disqualified by their positions, either. Sometimes his high-status partners in the dialogues advance views that serve their interests, but Socrates never takes issue on that ground. He doesn't care. An argument that serves their interests might be valid. Claims are judged strictly by the quality of the reasoning and evidence that supports them.

This rule is subject to exceptions on reasoned grounds. At one point in the *Republic*, for example, Socrates and Glaucon talk about which pleasures are greatest: those that come from material gain, from honor, or from wisdom. They decide that the question is best answered by someone who has experienced all three pleasures and can compare them. And they think that someone with wisdom is most likely to be in that position. So Glaucon is led to the conclusion that, in this respect, "the wise man speaks with authority when he approves of his own life." [16] This makes sense because the question on the table is not a matter of reason. They are asking which kind of pleasure is strongest, and this is a matter of observation. Those who have done the observing know more than those who haven't. They can see the evidence better.

These points can be turned into practical guidelines for those using the Socratic method, whether formally or informally. The internal consistency of someone who makes a claim is a central focus of the method. In other words, Socrates cares whether their claims are consistent with one another. But the *identity* of the person making a claim is irrelevant to the analysis. The Socratic vocabulary, that is, does not include the protest, "Who are *you* to argue *that*?" Anyone can be heard on anything. If an argument depends on a claim about evidence, someone who knows the evidence might be entitled to

---

15. *Apology* 21c–22e.   16. *Republic* 583a.

deference from those who don't. But a claim to deference on that or other grounds requires justification like any other. The Socratic method thus observes the priority of reason across the board.

Candor. Another rule of Socratic dialogue: say what you think, not what others want to hear.[17] It is a practice he claims for himself.

> SOCRATES. I have refused to address you in the way which would give you most pleasure. You would have liked to hear me weep and wail, doing and saying all sorts of things which I regard as unworthy of myself, but which you are used to hearing from other people. But I did not think then that I ought to stoop to servility because I was in danger, and I do not regret now the way in which I pleaded my case. I would much rather die as the result of this defense than live as the result of the other sort.

Apology
38de

It is also the practice he demands of his partners.

> SOCRATES. Could you tell me once and for all whether in your opinion the pleasant and the good are the same, or whether there's even one pleasure which isn't good?
> CALLICLES. I can't say they're different and still be consistent, so I'll say they're the same.
> SOCRATES. You're breaking your original promise, Callicles. If what you say contradicts what you really think, your value as my partner in searching for the truth will be at an end.

Gorgias
495a

"It does not appear to me," replied Protagoras, "so simple and obvious that justice and holiness are the same thing. There seems to me to be a difference; but let us call them the same thing, if you will."—"I have no use," said Socrates, "for 'if you will.' I do not desire to examine or confute an 'if you will,' or an 'if you think so,' but what you think, and what I think, leaving out the 'if.' "

Protagoras
331bc

Why do we need a rule about this? First, because insisting that the

---

17. Discussed well in Vlastos, *Socratic Studies*, 7–11; Irwin, "Say What You Believe"; Robinson, *Plato's Earlier Dialectic*, 78–79.

players say what they think keeps the focus where it's supposed to be: on the truth.[18] Speaking anything other than the truth of your own views also retards the care of the psyche. It is like lying to a doctor or therapist. It means you really can't be treated because you won't be affected by the experience. And if nobody is affected by a dialogue, it's a waste of time. The point is familiar from a teacher's standpoint. If you want students to be changed by their time in the classroom, it's best for them to put their true opinions on the line. If they say what they think the teacher wants to hear, there's not much learning.

But of course that happens all the time. People under interrogation are tempted to say things that aren't true. They want to please or impress the questioner, or be polite to the questioner, or avoid giving offense or feeling embarrassment. All these pressures make it easy to give false agreement, especially when a leading question invites a "yes" in reply. But the Socratic cross-examiner doesn't want a "yes" unless you mean it. Rather than pressuring his partner to agree, Socrates pressures him *not* to agree unless he's sure.

Crito
49de

SOCRATES. Now be careful, Crito, that in making these single admissions you do not end by admitting something contrary to your real beliefs.... I want even you to consider very carefully whether you share my views and agree with me, and whether we can proceed with our discussion from the established hypothesis that it is never right to do a wrong or return a wrong or defend oneself against injury by retaliation, or whether you dissociate yourself from any share in this view as a basis for discussion. I have held it for a long time, and still hold it, but if you have formed any other opinion, say so and tell me what it is.

Candor is also important for the sake of making ethical headway in a community. Callicles explains his view that the best life is the one most full of the satisfaction of desires. Socrates appreciates his expression of the point.

18. See Vlastos, *Socratic Studies*, 8–9.

SOCRATES. Thank you, Callicles, for this generous and frank elaboration of your position. You see, what you're doing here is giving a clear account of things which other people think, but are reluctant to voice out loud. Please, I beg you, do all you can to sustain the momentum.

Everyplace is like this. There are beliefs people talk about, and then others that they hold but do not want to speak. It is impossible to make serious progress in conversation until both kinds of beliefs are brought forth. So it is part of the Socratic questioner's job to encourage honesty. It is best done in the way that Socrates shows. The honest claim will be challenged and probed, but the maker of the claim will not be condemned. Quite the contrary: one who says something shocking should be thanked for putting the claim on the table so that it can be rationally talked about and tested. The act of doing so is a personal risk taken in part for the good of the community. Other people are probably having the same thought but not saying so. And the unspoken thing might be closer to the truth than the thing spoken.

The rule of candor in the Socratic method is no more absolute than most of the other rules.[19] Sometimes Socrates lets it go so that the argument can advance after his partner has given up or for other reasons.[20] And candor isn't required in the same way from the *questioner*; notwithstanding the passage from the *Apology* shown above, Socrates' own sincerity is sometimes in doubt.[21] That is inevitable. To be an effective Socratic questioner, you often have to push back against claims even if you agree with them—perhaps especially then, since the risk of self-serving confirmation is so high. The "devil's advocate" originally referred to the person in the Catholic Church whose job was to point out flaws in a candidate for sainthood. The Socratic questioner is often in that position with respect to a popular belief.

19. See Vlastos, 10–11; Kahn, "Vlastos's Socrates," 170–172.
20. See *Protagoras* 333bc; *Republic* 349a.
21. For discussion, see Fink, *Development of Dialectic from Plato to Aristotle*, 7; Brickhouse and Smith, *Plato's Socrates*, 14–16; Kahn, "Vlastos's Socrates," 169–73.

Candor has to be self-policed, and the policing can fail. You can cheat at Socratic inquiry without getting caught. And that can happen even when you test your own beliefs. Here a rule of candor might seem silly because of course you have no reason to be anything but frank when you talk to yourself. But there's no "of course" about it. It's common to falsely imagine you believe something that you don't but wish you did, and then no one is around to point out what claptrap it is. The self-image may be protected as cautiously as a public image; the urgency and difficulty of candor can be greatest when confronting oneself. Socrates worried about this.

Cratylus
428d

SOCRATES. There is nothing worse than self-deception—when the deceiver is always at home and always with you.

And Socrates notes how energetically we can try to convince ourselves of things that may not be true:

Phaedo
91a

SOCRATES. At this moment I am sensible that I have not the temper of a philosopher; like the vulgar, I am only a partisan. Now the partisan, when he is engaged in a dispute, cares nothing about the rights of the question, but is anxious only to convince his hearers of his own assertions. And the difference between him and me at the present moment is merely this—that whereas he seeks to convince his hearers that what he says is true, I am rather seeking to convince myself; to convince my hearers is a secondary matter with me.

The one-witness principle. Another rule for Socratic practice: numbers count for nothing. Having a majority in favor of an opinion, or for that matter having the whole world in favor of it, doesn't matter. The views that matter are those of the parties to the dialogue. A single witness to the truth is enough.

Gorgias
472bc

SOCRATES. I won't have accomplished anything important with regard to the issues we've been discussing, unless I get you yourself to act as my witness—albeit a single one!—to testify to the truth of my position; and I'm sure you won't think you've accomplished anything important either unless I testify for your position. It doesn't matter that there's only one of me; you'd let all the others go if you could get me as your witness.

POLUS. Don't you think the sheer eccentricity of what you're saying is enough of a refutation, Socrates? Why don't you ask anyone here whether they agree with you?

SOCRATES. I'm no politician, Polus.... My expertise is restricted to producing just a single witness in support of my ideas—the person with whom I'm carrying on the discussion—and I pay no attention to large numbers of people; I only know how to ask for a single person's vote, and can't even begin to address people in large groups.

Gorgias
473e–74a

The one-witness idea serves several purposes. First, you can't be expected to say what you think if you're worried that the world won't like it. The single-witness idea tries to keep such social pressure out of a dialogue by rule. Second, Socratic dialogue is supposed to rely on reasoning by the parties to it and nothing else. The one-witness rule keeps them from treating anyone else as a source of authority.[22] And it's a reminder that sound reasoning and popular reasoning are utterly different things.

SOCRATES. You're trying to use on me the kind of rhetorical refutation which people in law courts think is successful. There too, you see, people think they're proving the other side wrong if they produce a large number of eminent witnesses in support of the points they're making, but their opponent comes up with only a single witness or none at all. This kind of refutation, however, is completely worthless in the context of the truth, since it's perfectly possible for someone to be defeated in court by a horde of witnesses with no more than apparent respectability who all testify falsely against him.

Gorgias
471e–72a

So proving a point by saying that "everybody knows…" or "nobody thinks…" is out of bounds. Do *you* know it?

---

22. Robinson, *Plato's Earlier Dialectic*, 79.

Third, we've seen that Socratic inquiry is a personal process. The single-witness principle is another part of that approach. Waking up to some feature of the truth, or waking up someone else, is a momentous achievement. But the only test of wakefulness is recognition of it by the party awakened. That test keeps success in inquiry simple to measure. There's no need to bother about what bystanders think. The question is whether the partners agree.

Republic
348ab

SOCRATES. If we counter his claim by drawing up an alternative list of all the advantages of morality, and then he responds to that, and we respond to his response, we'll find ourselves in the position of having to add up advantages and measure the lengths of our respective lists, and before we know it we'll need jurors to adjudicate for us. On the other hand, if we conduct the investigation as we did just now, by trying to win each other's consent, then we'll be our own jurors *and* claimants.

Most of these points carry over to the use of Socratic thought without a partner. The Socratic type is in a constant dialogue with prevailing opinion, talks back fearlessly, and doesn't knuckle under to what everyone else says or would say. A remark like the following is as apt when going back and forth with oneself as it is when speaking with anyone else.

Gorgias
472ab

SOCRATES. If you feel like calling witnesses to claim that what I'm saying is wrong, you can count on your position being supported by almost everyone in Athens.... Nevertheless, there's still a dissenting voice, albeit a single one—mine. You're producing no compelling reason why I should agree with you; all you're doing is calling up a horde of false witnesses against me to support your attempt to dislodge me from my inheritance, the truth.

The crowd is not to be trusted. This point is especially important in current times when a "horde of false witnesses" can be summoned on demand by anyone online. (Notice, though, that although Socrates counts one witness as enough in a dialogue, the problem of reckoning with collective opinion gets more complex when that collective opinion takes the form of law and one must decide what to *do*—an issue he discusses in the *Crito*.)

Charity. Socrates generally treats his partners with charity. First, when he construes what his partners say, he tries to put it in the most reasonable light. Gorgias, for example, suggests that rhetoric is expertise in the use of speech, and nothing but speech, to produce results. Socrates means generally to challenge the way Gorgias thinks about rhetoric, but first he wants to help Gorgias do the best he can. Socrates points out that people use words to convey ideas and get things done in far-flung fields such as arithmetic and geometry. Gorgias agrees. The dialogue continues:

> SOCRATES. But I'm sure you wouldn't want actually to iden-   *Gorgias*
> tify rhetoric with any of them. I know that's what it sounded as   450e–451a
> though you were saying, when you defined rhetoric as the area
> of expertise which relies on speech to achieve its results, and if
> someone wanted to pick a quarrel he might take you up on this
> point and say, "So you're identifying rhetoric with mathematics,
> are you, Gorgias?" But I'm sure you're not actually identifying
> rhetoric with mathematics or geometry.
> GORGIAS. You're right, Socrates. You've correctly interpreted
> my meaning.

This is good general practice in a dialogue: try to help your partners, real or imagined, get clear about what they mean; and when their meaning isn't clear, assume they're smart, that they mean well, and that they're saying things that make more sense rather than less.[23]

Socrates follows the same practice, but with more vigor, in the *Theaetetus*. There he intends to challenge the views of Protagoras. Unfortunately Protagoras is dead, so Socrates has the job of

---

23. For more discussion of this approach from a Socratic standpoint, see Boghosian and Lindsay, *How to Have Impossible Conversations: A Very Practical Guide*, 26–27. The book contains many other useful practical pointers for good dialogue.

describing the ideas of Protagoras before tearing them down. He starts by attributing to Protagoras the view that "Man is the measure of all things." That claim can have several meanings, some of them plausible and some not. Socrates says of Protagoras that "he's a clever person, and unlikely to be talking nonsense; so let's follow in his footsteps." [24] Then he offers cases that make the Protagorean view seem as convincing as possible. Then he spends many pages showing that the Protagorean view is unconvincing. Then he spends many *more* pages imagining the vigorous and powerful responses that Protagoras would make if he were present. Then he spends still more pages going back the other way—etc. The reader of this dialogue or any other is usually struck by the ingenuity of Socrates in developing arguments against his position as well as in favor of it. That is a good test of Socratic progress: the extent of one's inclination and ability to come up with strong objections to one's own views, and indeed to do it better than one's opponents can.

In modern times the practices just described are sometimes summed up as a principle of charity: interpreting what others say in the most reasonable ways you can, and putting the arguments of others in their best light. That principle has been attributed to many authors; like most important intellectual procedures, though, it goes back to Socrates. When he challenges a position, he generally challenges it in its strongest and most appealing form, and sometimes that means doing the other side's job for them. Socrates, in short, runs *toward* the hard problems for his position. To state the point as practical advice for dialogue: consider the best case for your adversary or partner, not the best case for you.

Offense. The Socratic practitioner avoids giving offense and also avoids taking it. The risk of personal offense is serious if you're trying to find the truth in a dialogue with a partner. A dialogue about a topic that matters will often involve points that both sides feel strongly about. Those strong feelings are sensitive to the touch. Disagreement when such feelings are at stake, no matter how rational an argument

---

24. *Theaetetus* 152b.

may be, can be experienced as a personal attack or provoke indignation in reply. The inquiry is then derailed and the dialogue turns into something else.

Socrates talks about this problem. He cautions Gorgias about cases in which, when two people are arguing,

> One person tells the other that he's wrong or has expressed himself obscurely, and then they get angry and each thinks that his own point of view is being maliciously misinterpreted by the other person, and they start trying to win the argument rather than look into the issue they set out to discuss. Sometimes the argument finally breaks up in an appalling state, with people hurling abuse and saying the kinds of things to each other which can only make the bystanders cross at themselves for having thought these people worth listening to.

Gorgias 457d

(Observe how little has changed over the millennia.) Socrates spells out his worry because he is contradicting Gorgias and wants to make sure his partner knows that it's nothing personal. If Gorgias is feeling offended, they should stop and move on. Socrates sometimes takes similar steps elsewhere.

> I will say no more about your friend's speech lest I should give offense to you; although I think that it might furnish many other examples of what a man ought rather to avoid.

Phaedrus 264e

This shows sound judgment. If you want to get anywhere in a dialogue, avoid lines of argument that tweak personal sensitivities; use examples that don't strike too close to home; express yourself in ways that won't tempt your partner to get defensive. In other words, use good manners. There is an art to expressing a difficult point in a way that doesn't give offense, as discussed in chapter 10. It means choosing words and examples carefully and conveying personal respect. And if it's getting hot, there's nothing wrong with pointing that out and making clear that you mean X and not Y. This is what Socrates did.

So Socrates tries not to give offense. But there are two sides to the issue. If you want reasoned discourse, taking offense is as much a problem as giving it. So Socrates also makes clear that *he* won't take offense at being contradicted; he says that "I'm happy to have a mistaken idea of mine proved wrong."[25] Indeed, Socrates experiences refutation as a favor.

I'm certainly not *less* happy if I'm proved wrong than if I've proved someone else wrong, because, as I see it, I've got the best of it: there's nothing worse than the state which I've been saved from, so that's better for me than saving someone else.

He makes the same point later to Callicles:

If you do prove me wrong, I won't get cross with you as you did with me. No, I'll make sure the public register lists you as my greatest benefactor.

In a later dialogue where Socrates does not figure, Plato lets one of his other protagonists state the same point in plain and less dramatic language.

ATHENIAN. If, as is very likely, in our search after the true and good, one of us may have to censure the laws of the others, we must not be offended, but take kindly what another says.

This attitude is crucial to the success of Socratic inquiry. Offense isn't only a problem when it's given and taken in fact. The *risk* of offense is a problem in advance because it makes people dishonest. When they are worried about the other side taking offense, they don't say what they really think, and progress toward the truth is over. Everyone pretends to agree more than they do. That's a common problem now, as it was then. Pushing past that fear is part of the Socratic method. It takes courage, and a commitment on both sides not to treat the dispute as personal no matter where the ideas may go.

Some of this discussion might seem contrary to recollections the reader has of Socrates being obnoxious. But his approach depends on the context. We've seen that Socrates can be sarcastic with pompous

---

25. *Gorgias* 458a.

or combative discussion partners (and very harsh with himself), but many of his dialogues are conducted with friends in a good-natured spirit. He draws the distinction openly.

> MENO. If someone were to say that he didn't know what color was and was just as puzzled about color as he was about shape, what reply would have given him, do you think?
> SOCRATES. I'd tell him the truth. And if the person asking me the question was one of those clever, disputatious men who always try to win arguments, I'd say: "You've heard what I have to say. If I've made a mistake, it's up to you to challenge me and get me to explain myself." On the other hand, if people are willing to join in the kind of friendly conversation you and I are having now, a less aggressive reply, one better suited for conversation, is appropriate.

Meno
75cd

This approach can be carried over to examination of the self. The Socratic function in the mind, as in the dialogues, works like a gyroscope. It helps maintain orientation; it compensates. When his partners don't have confidence, Socrates encourages them. When they're inflated, he deflates them. The Socratic instinct in the self can operate the same way. In its caustic moments the Socratic function does some of the work of the fool or court jester in Shakespeare. Its job is to be offensive when the ego overrates itself. It pokes at self-importance and hubris when they need mockery; it looks long and hard for the emperor's clothes and doesn't find them. And it shows surprise and chagrin when the emperor is enraged.

11

Ignorance

THE Socratic dialogues are all about different topics but also about the same topic: the relationship between knowledge and ignorance. Whatever else he's doing, Socrates usually demonstrates that someone who looks like an expert doesn't have the knowledge that he thought he did. This helps us see that we don't have it, either. Socrates shows how hard it is to reach the truth, and with luck this makes us hungry to get closer to it and humbler in the meantime. Ignorance also can serve for Socrates as a tactical posture—as a way to approach questioning, a method for eliciting the views of others, and an openness to refutation. This chapter talks about these various roles that ignorance plays in the Socratic method.

Socratic ignorance generally. A philosophy can start in many places and end in many others. Socratic philosophy starts with "I don't know." It ends with "I don't know." Between those two points there is progress and improvement, but it isn't a journey from a question to an answer; it's a journey from one question to another. It's also a change in orientation. Instead of moving through a series of certainties, you get used to searching without certainty. There is a lump under the mattress and you toss and turn in trying to deal with it and finally accept that you will never fully come to rest and that's all right. The lump is ignorance. Ignorance is many things in Socratic philosophy: a shocking discovery, a chronic condition, a motivator, an enemy, perhaps an inevitability.

Socratic inquiry begins with awareness of your own ignorance— that is, awareness of how far short you fall from the wisdom you would like to have, and from conclusive answers to the most urgent questions. The point is established in the *Apology* (or "defense"), the speech at his trial in which Socrates recounts the beginnings of his efforts. A visitor to the Oracle of Delphi had been told by the

Pythia—the presiding High Priestess—that no man was wiser than Socrates. Socrates describes his reaction when he heard this report.

> I said to myself, What can the god mean? and what is the inter-
> pretation of his riddle? for I am not aware of being wise in any-
> thing, great or small.... I reflected that if I could only find a man
> wiser than myself, then I might go to the god with a refutation in
> my hand.... Accordingly I went to one who had the reputation
> of wisdom, and observed him—his name I need not mention;
> he was a politician whom I selected for examination—and the
> result was as follows: When I began to talk with him, I could
> not help thinking that he was not really wise, although he was
> thought wise by many, and still wiser by himself; and thereupon
> I tried to explain to him that he thought himself wise, but was not
> really wise; and the consequence was that he hated me, and his
> enmity was shared by several who were present and heard me.
> So I left him, saying to myself, as I went away: Well, although I
> do not suppose that either of us knows anything really beautiful
> and good, I am better off than he is,—for he knows nothing, and
> thinks that he knows; I neither know nor think that I know.

Apology
21bd

Socrates continues questioning others with the same result. The singular wisdom of Socrates turns out to be this: not thinking that he has it. This is a recurring theme in the dialogues. He reiterates his ignorance often.[1]

> SOCRATES. I share the poverty of my fellow countrymen in
> this respect, and confess to my shame that I have no knowledge
> about virtue at all.

Meno
71b

Socrates regards it as his mission to expose false feelings of wisdom wherever they may be found.

> I go about the world, obedient to the god, and search and make
> enquiry into the wisdom of any one, whether citizen or stranger,

Apology
23b

---

1. For a review of all of Socrates' professions of ignorance, and of theories offered to explain them, see McPartland, "Socratic Ignorance."

who appears to be wise; and if he is not wise, then in vindication of the oracle I show him that he is not wise.

If we treat Socrates as an internalized feature of the mind, then this is its first and constant order of business: uprooting false conceits of knowledge. Otherwise those conceits, like weeds, block the growth of anything better. Socrates regards the actual presence of wisdom and the feeling of having it as inversely related.

Irony. Scholars have spent a lot of time wondering about the claims of ignorance that Socrates makes. The claims are hard to take literally for two reasons. The first is that they sometimes sound ironic. In Socrates there is a frequent undercurrent of playfulness, of mockery, of games between him and his partners—and between him and the reader, since the comings and goings of his irony are hard to judge.[2] (The passages from the *Apology* just shown can be taken as examples.) The irony is clearest when Socrates deals with a partner who claims to have knowledge. Socrates will congratulate him in fulsome terms before asking a few questions, and then flatter him more later after he can't answer them. When Euthyphro claims to know the difference between piety and impiety, Socrates says that "the best thing I can do is to become your pupil."[3] Some pages later, after the demolition of Euthyphro's arguments, Socrates goes on:

Euthyphro
15e–16a

SOCRATES. I am sure that you think you know exactly what is holy and what is not. So tell me, peerless Euthyphro, and do not hide from me what you judge it to be.

EUTHYPHRO. Another time, then, Socrates, for I am in a hurry, and must be off this minute.

SOCRATES. What are you doing, my friend? Will you leave, and dash me down from the mighty expectation I had of learning from you what is holy and what is not?

It's the same when Socrates seeks lessons from Hippias about beauty

---

2. See Vlastos, *Socrates, Ironist and Moral Philosopher*, 21–44.
3. *Euthyphro* 5a.

or the "fine," a subject that Socrates says he can't discuss intelligently when he's called on to do so. He says to Hippias, "Of course you know it clearly; it would be a pretty small bit of learning out of the many things you know." [4] They talk it out for many pages, at the end of which Hippias becomes exasperated. Socrates is sad.

> SOCRATES. Hippias, my friend, you're a lucky man, because you know which activities a man should practice, and you've practiced them too—successfully, as you say. But I'm apparently held back by my crazy luck.

Hippias Major 304bc

Socrates comes off as unappealing in these moments. Nobody, except maybe Hippias, would think his praise was earnest. It's easiest to make peace with this style by supposing that it was not how the real Socrates talked—though if he did, it might help explain his lack of popularity. And it need not be taken as a suggestion by Plato of how anyone else should talk, either. We do better to remember that the characters who get Socratic skewerings are the self-important windbags (he's nicer to others). We can read his treatment of them as a model of the contempt with which we should regard the pomposity in ourselves, as noted in chapter 4.

In any event, it is apparent that Socrates doesn't always mean exactly what he says. Some think that his claims of ignorance are more of the same and are pedagogical tricks.[5] "Socratic irony" is a stock expression for pretending that you're ignorant in order to get someone else to talk. And Socrates does sometimes exaggerate his ignorance for the sake of discussion. Yet his more usual claims to lack knowledge seem serious at their core.[6] Socrates seems ironic because he claims to be ignorant but then shows that other people are more so, which makes him look not so ignorant. But ridiculing others who claim to know something doesn't imply that he knows what they don't. He draws this distinction openly.

---

4. *Hippias Major* 286e.

5. Gulley, *Philosophy of Socrates*, 39.

6. The view pursued in, e.g., Irwin, *Plato's Moral Theory*, 39–40; Bett, "Socratic Ignorance," 218; and Benson, *Socratic Wisdom*, ch. 8.

SOCRATES. I am called wise, for my hearers always imagine that I myself possess the wisdom which I find wanting in others: but the truth is, O men of Athens, that God only is wise; and by his answer he intends to show that the wisdom of men is worth little or nothing; he is not speaking of Socrates, he is only using my name by way of illustration, as if he said, He, O men, is the wisest, who, like Socrates, knows that his wisdom is in truth worth nothing.

Socrates really does have a low opinion of his wisdom. He just has an even lower opinion of everyone else's because they don't have a low opinion of their own.

Another reason we smell irony is that Socrates claims not to know anything but then goes on to show that he is full of thoughts and insights that never occurred to his partners. But being full of thoughts isn't the same as having answers. If Socrates has the answers that he claims he doesn't, we might expect him to tell us about them in a roaring proof at the expense of his most puffed-up partners. He doesn't. In the dialogues (at least the ones that interest us here) Socrates never does resolve the main questions at issue. If he could have, he probably would have.

Imagine that a chess master, perplexed by a hard position, meets a kibitzer who says the solution is obvious. The chess master says: "What a relief! I certainly don't know what it is. Enlighten me." The kibitzer makes a half-baked suggestion, and the chess master gives a dazzling explanation of its inadequacy. Was he being ironic at the outset? Only in part. He meant it when he said that he didn't have the answer and would be delighted to learn what it was, though he was sure the kibitzer would be wrong. But he does understand the question (and the problems with many answers to it) better than most. He's spent time looking ahead and sees twelve moves deep. That's one way to imagine what Socrates has in mind. When he goes around talking to others as if he expects them to understand anything that he doesn't, he's playing. But he means it when he says that he doesn't know the answers himself.

So when Socrates says that he doesn't know the things he wishes he did, suppose he's being sincere. Still: what does he mean?

Kinds of knowledge. I said there are two reasons why scholars puzzle over Socrates' claim of ignorance. The first is the nearby presence of irony just discussed. The second is that, often enough, he talks as though he does have some knowledge. Sometimes he distinguishes between the little things he knows and the big things he doesn't.

I know many things, but not anything of much importance.

Euthydemus 293b

But he also makes claims here and there that suggest knowledge about big things after all.

I do know that injustice and disobedience to a better, whether God or man, is evil and dishonorable.

Apology 29b

I certainly don't think the distinction between knowledge and true belief is just a plausible inference. There's not a lot I'd say I know, but I'd certainly say it about this; I'd count this as one of the things I know.

Meno 98b

There have been efforts to round up all the cases where Socrates says that he knows things (Vlastos finds nine), to generalize about them, and to square them with his disavowals of knowledge elsewhere.[7] And there is scholarly debate about the meaning of those occasional claims of knowledge. They might be things that Socrates considers true until such time as they may be refuted, or things he claims to know outright.[8] Or maybe his claims of knowledge are slips. Or maybe they're claims about his own experience, not about any universal truths. Or he lacks systematic moral knowledge but has piecemeal knowledge.[9]

---

7. See Vlastos, *Socratic Studies*, 43–66; Bett, "Socratic Ignorance"; Lesher, "Socrates' Disavowal of Knowledge"; Wolfsdorf, "Socrates' Avowals of Knowledge."

8. Compare Vlastos, *Socratic Studies*, 48–56, and Lesher, "Socrates' Disavowal of Knowledge," 279.

9. See C. C. W. Taylor, "Plato's Epistemology," 166; Bett, "Socratic Ignorance," 225–228.

Or he means something different by knowledge when he talks about "knowing" this or that but then also about "knowing" nothing.[10]

This last idea seems most promising. Socrates has the kind of confidence in his views that we discussed in chapter 6 (on the elenchus). His knowledge is what has seemed true to him so far in his reasonings and has yet to be refuted. Or he has the kind of knowledge that we all claim about things on which we aren't experts.[11] We *feel* sure about it and act accordingly. But he doesn't have the sort of knowledge to which others should defer, and he can't find anyone else who does, either. Regardless of which of these variations is correct (if any of them are), the result is the same in this respect: his knowledge is not the kind that ends the need for more inquiry.

The interpretation just noted, incidentally, helps to make sense out of a problem. Socrates says that virtue is a kind of knowledge (see chapter 14). He also denies that *he* has any important knowledge. Does this mean that he's devoid of virtue? Not if he uses "knowledge" in the mixed way just discussed. Knowledge in the sense of final, inquiry-ending certainty is what he doesn't have and can't find. But he has a lot of "for now" knowledge that has been tested for consistency many times over and has yet to fail, and this allows him a measure of virtue. "Knowing," on this view, is a matter of degree. Socrates is making all the progress he can: not much, perhaps, but more than most.

Ignorance of ignorance. Having found—provisionally!—that Socrates means it when he claims ignorance, we can consider why the ignorance receives such emphasis in the dialogues and how it might be useful.

First, Socrates regards unconscious ignorance as the source of great evils. Ignorance is why we go wrong in general. People have vices, do wrong, and make themselves wretched because they don't really

---

10. Vlastos, *Socratic Studies*, 39–66, is the most famous theory of this kind; for a discussion relating this possibility to the work of more contemporary philosophers, see Goldstein, *Plato at the Googleplex*, 366–67.

11. See Woodruff, "Plato's Early Theory of Knowledge," for discussion.

understand what they are doing and why. They haven't thought hard enough about it. But there's a special tier of Socratic dread and contempt for *double* ignorance—the ignorance of those who don't know but think they do. Everyone is in that position sometimes. We have a felt sense of confidence built on sand. It wouldn't survive cross-examination but doesn't receive any. Those in that position are badly off and also dangerous to others, like drunk drivers who think they are sober.

We saw this idea in passages from the *Apology* where Socrates says that knowing you're ignorant is at least better than being ignorant without knowing it. But the point is made more firmly in later dialogues, including some where Socrates doesn't figure much.

STRANGER. I do seem to myself to see one very large and bad sort of ignorance which is quite separate, and may be weighed in the scale against all other sorts of ignorance put together. *Sophist* 229cd

THEAETETUS. What is it?

STRANGER. When a person supposes that he knows, and does not know; this appears to be the great source of all the errors of the intellect.

THEAETETUS. True.

STRANGER. And this, if I am not mistaken, is the kind of ignorance which specially earns the title of stupidity.

THEAETETUS. True.

STRANGER. What name, then, shall be given to the sort of instruction which gets rid of this?

THEAETETUS. The instruction which you mean, Stranger, is, I should imagine, not the teaching of handicraft arts, but what, thanks to us, has been termed education in this part of the world.

This principle is a worthy one as the starting point for a philosophy, or, as the passage says, for an education. Double ignorance can be linked to a more basic problem of human nature: self-serving bias, one form of which is thinking of oneself as the center of the universe. Freud described the discoveries made by Copernicus, by Darwin, and by himself as a tradition of assaults on the "naïve self-love" of mankind.[12] The points of intersection between Socratic inquiry and psychoanalysis (itself an attack on a kind of double ignorance) are a tale for another time; but we at least can see now that the tradition at issue dates back to Plato.

Laws 731e–32a ATHENIAN. The excessive love of self is in reality the source to each man of all offences; for the lover is blinded about the beloved, so that he judges wrongly of the just, the good, and the honorable, and thinks that he ought always to prefer himself to the truth. But he who would be a great man ought to regard, not himself or his interests, but what is just, whether the just act be his own or that of another. Through a similar error men are induced to fancy that their own ignorance is wisdom, and thus we who may be truly said to know nothing, think that we know all things.

Double ignorance has practical consequences. Being wrong isn't a terrible problem if you know it's a risk and account for it. But when people are wrong but feel unshakably right it takes away their will to learn and eventually involves them in disaster. And if they are put in charge of anything, their double ignorance produces disaster for everyone else, too. Most political calamities can be seen that way. Plato comes back to this idea repeatedly.

Laws 863cd ATHENIAN. Ignorance ... may be conveniently divided by the legislator into two sorts: there is simple ignorance, which is the source of lighter offences, and double ignorance, which is accompanied by a conceit of wisdom; and he who is under the influence of the latter fancies that he knows all about matters of which he knows nothing. This second kind of ignorance, when possessed of power and strength, will be held by the legislator to be the source of great and monstrous crimes, but when attended with weakness, will only result in the errors of children and old men.

Philebus 49ac SOCRATES. Ignorance in the powerful is hateful and horrible,

---

12. Freud, *General Introduction to Psychoanalysis*, 246–47.

because hurtful to others both in reality and in fiction, but powerless ignorance may be reckoned, and in truth is, ridiculous.

Socratic philosophy starts with a love of truth, but as a matter of *action* its first task is negative: shaking off the delusion of wisdom. Before worrying about adding to your knowledge, you have to get clear—clearer than anyone naturally wants to be—about what you don't know and where your false certainties lie. They're hard to see and they resist attack. The best strategy against them is an internalized Socrates who says that you're not as wise as you seem to yourself. That is as close as we can get to the feeling and the posture of the wise. Professor Guthrie said it well:

> To be a Socratic is not to follow any system of philosophical doctrine. It implies first and foremost an attitude of mind, an intellectual humility easily mistaken for arrogance, since the true Socratic is convinced of the ignorance not only of himself but of all mankind.[13]

Midwifery. A posture of ignorance can have another kind of value besides being a defense against your own foolishness. It encourages experiments. In effect you say to a discussion partner: "Assume I know nothing. Spin out your idea and develop it fully. I'll ask questions. Some of them will be naïve. We'll see where the answers go." This gives new ideas a chance at acceptance. They aren't up against the prejudice that comes naturally when an old conviction is in place and is defended by territorial instincts and force of habit. The listener gives up those convictions for a while, and so is free to believe the new idea and also to contradict it. Think of this as an effort at a fair election. While the new idea doesn't go unchallenged, it at least goes unopposed by an incumbent.

This use of ignorance gets its most famous depiction in the *Theaetetus.* Socrates describes himself as a midwife. He can't bear children himself, but he can help his partner toward the birth of an idea or toward a miscarriage, as needed.

---

13. Guthrie, *History of Greek Philosophy*, 449.

SOCRATES. My midwifery has all the standard features, except that I practice it on men instead of women, and supervise the labor of their minds, not their bodies. And the most important aspect of *my* skill is the ability to apply every conceivable test to see whether the young man's mental offspring is illusory and false or viable and true. But I have *this* feature in common with midwives—I myself am barren of wisdom. The criticism that's often made of me—that it's lack of wisdom that makes me ask others questions, but say nothing positive myself—is perfectly true. Why do I behave like this? Because the god compels me to attend to the labors of others, but prohibits me from having any offspring myself. I myself, therefore, am quite devoid of wisdom; my mind has never produced any idea that could be called clever....

There's another experience which those who associate with me have in common with pregnant women: they suffer labor-pains. In fact, they are racked night and day with a far greater distress than women undergo; and the arousal and relief of this pain is the province of my expertise.

With help from Socrates, Theaetetus comes up with a definition of knowledge—that it amounts to perception. The theory is put through a long examination. It doesn't survive.

SOCRATES. Well, are we still pregnant? Is anything relevant to knowledge still causing us pain, my friend, or have we given birth to everything?

THEAETETUS. *I* most certainly have: thanks to you, I've put into words more than I had in me.

SOCRATES. And does our midwifery declare that everything we produced was still-born and that there was nothing worth keeping?

THEAETETUS. Absolutely.

SOCRATES. Well, Theaetetus, if you set out at a later date to conceive more ideas, and you succeed, the ideas with which you'll be pregnant will be better because of this inquiry of ours;

and even if you don't get pregnant, you'll be easier to get on with, because you won't make a nuisance of yourself by thinking that you know what you don't know. This self-responsibility is all my skill is capable of giving, nothing more.

This is one of the best-known metaphors in the dialogues.[14] It is open to many interpretations. I give it here as an image of Socratic ignorance and how it can draw out ideas that might have stayed un-developed. Socrates overstates the emptiness of his mind for good reason. He's taking on the role of midwife: a state of receptivity followed by testing. In a sense he's *aspiring* to a type of ignorance because it lets his partner bring forth an idea. This isn't the only way that Socrates conducts a dialogue. He generally isn't a very scrupu-lous midwife; he introduces ideas of his own, and he does some of that in the *Theaetetus*, too.[15] But intellectual midwifery is an aspect of the Socratic method.

The midwife comparison suggests a way to listen to someone else. But its more likely use, as with most of what Socrates offers, is inter-nal. Think of it as a posture of mind when you're looking at an idea or a hard question. You want to see the idea in full and at its best before you criticize it. Socrates spends the time needed to help Theaetetus work out what he means and how to say it—*then* he takes it apart. This is much better than the usual habit of shading an opponent's argument to make it look bad before you argue against it. It's also a form of self-discipline when you weigh an idea that goes against your own beliefs. You don't just try to remember that you might be wrong. You try to forget for a while whatever you already think.

---

14. Robinson suggests that the metaphor "has so gripped our minds that we usually think of it as a feature of all the Socratic literature and of the real Socrates." Robinson, "Forms and Error in Plato's Theaetetus," 4. See also Burnyeat, "Carneades Was No Probabilist," 8: "At a superficial level it is a metaphor like any other, based on a sense of resemblance between mental and physical creativity. The resemblance seems so fitting, however, so familiar even, as to invite the thought that the metaphor corresponds, in some deeper sense, to psychological reality."

15. For discussion, see Annas, "Plato the Skeptic," 325.

12

Aporia

IF you were questioned by Socrates, he would eventually convince you that nothing you say is good enough. After getting the hang of Socratic thinking, you may reach the same conclusion yourself. Any statement you make about a big question can be revealed as wrong, incomplete, or otherwise inadequate in some way. This discovery can ultimately lead to a sense of skepticism (see chapter 16). But most immediately it leads to *aporia* (pronounced ap-or-*ee*-ah). Aporia is a kind of impasse; literally it means "without a way." It is the state reached when your attempts to say something true have all been refuted and you don't know what else to do or think. Sometimes it is described as a state of mind—a sense of disorientation and perplexity; but strictly speaking those states are a reaction to the impasse. They are what you feel when you run out of resources for answering a question. Your feet are trying to find something solid to stand on and can't. This chapter considers the meaning and value of aporia.

Definitions. Aporia, and the way it feels, are described in different ways at different points in the dialogues. It's usually explained with a metaphor, as in this account from Meno to Socrates:

Meno
79e–80b

MENO. At this moment I feel you are exercising magic and witchcraft upon me and positively laying me under your spell until I am just a mass of helplessness. If I may be flippant, I think that not only in outward appearance but in other respects as well you are exactly like the flat sting ray that one meets in the sea. Whenever anyone comes into contact with it, it numbs him, and that is the sort of thing that you seem to be doing to me now. My mind and my lips are literally numb, and I have nothing to reply to you. Yet I have spoken about virtue hundreds of times, held forth often on the subject in front of large audiences, and very well too, or so I thought. Now I can't even say what it is.

Some other accounts of such moments:

> EUTHYPHRO. I simply don't know how to tell you what I think.   *Euthyphro*
> Somehow everything that we put forward keeps moving about   11b
> us in a circle, and nothing will stay where we put it.

> SOCRATES. All right, then, Nicias. If you have any resources   *Laches*
> at your command, please could you help your friends who've   194c
> been caught in a storm of words and can find no way through.

The most familiar encounter with aporia for many people comes from thinking about death. If they dwell on the end of their own consciousness, they sometimes end up at a loss. Thinking about anything infinite, or any paradox, can also bring on this kind of feeling. Reason has been exhausted. You can't advance but aren't in a position of stability, and you might feel speechless.[1]

Aporia is a common way for Socratic dialogues to end. Producing aporia is sometimes thought to be their purpose. That may be another reason why Plato writes in the way he does. Aporia is more likely to be produced by participating in a dialogue, or by reading one, than by direct exposition. A dialogue that seems to go nowhere can be very productive if its goal was to produce aporia instead of a conclusion.

Double ignorance. Aporia can be a sign that its holder is departing a state of compound ignorance. You thought you knew something, but it turns out that you don't understand it; you were ignorant of your ignorance, and now it's clear. That is how Socrates speaks of aporia in the *First Alcibiades*. People aren't alarmed when they are questioned and know the answer. They aren't alarmed when they know that they *don't* know the answer. They are alarmed when they thought they knew and then realize that they don't.

> ALCIBIADES. I solemnly declare, Socrates, that I do not know   *First*
> what I am saying. Verily, I am in a strange state, for when you   *Alcibiades*
> put questions to me I am of different minds in successive instants. 116e–17d

---

1. See Szaif, "Socrates and the Benefits of Puzzlement," 33.

SOCRATES. And are you not aware of the nature of this perplexity, my friend?

ALCIBIADES. Indeed I am not.

SOCRATES. Do you suppose that if some one were to ask you whether you have two eyes or three, or two hands or four, or anything of that sort, you would then be of different minds in successive instants?

ALCIBIADES. I begin to distrust myself, but still I do not suppose that I should.

SOCRATES. You would feel no doubt; and for this reason—because you would know?

ALCIBIADES. I suppose so....

SOCRATES. Ask yourself; are you in any perplexity about things of which you are ignorant? You know, for example, that you know nothing about the preparation of food.

ALCIBIADES. Very true.

SOCRATES. And do you think and perplex yourself about the preparation of food: or do you leave that to some one who understands the art?

ALCIBIADES. The latter.

SOCRATES. Or if you were on a voyage, would you bewilder yourself by considering whether the rudder is to be drawn inwards or outwards, or do you leave that to the pilot, and do nothing?

ALCIBIADES. It would be the concern of the pilot.

SOCRATES. Then you are not perplexed about what you do not know, if you know that you do not know it?

ALCIBIADES. I imagine not.

SOCRATES. Do you not see, then, that mistakes in life and practice are likewise to be attributed to the ignorance which has conceit of knowledge?

As we saw in chapter 11, double ignorance is, for Socrates, a kind of sleep through which everyone walks to some extent. Then you walk into a wall. The wall is aporia. The awakening is a rude one, but deeply valuable. The sensation of ignorance—of realizing that you know less than you had thought—is unpleasant, at least at first. It is experienced as loss by the ego, which has a built-in good opinion of its own wisdom. But Socratic study helps make that discovery feel more welcome. One comes to see that such a discovery isn't really the loss of wisdom. It's the arrival of it.

Aporetic cleansing. Aporia may be seen as a necessary stage before real learning can happen. You realize that you've been pushing words around as if their meaning were obvious but that you don't really understand them.[2] Now you have a sense of something missing. Your confidence in your knowledge is gone. It needed to go to make room for something better. A good account of this vision is given in the *Sophist*, a Platonic dialogue in which Socrates does not serve as the protagonist.

> STRANGER. As the physician considers that the body will receive no benefit from taking food until the internal obstacles have been removed, so the purifier of the soul is conscious that his patient will receive no benefit from the application of knowledge until he is refuted, and from refutation learns modesty; he must be purged of his prejudices first and made to think that he knows only what he knows, and no more.
> THEAETETUS. That is certainly the best and wisest state of mind.
> STRANGER. For all these reasons, Theaetetus, we must admit that refutation is the greatest and chiefest of purifications, and he who has not been refuted, though he be the Great King himself, is in an awful state of impurity; he is uninstructed and deformed in those things in which he who would be truly blessed ought to be fairest and purest.

Sophist
230ce

Aporia in this sense can also cleanse you of obnoxious qualities. Recall the discussion of the *Theaetetus* in chapter 11. Theaetetus had given birth to an idea that was pronounced stillborn. Socrates encourages him to keep trying, but says that Theaetetus will be better off even if his ideas never improve. Aporia will have made him

---

2. Desjardins, "Why Dialogues? Plato's Serious Play," 116–17.

easier to put up with. Such humility may not seem a very exciting reward at first. But then think about how often people are too sure of themselves, and feel smart when they're not, and how unendurable they are, and how dangerous, and how likely we are to be just as insufferable to others for the same reasons, and how many problems arise from nothing but this. Other people, it seems clear, would be better off if they realized how little they know, and with a suspicion that in the long run they show themselves to be fools in most of what they say. So would we all. Some shock therapy is a small price to pay for relief from those curses.[3] Aporia is a form of it.

The aporetic spur. Aporia can not only prepare you to learn but make you *want* to learn.[4] It feels frustrating. In effect Socrates says: good— now get going on the search for an answer, this time with a better sense of the work it takes. You are made hungry for knowledge by discovering how little you have. Socrates suggests this when he talks about the slave he questioned in the *Meno*.

Meno
84bc

SOCRATES. He didn't think he was stuck before, but now he appreciates that he *is* stuck and he also doesn't think he knows what in fact he doesn't know.
MENO. You're right....
SOCRATES. It would seem that we've increased his chances of finding out the truth of the matter, because now, given his lack of knowledge, he'll be glad to undertake the investigation, whereas before he was only too ready to suppose that he could talk fluently and well to numerous people on numerous occasions about how a double-size figure must have double-length sides.
MENO. I suppose so.
SOCRATES. Do you think he'd have tried to enquire or learn about this matter when he thought he knew it (even though he didn't), until he'd become bogged down and stuck, and had

---

3. See Robinson, *Plato's Earlier Dialectic*, 18.
4. See ibid., 17: "The aim of the elenchus is to wake men out of their dogmatic slumbers into genuine intellectual curiosity."

come to appreciate his ignorance and to long for knowledge?
MENO. No, I don't think he would, Socrates.
SOCRATES. The numbing did him good, then?
MENO. I'd say so.

The feeling described here by Theaetetus might be considered a similar reaction to aporia:

SOCRATES. I suspect that you have thought of these questions before now.
THEAETETUS. Yes, Socrates, and I am amazed when I think of them; by the Gods I am! and I want to know what on earth they mean; and there are times when my head quite swims with the contemplation of them.
SOCRATES. I see, my dear Theaetetus, that Theodorus had a true insight into your nature when he said that you were a philosopher, for wonder is the feeling of a philosopher, and philosophy begins in wonder.

Theaetetus
155cd

Aporia as continuous. We've just talked as though there are right answers to the questions under pursuit, and that aporia might inspire a harder search for them. But suppose you conclude, after many rounds of all this, that the answers will never be found. It still wouldn't be time to give up. On a Socratic view it's *never* time to give up. We do better by accepting that the search probably has no end but going on anyway as if it might. For even if you can't possess the truth, you can get closer to it. Discourse that improves understanding becomes the valuable thing, but it works best if you forget that and act as though you're in it to capture the truth.

SOCRATES. If I say again that daily to discourse about virtue, and of those other things about which you hear me examining myself and others, is the greatest good of man, and that the unexamined life is not worth living, you are still less likely to believe me. Yet I say what is true, although a thing of which it is hard for me to persuade you.

Apology
37e–38a

SOCRATES. There's one proposition that I'd defend to the death, if I could, by argument and by action: that as long as we think we should search for what we don't know, we'll be better people—less faint-hearted and less lazy—than if we were to think that we had no chance of discovering what we don't know and that there's no point in even searching for it.

Aporetic truths. A more radical view of aporia regards it as sometimes inspiring speechlessness because you have arrived at a truth that can't be spoken. The idea goes: there are unspeakable truths—that is, truths that defy language, and so can be called ineffable.[5] Perhaps they are verbal analogues of irrational numbers. But they sometimes can be perceived without words. It may be that justice, for example, can't be captured by a definition. But it can be encircled by the close failure of many efforts at definition. Instead of that result seeming to be a mess and therefore a failure, the mess is the thing sought. The goal of the effort at reasoning isn't a conclusion based on the reasoning but a grasp of something larger. We learn that the truth isn't coextensive with our ability to talk about it or with our powers of comprehension.

This way of looking at aporia might be inferred from the approach of the early dialogues. Why is the truth always sought and never discovered? Perhaps because it can't be; *that* is the discovery. This idea finds some support in Plato's Seventh Letter. The authenticity of the letter is debated,[6] so it shouldn't be asked to bear too much weight, but it's worth seeing the passage regardless. If it's authentic, it gives us a direct account of Plato's thinking. If not, it's an interesting ancient stab at how he might have thought about philosophical discovery.

This much at least, I can say about all writers, past or future, who say they know the things to which I devote myself, whether by hearing the teaching of me or of others, or by their own discoveries—that according to my view it is not possible for them to have any real skill in the matter. There neither is nor

---

5. Versions of this view are advanced in Friedlander, *Plato*, 169–70, and Sayre, "Plato's Dialogues in Light of the Seventh Letter."

6. See discussion and references in chapter 1.

ever will be a treatise of mine on the subject. For it does not admit of exposition like other branches of knowledge; but after much converse about the matter itself and a life lived together, suddenly a light, as it were, is kindled in one soul by a flame that leaps to it from another, and thereafter sustains itself.

Mill offered this comment and paraphrase, after talking about the difficulties raised in the dialogues:

[Plato] had ceased to care about solving them, having come to think that insoluble difficulties were always to be expected. He certainly, if we trust his Seventh Epistle, was then of opinion that no verbal definition of anything can precisely hit the mark, and that the knowledge of what a thing is, though not attainable till after a long and varied course of dialectic debate, is never the direct result of discussion, but comes out at last (and only in the happier natures) by a sort of instantaneous flash.[7]

Others have been more restrained in reading the Seventh Letter and drawing conclusions about whether Plato thought there were truths that defied wording.[8] The reader might consider from experience whether the dialogues, or any process of dialectic modeled after them, can succeed in the way just described. A single or general answer is likely not possible. As Mill suggests, any such results are likely to depend on the capacity and disposition of the person seeking them.

False aporia. Aporia has been said to arrive when we have a philosophical problem and can't solve it.[9] But notice how subjective that is. Those who reach such a point might be reacting to a lack of ability in themselves, not to anything so hard in the problem (maybe aporia always includes some of both elements). Most teachers and students can think of cases where a student was reduced to an aporia-like state by bad instruction. Those risks appear in the dialogues. Sometimes we see Socrates defeat or at least flummox his partners with fallacies.[10]

---

7. Robson, *Collected Works of John Stuart Mill*, 11:431.

8. See Kahn, *Plato and the Socratic Dialogue*, 388–92.

9. Szaif, "Socrates and the Benefits of Puzzlement," 30–31.

10. See ibid., 35–35, 40–41.

And sometimes Socrates is said by his partners to confuse them with word games or bad arguments.

Gorgias
489bc
CALLICLES. Won't he ever stop talking rubbish? Tell me, Socrates, doesn't it embarrass you to pick on people's mere words at your age and to count it a godsend if someone uses the wrong expression by mistake?

In these moments Plato may be warning the reader about traps but also challenging himself to avoid them. He is keeping himself honest.

Since the Socratic approach to aporia never involves giving up in response to it, the risks of an unearned sense of aporia might not be too serious. If aporia makes people work harder to find the truth, perhaps it doesn't matter whether it was brought on by a bad argument. And if aporia creates a more humble and accurate impression of your own wisdom, again it might be good no matter how it arrives. But unearned aporia still seems as objectionable as any other false state from a Socratic standpoint (you wouldn't want it for yourself, would you?). Maybe a claim of aporia should be subject to the same testing as every other claim.

Self-induced aporia. This book treats the Socratic method as useful for your own thinking. Socrates' way of speaking about aporia fits that account. It isn't a trap he sets for other people while he stands separate. He runs up against it and then shares it with others.

Meno
80c
SOCRATES. It isn't that, knowing the answers myself, I perplex other people. The truth is rather that I infect them also with the perplexity I feel myself.

Charmides
169c
SOCRATES. He could see that I was stuck, and I got the impression that, thanks to my puzzlement, he too found himself, against his will, in the snares of perplexity—much as people who see others yawning in their presence find themselves yawning too.

If Socrates infects others with his reaction to aporia, how did he come to acquire that reaction in the first place? By self-examination.

Squandered aporia. The accounts of aporia's good effects generally come from Socrates himself, not from his partners. They tend not to thank him for the help. True, aporia sometimes leads to a friendly agreement to undertake additional learning.[11] But more often his partners step aside to be replaced by others, or they try to get away from him.[12] What are we to make of this? Possibly that aporia is fragile and can be squandered.[13] It is easily evaded and easily forgotten. The energy needed to generate aporia is also needed to endure it and get benefits from it. And if Socrates describes aporia in positive terms but his partner runs off and doesn't get the benefits, remember that the real candidate for an experience of aporia isn't the partner. It's the reader.[14]

---

11. See *Laches* 194ab.
12. See *Gorgias* 461b, *Euthyphro* 15e.
13. Szaif, "Socrates and the Benefits of Puzzlement," 43.
14. As discussed in ibid., 42–43.

13

Socratic Goods

WHY bother? That is the question pursued in this chapter. Most students of philosophy, putting aside professional academics, turn to the subject because they have challenges in their lives or their thinking. They're looking for helpful ideas. Neither Socrates nor Plato (if they can be distinguished) seems at first to offer promising candidates. Many philosophers don't *claim* to offer anything to the ordinary person, but Socrates isn't one of them. He's interested in how to live well and care for the psyche. He viewed these as problems for everyone. Yet the Socratic method doesn't meet needs that most people feel. It doesn't promise to improve anyone's mood. It doesn't offer better prospects for wealth or popularity; it might tend the other way. Nor does it seem to have produced much progress over the centuries in collective certainty about moral questions. And while the mind may need an internalized Socrates, it already has a well-developed anti-Socrates who will be eager to suggest that philosophy is a waste of time and that it's better to get on with the real business of living. So what's the case—the *Socratic* case—for troubling yourself about Socrates and his methods?

Socratic goods. An answer is suggested by one of Plato's most celebrated passages: the allegory of the cave. It's in a part of the *Republic* probably written in the later half of Plato's career, but it still sheds light on the point of the Socratic method.

The allegory starts by depicting people imprisoned in a cave. They spend their lives chained in place and can only look forward. Behind them is a fire that throws light in their direction and onto the wall in front of them. Between the fire and the prisoners there is a walkway where other people hold up figures—statuettes—of humans and animals. The shadows of those statuettes are thrown onto the wall in front of the prisoners; the shadows are the only things that the prisoners ever see. Socrates asks Glaucon to imagine what it would be like for one of the prisoners to be unchained and to walk out of the cave through an opening at the far end of it. Socrates begins:

Imagine that one of them has been set free and is suddenly made to stand up, to turn his head and walk, and to look towards the firelight. It hurts him to do all this and he's too dazzled to be capable of making out the objects whose shadows he'd formerly been looking at. And suppose someone tells him that what he's been seeing all this time has no substance, and that he's now closer to reality and is seeing more accurately, because of the greater reality of the things in front of his eyes—what do you imagine his reaction would be? And what do you think he'd say if he were shown any of the passing objects and had to respond to being asked what it was? Don't you think he'd be bewildered and would think that there was more reality in what he'd been seeing before than in what he was being shown now?

Republic
514a–17a

"Far more," he said....

He wouldn't be able to see things up on the surface of the earth, I suppose, until he'd got used to his situation. At first, it would be shadows that he could most easily make out, then he'd move on to the reflections of people and so on in water, and later he'd be able to see the actual things themselves. Next, he'd feast his eyes on the heavenly bodies and the heavens themselves, which would be easier at night: he'd look at the light of the stars and the moon, rather than at the sun and sunlight during the daytime.

"Of course." ...

If he went back underground and sat down again in the same spot, wouldn't the sudden transition from the sunlight mean that his eyes would be overwhelmed by darkness?

"Certainly," he replied....

And suppose that before his eyes had settled down and while he wasn't seeing well, he had once again to compete against those same old prisoners at identifying those shadows. Wouldn't he make a fool of himself? Wouldn't they say that he'd come back from his upward journey with his eyes ruined, and that it wasn't even worth trying to go up there? And wouldn't they—if they could—grab hold of anyone who tried to set them free and take them up there, and kill him?

"They certainly would," he said.

The allegory has been interpreted in many ways, most often as illustrating Plato's Theory of Forms.[1] I offer it for a more modest purpose: to describe the value of philosophical progress despite the unpromising properties of it noted a moment ago. Departure from the cave doesn't meet any felt need of the inmates. It doesn't make them any cheerier, and doesn't make them better off in any worldly way. But few who assess the story from the outside would rather be in the cave than out of it. We might call getting out of the cave a Socratic good: something assigned not much value (or maybe negative value) by those who haven't done it, but regarded as very valuable once they have.

Ignoti nulla cupido. The lack of desire for a Socratic good usually has this circular quality: the absence of the good keeps you from seeing why you would like it. You don't understand what you're missing. Plato has another character make the point to Socrates:

Symposium 204a

Herein is the evil of ignorance, that he who is neither good nor wise is nevertheless satisfied with himself: he has no desire for that of which he feels no want.

It isn't easy to persuade others, or sometimes oneself, that such goods exist or are worth much effort to get. All of our usual reasons to desire something are missing. Students of Socrates have come back to this point often. Montaigne writes:

That every man is seen so resolved and satisfied with himself, that every man thinks himself sufficiently intelligent, signifies that every one knows nothing about the matter, as Socrates gave Euthydemus to understand.[2]

---

1. See, e.g., *Plato at the Googleplex*, 382–85.

2. Hazlitt, *Essays of Montaigne*, 3:390. The reference is not to Plato, however; it is to Xenophon's *Memoirs of Socrates* 4.2.24.

Kierkegaard:

> It never occurs to anybody that what the world now needs, confused as it is by much knowing, is a Socrates. But that is perfectly natural, for if anybody had this notion, not to say if many were to have it, there would be less need of a Socrates. What a delusion most needs is the very thing it least thinks of—naturally, for otherwise it would not be a delusion.[3]

Mill:

> The benefit which [logic] affords consists in being freed from a defect, which no man who possesses it ever knows that he possesses.... Hence it is, that they who are ignorant of logic, never can be made, by any efforts, to comprehend its utility. They either reason correctly without it, or they do not: if they do, they are in no need of it; and as for those who reason incorrectly for want of it, they never find out their deficiency until it is removed.[4]

Ovid also expressed a version of this idea: *ignoti nulla cupido* (there is no desire of the unknown).[5] However it is expressed, the point describes a great impediment to progress in wisdom. It's hard to get fired up about searching for something that you haven't had and therefore don't miss.

Milder forms of this pattern are sometimes described in modern times as the Dunning-Kruger effect (after two psychologists who have studied it): idiocy tends not to fully recognize its own existence; incompetence prevents you from being aware of your own incompetence.[6] Socrates regards the spirit of that idea as having broad and deep application. Our ignorance makes us unconscious of our ignorance. We are philosophically feeble, and too philosophically feeble to know it.

---

3. Kierkegaard, *Sickness Unto Death*, 149.
4. Mill, "Whately's Elements of Logic," 5.
5. *Ars Amatoria* 3.397.
6. Dunning and Kruger, "Unskilled and Unaware of It."

Looking back. A Socratic defense of its own enterprise wouldn't tell others to care about philosophy. It would ask questions that cause them to conclude that they already care about it. But sometimes those questions are hard to devise. Suppose Socrates asks you to imagine how much better off you will be with an improvement in your own wisdom. You say this doesn't seem very exciting. You feel that you have a good share of wisdom already, and can't easily imagine understanding what you don't now grasp; if you could, you would be grasping it already. What to do?

Socrates might reply by coming at the problem from the other direction. Think about Socratic goods that are *already* yours and whether you're glad to have them. How highly do you value whatever wisdom you can claim now? Or think of people you know who seem happier than you because they're self-satisfied or otherwise ignorant of things that you understand but they don't. If you can't imagine anyone like that, praise your good fortune; but you probably can. Now ask how you would feel about trading places with them to improve your mood. It's probably a repulsive idea. It certainly didn't appeal to Socrates. In the *Apology* he describes meeting people, all enjoying worldly success, who thought they were wise but weren't.

Apology
22de

> I asked myself on behalf of the oracle, whether I would like to be as I was, neither having their knowledge nor their ignorance, or like them in both; and I made answer to myself and to the oracle that I was better off as I was.

If you wouldn't make the trade either, then evidently you value the fruits of Socratic thinking: you wouldn't want to give up even a bit of whatever wisdom and knowledge of the truth you already have.

You can run the same kind of experiment by thinking about animals.

Republic
586ab

> People to whom intelligence and goodness are unfamiliar, whose only interest is self-indulgence and so on, spend their lives moving aimlessly to and fro between the bottom and the halfway point, which is as far as they reach. But they never travel any further towards the true heights: they've never even looked up there, let alone gone there; they aren't really satisfied by any-

thing real; they don't experience steady, pure pleasure. They're no different from cattle.

Mill thought it clear that trading places with those creatures, no matter how pleased they seem, was unappealing.

> Few human creatures would consent to be changed into any of the lower animals, for a promise of the fullest allowance of a beast's pleasures; no intelligent human being would consent to be a fool, no instructed person would be an ignoramus, no person of feeling and conscience would be selfish and base, even though they should be persuaded that the fool, the dunce, or the rascal is better satisfied with his lot than they are with theirs.[7]

These passages invite the reader to stand over here, to reflect on people over there who are like farm animals, and to contemplate their wretchedness. And then they invite consideration of the extent to which we are fooling ourselves by assuming that distanced perspective, because we too are part of the herd. Call these cases of looking back, or down: using what you can see to help think about what you can't. It's hard to see the value of insight that you don't have—to see it, that is, by looking forward, or up. It's easier to appreciate the value of whatever insight you *do* have that others don't. Then you can think about the horror of not having it. Then you think about the possibility that, from a different point of view, you *don't* have it. Then you realize it's more than a possibility; it's certain. Then you get to work.

The best example of this approach in the dialogues comes in a part of the cave allegory that was left out earlier so that we could look at it here. Socrates is talking about the thoughts of the inmate who escaped the cave.

> If he recalled the cell where he'd originally lived and what passed for knowledge there and his former fellow prisoners, don't you think he'd feel happy about his own altered circumstances, and sorry for them?

Republic
516ce

---

7. Robson, *Collected Works of John Stuart Mill*, 10:212.

"Definitely."

Suppose that the prisoners used to assign prestige and credit to one another, in the sense that they rewarded speed at recognizing the shadows as they passed, and the ability to remember which ones normally come earlier and later and at the same time as which other ones, and expertise at using this as a basis for guessing which ones would arrive next. Do you think our former prisoner would covet these honors and would envy the people who had status and power there, or would he much prefer, as Homer describes it, "Being a slave laboring for someone else—someone without property," and would put up with anything at all, in fact, rather than share their beliefs and their life?

"Yes, I think he'd go through anything rather than live that way."

This passage describes a feeling that is familiar to everyone. When you get out of a cave, you don't want to go back. The revulsion at the thought of going backward can drive a desire to go forward. For after enough experience with caves, you realize that we're all trapped in some and we've all escaped from others. Backward and forward movement are both possible; why should movement one way be more important than the other? The value of understanding is the same whether we're gaining it or losing it. So our attachment to whatever wisdom we have should generate an equivalent appetite for more. Put differently, your understanding is currently in a state that you would, with some progress, regard with horror. Best, then, to make haste now.

In practice, of course, the mind doesn't tend to work this way. It is more likely to be pleased with what it has and unmoved to seek more. Another relevant topic psychologists study is the endowment effect, which is the tendency of people to value the same thing more highly once it belongs to them than they do before they have it. The endowment effect evidently applies to truth, too. We're very attached to whatever amount of it we possess. We don't feel quite the same attachment to getting more. But thinking about the value of what we have can help motivate the work needed to add to it.

Comparisons. Our topic in this chapter is the rationale for doing Socratic work—some ways to think about the value of it, and some reasons why the value can be hard to see. Socrates had another idea about how to illustrate the point: invite comparisons, by those who are in a position to make them, between wisdom and other things. As we saw in chapter 10, Socrates suggests that there are three kinds of people: lovers of wisdom, lovers of honor, and lovers of gain. He asks which of those goods produces the best pleasures. It's a hard question because everyone might be expected to say that the pleasures they know are the best. But we can get traction by finding people who know *all* such pleasures and asking which they prefer. Socrates questions Glaucon as follows:

> Of the three individuals, which has the greatest experience of all the pleasures which we enumerated? Has the lover of gain, in learning the nature of essential truth, greater experience of the pleasure of knowledge than the philosopher has of the pleasure of gain?
>
> The philosopher, he replied, has greatly the advantage; for he has of necessity always known the taste of the other pleasures from his childhood upwards: but the lover of gain in all his experience has not of necessity tasted—or, I should rather say, even had he desired, could hardly have tasted—the sweetness of learning and knowing truth.
>
> Then the lover of wisdom has a great advantage over the lover of gain, for he has a double experience?
>
> Yes, very great....
>
> His experience, then, will enable him to judge better than any one?
>
> Far better....
>
> And so we arrive at the result, that the pleasure of the intelligent part of the soul is the pleasantest of the three, and that he of us in whom this is the ruling principle has the pleasantest life.

Republic
582a–83a

Mill borrowed that Socratic idea in one of his arguments about utilitarianism:

It is better to be a human being dissatisfied than a pig satisfied; better to be Socrates dissatisfied than a fool satisfied. And if the fool, or the pig, is of a different opinion, it is because they only know their own side of the question. The other party to the comparison knows both sides.[8]

So if you want to judge two states of mind, and the value of moving from one to the other, don't ask someone who only knows the first. Ask someone who knows them both. Who might that be? The most convenient candidate is you. We've all made some progress, and all have progress yet to make, so we all have a partial ability to make the comparisons that Mill describes. Insofar as we're pigs, we don't care much about being more Socratic. But insofar as we're Socratic, we strongly wish not to regress into pigs. Anytime we're in a position to compare, in other words, our preference is strongly the Socratic way. That preference is instructive.

Comparisons can also be drawn from the observation of others. It's easy to imagine being richer because we can observe tycoons. The Socratic equivalent is to ogle the powers of those who see farther than we do. Help with this process is another of the services provided by Plato. He recorded a method for the pursuit of understanding and wisdom, but he also showed what the process can look like when carried out with astonishing energy and talent. If you don't find the dialogues useful in that way, you probably have other models that can serve such a purpose. It is worthwhile in any event to remember this feature of Plato's writings: they show what can be done with dialectic, and remind us of the extent to which we're still in caves.

Such reminders are useful. People rarely *feel* as though they're in caves. They don't notice until they've gotten out and can look back. (The simplest way to illustrate this for yourself is to think about what a fool your younger self was.) So it helps to have provocations that suggest how much we don't understand but might. To put it more plainly, nobody walks through life feeling like an idiot, though you

---

8. Ibid.

can no doubt think of plenty of people who fit that description, and it fits all of us from a certain point of view. Idiocy is a relative state and an invisible one to its occupant. People vary widely in how much wisdom they have, but not in their *sense* of how much they have; anyone's felt sense of wisdom at any given time tends to be high and stable. It's tempting to describe that feeling as a constant in the workings of the mind, because that is how it usually seems—but Socrates himself shows that it can vary between people. So let's just call that sensation of one's own wisdom a deceptive, insidious, and stubborn feature of human nature. This is the root of the problem that Socrates means to address; it is the master mistake that makes all other mistakes more likely, over a lifetime and by the hour. The Socratic method is a way to correct for it.

Socratic injuries. The notion of Socratic goods can be turned around and seen as a parallel problem of *injuries*. Suppose you go through your life enjoyably enough, only to discover toward the end that you've been laboring under a mistake. You think you're surrounded by friends and family who love you, but then you find out that they've always hated you, so you become miserable. A sad story. Now suppose instead that you're in a situation of this kind but never learn the truth. What kind of harm you have suffered? Or take a side view of the problem once more: you see someone else in a situation like that—a dupe—cheerfully engaged in a way of life that would disgust him if he knew the truth of it, but he doesn't. Should you envy such a person? Again, Plato thought not.

> ATHENIAN. He is not to be trusted who loves voluntary false-hood, and he who loves involuntary falsehood is a fool. Neither condition is enviable, for the untrustworthy and ignorant has no friend, and as time advances he becomes known, and lays up in store for himself isolation in crabbed age when life is on the wane: so that, whether his children or friends are alive or not, he is equally solitary.

Laws 730cd

There isn't a common label for this situation: misfortunes of which the bearers are unconscious, and that cause them no felt suffering, but that everyone—including them—would want to avoid if they knew of it. (In effect these amount to cases in which there is a big gap between someone's subjective happiness and their *eudaimonia*, an idea we will explore in the next chapter.) We might as well call such misfortunes Socratic injuries, because they have a symmetrical relationship to Socratic goods. You don't know what you're suffering.

Socratic injuries are pervasive; we bear them as part of the human condition. Think of someone who acts unethically or without reflection but gets away with it and is pleased. Such a person can be viewed like a patient with dementia—not necessarily a deteriorating patient, but one who is steadily feeble-minded, oblivious to the problem, and indifferent or hostile when informed of it. Such people will often be in good spirits, yet to know them is to dread their condition. It is useful to reflect on that sense of dread, and to realize that Socrates would feel some of the same if he were to watch you. His function is to wake us from the degrees of dementia in which we're all submerged. The more we need the help, the less we want it. As Socrates said to his jury:

Apology
31a

> If you take my advice, you will spare me. But you, perhaps, being angry, like sleepers awakened, will strike at me, and being persuaded by Anytus, will inconsiderately put me to death; and then pass the remainder of your lives in slumber, unless the god in his care for you should send to you some one else.

The mind with a Socratic bent looks at itself with some of the same horror and urgency you would feel if you realized you were in the early stages of dementia but might be able to reverse it with effort. In that case you would apply yourself energetically. That *is* your case, more or less, and everyone else's.

Everyone bears Socratic injuries. We say things, do things, and otherwise live in ways that would probably cause us embarrassment and horror if we honestly gave or learned answers to every hard question about them, so we don't. The injuries can become more severe and harder to see as life goes on. We get invested in the defense of bad choices after making them. (As an exercise, define "bad choice" from a Socratic standpoint.) Earlier we considered cases where people discover late in life that they've been wrong about something all along. Real cases like that are rare, not because people are rarely in that position but because late in life it's too costly to see. Thus Socrates' biting description of orators in the law courts who have spent too much of their lives learning to say what they're paid to say or what clients or juries want to hear:

> They have become tense and neurotic. They know how to speak *Theaetetus* flatteringly to their master and how to behave to get into his good 173ab books, but their minds are narrow and crooked. They became slaves when they were young, and slavery prohibits growth, integrity and freedom, makes devious deeds inevitable, and puts minds that are still impressionable through extremes of danger and fear, which cannot be dealt with honestly and truthfully. So in no time at all they turn to deceit and repaying wrong with further wrong; they become warped and stunted in many ways. In the end, when they become adults, they are left with minds which are incapable of a single wholesome thought. They have become highly skilled and intelligent—or so they think.

The Socratic light is easier to bear when it's directed at smaller things or when we're younger and haven't yet made so many choices that are painful to think about or would be if we did. But there's no need to dwell here on the difficulty of lifting the heaviest of all rocks. There are always fresh chances to acquire Socratic goods and avoid Socratic injuries. That is another way to think about what the Socratic method is for.

Socratic injuries may be suffered culturally as well as individually. A society can be wretched in ways that are invisible to itself, but perhaps clear to outsiders or clear to the society's own members when they later view themselves in retrospect. The injuries can be matters of regress as well as failures of progress; a culture can be slow in learning, or can forget truths that it once knew and why it ever cared about them. These general patterns are familiar to all. I mention them here because they can sometimes be viewed in the Socratic way we have been considering. Wretchedness can occur because points of tension in the values of the society have not yet been brought to its collective awareness in a clear enough way. Either few can see those points or few are willing to hear about them. The truth may seem too uncomfortable to bear study or not uncomfortable enough to require adjustment. Economics, and technologies that change economics, do much to shape people's willingness to take such tensions seriously. When the cost of confronting a truth goes down (or the cost of ignoring it goes up), people get more willing to ask and answer questions about it. And vice versa.

14

Socratic Ethics

OUR principal topic in this book is the Socratic *method*, a set of ideas more about how to think than what to think. But in the earlier dialogues where the method is best displayed, Socrates does make some claims about how to live well. Those claims are interesting in their own right, and also because they help answer a natural question: toward what conclusions, if any, might Socratic reasoning lead? To what views did the Socratic method take Socrates?

Virtue and happiness. Socratic philosophy treats *eudaimonia* as its final goal. That word will be translated here as *happiness*, which is most common.[1] Some say eudaimonia is better translated as well-being, or as living well. The issue arises because in English it's natural to think of happiness as a subjective state: it means feeling good. But eudaimonia has an objective aspect. It implies a judgment from the outside that someone is doing well. It means a good life, not just a good mood; a good life is one to which felt happiness is the right response. People can enjoy themselves in despicable ways and so not be described as happy in this Greek sense even if they seem to be having a good time. The opposite of happy, on this view, wouldn't be *gloomy* or *depressed*; it would be a word like *wretched* or *pitiable*.

This way of thinking about happiness sometimes takes adjustment now (and the adjustment is useful), but it seemed ordinary in ancient times. Socrates treats the achievement of happiness, in the sense just described, as the purpose of life. Everybody wants to live well; if a philosophy leads to that result, nothing more need be said in defense of it. As Plato has one of his characters put the idea:

---

1. Vlastos, *Socrates, Ironist and Moral Philosopher*, 200–203, makes a convincing case for "happiness" as a better translation than any alternative.

Symposium
205a Of one who wants to be happy there is no longer any point in asking, "*Why* does he want to be happy?" There, it seems, the question stops.

Socrates more or less equates happiness with the good, or with virtue (we will consider the extent of the "more or less" in a moment).

Crito
48b SOCRATES. Do we still hold, or do we not, that we should attach the highest value not to living, but to living well?
CRITO. We do.
SOCRATES. And that to live well is the same as to live honorably and justly; do we hold that, too, or not?
CRITO. We do.

Euthydemus
282a SOCRATES. Seeing that all men desire happiness, and happiness, as has been shown, is gained by a use, and a right use, of the things of life, and the right use of them, and good-fortune in the use of them, is given by knowledge,—the inference is that everybody ought by all means to try and make himself as wise as he can?
CLEINIAS. Yes.

Gorgias
470e SOCRATES. In my opinion, it takes true goodness to make a man or a woman happy, and an immoral, wicked person is unhappy.

It's clear that Socrates saw happiness as closely related to virtue, but scholars debate the precise relationship between them in his thinking. The most literal reading of what he says is this: virtue is the only real good. It is necessary for happiness and enough for it. This is sometimes called the "identity thesis" because it states that virtue and happiness are the same.[2] On this view we shouldn't treat money or even health as true goods because they are just means to other ends. Think of a politician or judge who is praised for being persuasive. Is persuasiveness really a virtue? That depends on how it gets used, doesn't it? Persuasive powers can make a good leader more effective; in the hands of someone evil, though, they make

---

2. Vlastos, 214.

the evil worse and make the holder of the powers more wretched. That is how Socrates thinks about most things that people describe as good—money, power, even health. They're good if you use them in wise ways and bad if you use them in bad ways. So wisdom, or virtue—these are the things that really matter (and Socrates is not inclined to distinguish between those words, as we shall see). They are the only things that are good no matter what; they are the only certain sources of the good life or, in a word, happiness. In a well-known passage from the *Euthydemus*, for example, Socrates begins:

> The sum of the matter appears to be that the goods of which we spoke before are not to be regarded as goods in themselves, but the degree of good and evil in them depends on whether they are or are not under the guidance of knowledge: under the guidance of ignorance, they are greater evils than their opposites, inasmuch as they are more able to minister to the evil principle which rules them; and when under the guidance of wisdom and prudence, they are greater goods: but in themselves they are nothing?
>
> That, Cleinias replied, is obvious.
>
> What then is the result of what has been said? Is not this the result—that other things are indifferent, and that wisdom is the only good, and ignorance the only evil?
>
> Cleinias assented.

Euthydemus
281de

Some readers don't think Socrates really equates virtue and happiness so completely. They find other passages where he refers to things besides virtue as good or suggests that even a life of virtue is not worth living under certain conditions.[3] The resulting controversy is subtle and probably also inevitable because it is hard to reconcile everything Socrates says about these issues at various points in the dialogues. An especially frequent subject of debate is whether Socrates regards virtue as entirely sufficient for a good life or whether

---

3. See, e.g., *Apology* 30ab and *Crito* 47e; for discussion, see Brickhouse and Smith, "Socrates on Goods, Virtue, and Happiness," 4:204–15.

anything else makes a contribution as well. The back-and-forth on these points is too much to explain in a short space. But let me quote a leading alternative to the identity thesis; it is offered by Gregory Vlastos after long argument:

> Keeping virtue in its place as the sovereign good, both necessary and sufficient for happiness, let us allow happiness a multitude of lesser constituents in addition to virtue. Everything on Socrates' list of non-moral goods [health, wealth, etc.] would come in under this head. *In isolation from virtue each would be worthless.* But when conjoined with virtue (i.e., when used virtuously) they would enhance happiness in some small degree.[4]

The difference between the identity thesis and this runner-up is interesting but practically modest. Everyone agrees that Socratic philosophy identifies happiness with virtue—and thus with wisdom, and thus with knowledge—either closely or completely. Meanwhile there is also a controversy about whether Socrates regards virtue as a *means* to achieving happiness or as the critical *component* of happiness. I will not pursue that debate here, either, but put references in the notes for the interested reader.[5]

The Socratic vision of happiness, in whichever version you prefer, makes the Socratic practitioner immune from most sorts of injury. Socrates says at his trial:

Apology
30cd

Neither Meletus nor Anytus [the prosecutors] can do me any harm at all; they would not have the power, because I do not believe that the law of God permits a better man to be harmed by a worse. No doubt my accuser might put me to death or have me banished or deprived of civic rights, but even if he thinks—as he probably does, and others too, I dare say—that these are great calamities, I do not think so. I believe that it is far worse to do what he is doing now, trying to put an innocent man to death.

---

4. Vlastos, *Socrates, Ironist and Moral Philosopher*, 216.

5. The view that virtue (on a Socratic view) is instrumental to happiness is argued in Irwin, *Plato's Moral Theory*, and disputed by Vlastos, *Socrates, Ironist and Moral Philosopher*, 7–10.

The ordinary provocations of life, or for that matter the extraordinary ones, don't really touch a Socrates. He may be physically harmed, of course. But since his happiness—that is, the goodness of his life—depends on his own virtue (or wisdom, or understanding), it's up to him. This idea powerfully influenced the Stoics, as we will see soon.

Virtue as knowledge. Suppose the good life amounts to a life lived virtuously. But then what *is* virtue?[6] Socrates holds that it's a form of knowledge and that vice is a kind of ignorance. This idea and the previous one, taken together, can be simplified into a Socratic equation with three elements: happiness is virtue is knowledge.[7]

It can be startling to hear Socrates treat knowledge and virtue as the same. Knowledge sounds like something you have in your mind. Virtue sounds like a property of actions you might take. So it seems easy to have one without the other. It's a familiar experience for anyone, for example, to think that an act would be virtuous but not do it. The old word for that is *akrasia*: acting against your better judgment, or having a failure of will. Our experience of such moments makes knowledge and virtue seem to be very different things. But Socrates thought otherwise.

> The rest of the world are of opinion ... that a man may have knowledge, and yet that the knowledge which is in him may be overmastered by anger, or pleasure, or pain, or love, or per-haps by fear,—just as if knowledge were a slave, and might be dragged about anyhow. Now is that your view? or do you think that knowledge is a noble and commanding thing, which cannot be overcome, and will not allow a man, if he only knows the difference of good and evil, to do anything which is contrary to knowledge, but that wisdom will have strength to help him?

Protagoras 352bc

Socrates evidently takes the latter view: if you seem to have a failure

---

6. For excellent discussion of the linguistic meanings of virtue and aretē, see Goldstein, *Plato at the Googleplex*, 139–42.

7. The equation is stated in something like this way and discussed by Irwin; see Prior, *Socrates: Critical Assessments*, 4:231. See also Santas, "Socratic Goods and Socratic Happiness."

of will, it's really a failure of knowledge. There is no such thing as akrasia.

That claim is a controversial one that can't be treated here in detail, but let's try to understand, at least briefly, what Socrates might have meant by it. It is the long-standing policy of this book not to argue in the abstract when we can instead approach a question Socratically—that is, by asking how a claim might be supported in your own knowledge and experience. Look at it this way, then: There are probably temptations that you now resist easily just because you understand them. There are drugs you don't take and things you don't eat. You know they would feel good or taste good, and yet you don't even experience them *as* temptations. Why not? Because you know too much. You know where they lead and how you will feel if you go there. If someone were to congratulate you on your willpower in declining to take those drugs, you would likely shrug and say that willpower doesn't really enter into it. You just know better.

Socrates thinks everything is like that, or could be. When you have a failure of will, it's really a failure to reach the state just described: a failure to know better. If you say, "I *did* know better, but I couldn't stop myself," he would reply that some of your knowledge got away from you. Of course this implies a certain view of what it means to "know" something. When you avoid dangerous drugs or other things, it isn't only because you can recite their dangers. It is because you know about those dangers in a deeper sense. You are completely conscious of them; they register in full. Sometimes we don't have that kind of knowledge; we only have the kind that is associated with recital. We have faux knowledge, and we are weak.

Socrates has more to say about failures of knowledge that look like failures of will. The "knowledge" you are missing in a moment of weakness often turns out to be an understanding of costs and benefits—that is, a complete and enlightened understanding of them. Socrates speaks in the *Protagoras*, for example, of temptations as giving us pleasure now and making us unhappy later. When that's a bad trade, it's a kind of measurement error caused by the hard time we have giving due weight now to how we will feel in the future.[8] You would act differently if all those future consequences were right in front of you. But you don't see the future that accurately or vividly. And this is, indeed, a problem of knowledge.

The Socratic equation of virtue and knowledge has this implication: people who do wrong are mistaken. The sense of this idea is easiest to see by thinking about self-interest. On a Socratic view, people always *try* do whatever they think will be best for themselves, all in all; their master desire is for their own good. If "good" is defined a certain way, that has to be true. It seems crazy to suppose that anyone would deliberately do something that they didn't think was best for themselves as they understood it. Someone who jumps off a bridge just has an unusual idea about what is best: death. If you seem to want something that is bad, it doesn't seem bad to you when you want it, at least compared to the alternatives.

SOCRATES. Don't you think that everyone desires good things, my friend?

MENO. No, I don't.

SOCRATES. Some people desire bad things, then?

MENO. Yes....

SOCRATES. Do you also think that people who think that bad things do them good are recognizing the bad things as bad?

MENO. No, I don't think that.

SOCRATES. Obviously, then, in these cases, when people don't recognize something bad as bad, it's not that they're desiring something bad; they desire what they take to be good, even though in actual fact it's bad. And this means that people who fail to recognize something bad as bad, and take it to be good, are obviously desiring something good, aren't they?

Meno
77be

Socrates famously put the implication of these points in the following way: no one willingly does wrong.[9]

---

8. *Protagoras* 356ae.

9. See *Gorgias* 509e; *Protagoras* 358cd; for discussion, see Gulley, "Interpretation of 'No One Does Wrong Willingly'"; Walsh, "Socratic Denial of Akrasia."

We've been talking only about choices between acts that are better or worse for *you*—i.e., things that might seem appealing but would make you worse off in the long run or, if you understood them more completely, now. It's easy enough in that setting to see that people all try to do what's best for themselves as they understand it. But what about cases where virtue, or "doing the right thing," means looking out for other people? It might seem crazy to do something you think is bad for *you*, but it doesn't seem crazy (though it might be selfish) to prefer what's best for you to what would be best for your neighbors. Yet Socrates looks at those two cases the same way.[10] If you do the wrong thing and it hurts someone else, it's worse for you, not just for them. And in the largest sense no one willingly does wrong even here—even, that is, to others. The most vicious wrongdoers have stories to tell themselves in which what they do seems right, all in all. They're in the grip of mistakes and bad understandings.

This point can be made most Socratically, again, by thinking of cases where you already feel its truth. There are probably horrible things you could do to others that would seem to make you better off by leaving you with their money or something like that. But you don't want to do those things, and not only because you'd be afraid of getting punished. That just isn't who you want to be; doing them wouldn't really make you feel that you *were* better off, all in all. An extreme example might make this more clear. Imagine that you travel back in time to an era where slavery is common, and you're offered a chance to own slaves yourself. You don't want any; you aren't tempted. Your hosts think that you're either a fool or making a great sacrifice because you're passing up a chance to be better off. What willpower! But you don't see it that way. It's not a question of willpower or sacrifice. You just have a different understanding

---

10. For more on this, see Santas, "Socratic Paradoxes" (reprinted with minor revisions in Santas, *Socrates*, 183–94). Santas suggests that there are two paradoxes at issue. The first is the "prudential paradox": people always want what is best for themselves (despite not always appearing to act that way—hence the paradox). Socrates assumes this. The second is the "moral paradox," which is that no one willingly does wrong (despite the fact that people sometimes do seem to deliberately do things that they know they shouldn't). Socrates views this claim as requiring defense by argument, which it receives in the *Gorgias* and elsewhere.

than they do of what "better off" means. (Someday in the future, people will tell stories like this in which they imagine visiting our time and feeling a comparable sense of revulsion at our ideas about the good life.)

Turn that vision around, make it less extreme, and you have the general Socratic interpretation of moral failure. When you fail to do the right thing—even for the sake of others—it's not really a question of will. It happens because you aren't seeing the situation "all in all," or you aren't seeing the effect on other people up close, or you aren't understanding that they are just as important as you are. It's a failure of knowledge.

Knowledge and emotion. Saying that virtue is knowledge has bothered many readers because it makes human motives sound entirely rational—an "intellectualist" position, as it sometimes is called. Aren't emotions different from knowledge, and just as important or more?[11] Later works of Plato's make more room for emotions, which some readers consider an improvement.[12] But it's also possible to look at emotions as *responses* to knowledge or beliefs.

Fear is a good example. Socrates sometimes teaches that courage is a kind of knowledge and that cowardice is a form of ignorance. This sounds strange at first because courage and cowardice involve fear, and fear seems to be a feeling or emotion rather than a matter of knowledge. But when people fear what they *should* fear, we don't call them cowards. Cowardice is when people fear what isn't worth fearing. The onlooker who sees the cowardice understands that there's nothing to be afraid of. The person in the grip of the cowardice doesn't see this. True, the onlooker and the coward *feel* different things. But their different feelings result from a difference in what they understand, or how deeply the understanding has sunk in. Here is how Socrates put it (the party responding to him is Protagoras):

> In general when the brave feel fear, there is not disgrace in their fears, nor in their confidence when they are confident?

Protagoras
360bd

---

11. See Nehamas, *Virtues of Authenticity*, 27; Grote, *Plato and the Other Companions of Sokrates*, 399–400.

12. See Cooper, "Plato's Theory of Human Motivation."

True....

Cowards on the other hand, and likewise the rash and the mad, feel fears or cowardice which are discreditable, and can they exhibit discreditable fear or confidence from any other cause than ignorance?

No....

Ignorance of what is and is not to be feared must be cowardice.

[Protagoras] nodded.

Well, courage is the opposite of cowardice.

He agreed.

And knowledge of what is and is not to be feared is the opposite of ignorance of these things.

He nodded again.

Which is cowardice.

Here he assented with great reluctance.

Therefore knowledge of what is and is not to be feared is courage.

Socrates thus turns all apparent problems of ethics—of how to live and act—into problems of knowledge and intelligence. Or perhaps he turns them into *one* problem of knowledge, since he seems to argue at points for the "unity of virtues": the idea that if you have any of the virtues in full, you will have them all. They amount to the same deep understanding of the good and the bad, just dressed in different forms.[13]

Turning to the practical, it is a good Socratic exercise to try interpreting every wrongful or unvirtuous act done by anyone in the way we've seen: as a failure of knowledge or understanding. Some cases are challenging to view this way, as when people are up against physical addictions or are otherwise acting without any kind of thought at all. But it's usually possible to at least look at any bad *decision* from the Socratic angle. Sometimes it helps to ask why an omniscient person

13. See Vlastos, "Unity of Virtues in the 'Protagoras'"; Penner, "Unity of Virtue"; Woodruff, "Socrates on the Parts of Virtue"; Devereux, "Unity of the Virtues in Plato's Protagoras and Laches"; Brickhouse and Smith, "Socrates and the Unity of Virtues."

wouldn't have done it—that is, someone who had perfect knowledge of the future, of others and their experiences, and so forth. If the decision was emotional, you can ask whether the emotions would have been the same if the understandings and knowledge that provoked them were different. The Stoics worked out this last idea in more detail, as the next chapter will show.

Boiling virtue down to a matter of understanding is, from a Socratic standpoint, a source of encouragement. It suggests that progress is possible, and that studying philosophy in the right way can make you a happier person at least in the ancient sense. If the Socratic method doesn't leave you in a good mood, in other words, it at least leaves you better entitled to one.

Teachability. And yet Socrates regarded the teaching and learning of virtue as a difficult problem, too. Knowledge can be taught. So if virtue is inseparable from knowledge, that implies *virtue* can be taught by one person to another. But can it really?

On the negative side of that question: Socrates points out in the *Protagoras* that when people want opinions about how to build something, they ask experts who have credentials. But when it comes to moral matters, everyone seems to get a say; nobody asks what credentials they have. This suggests that nobody thinks there are experts on those questions. And *that* suggests that the kind of knowledge needed to answer them well can't be taught. If it were teachable, those who had spent the most time studying it would get deference. People don't defer to philosophy professors when they think about questions of morality. They might defer to parents or other authority figures, but that doesn't make wisdom teachable. There are lots of examples of parents trying to make their children wise or teachers trying to make their students wise but having no success. Socrates viewed these cases as casting doubt on whether virtue can be transmitted from one person to another.

SOCRATES. I could mention numberless other instances of persons who were good themselves, and never yet made any one else good, whether friend or stranger. Now I, Protagoras, hav-

Protagoras
320b

ing these examples before me, am inclined to think that virtue cannot be taught.

Protagoras makes many replies. He points out that we don't punish people who are blind or have physical disabilities, but we do punish those who act immorally. Evidently we think they could do better if they applied themselves, which makes morality seem like something that can be learned, and perhaps therefore something that can be taught. And we do spend a lot of time trying to educate children and others in virtue. Some of that effort is embedded in customs so familiar that they are barely visible to us.

Protagoras
328a

PROTAGORAS. You, Socrates, are discontented, and why? Because all men are teachers of virtue, each one according to his ability; and you say Where are the teachers? You might as well ask, Who teaches Greek?

True, some people turn out to have more aptitude for virtue than others do, just as some have more natural aptitude for playing the flute. Imagine that playing the flute were considered important for everyone, and that everyone were instructed in it. Some would play well and some wouldn't. But we wouldn't therefore say that playing the flute is unteachable. The mistake Socrates commits (according to Protagoras) is not making enough comparisons. People who are *really* untaught in virtue are easy to find, and they are horrifying.

Protagoras
327cd

PROTAGORAS. I would have you consider that he who appears to you to be the worst of those who have been brought up in laws and humanities, would appear to be a just man and a master of justice if he were to be compared with men who had no education, or courts of justice, or laws, or any restraints upon them which compelled them to practice virtue—with the savages, for example, whom the poet Pherecrates exhibited on the stage at the last year's Lenaean festival. If you were living among men such as the man-haters in his Chorus, you would be only too glad to meet with Eurybates and Phrynondas, and you would sorrowfully long to revisit the rascality of this part of the world.

So maybe virtue *is* teachable. The process of teaching is just so diffuse, and the capacity to learn so varied, that we can't easily perceive them with our crude sensibilities. Socrates doesn't quarrel with these arguments (he changes the subject), so maybe he thought they had promise. But the Socratic puzzlement about the teachability of virtue, like most Socratic difficulties, never gets fully resolved. Plato probably wasn't sure how to answer it himself. It's still a hard problem. The activity of Socrates suggests what his own real answer to the question might have been: let's hope that it's teachable and try.

Incompleteness. Socrates offered a method and some principles that the method helped him produce. They don't add up to a complete philosophy of ethics. There are many questions that he doesn't try to analyze, at least not directly. There are others on which his analysis seems unfinished. Some readers treat his claims as a single theory and then say it doesn't work because it doesn't explain enough.[14] If virtue is a kind of knowledge, then what is it knowledge *of*? If the answer is measurement of "what's good for you," or what tends toward eudaimonia, then we might seem to have gotten nowhere, because what's good for you is—virtue. We need a better idea of what this knowledge is about, besides being knowledge that knowledge is everything.

Maybe the answer involves the enlightened measurement of costs and benefits discussed a few pages ago.[15] Plato's later writings can be read as filling in some other possible answers to that question; so can the writings of the Stoics. Both Plato and the Stoics are subject to criticisms that their reasoning, too, is circular;[16] as Socrates showed, it is difficult—maybe more than difficult—for reason to close the loop decisively on deep moral questions. But those examples also show a way in which the incomplete character of Socratic ethics might be considered an advantage. It can make his method compatible with a range of other philosophical projects and approaches.[17] Socratic

14. A concise discussion is C. C. W. Taylor, *Socrates: A Very Short Introduction*, 68–70.
15. The argument of Prior, *Socrates*, 81.
16. A good discussion is Sidgwick, *Methods of Ethics*, 376–79.
17. As Terence Irwin puts it: "Socrates' views about the relation of happiness, virtue and

philosophy is like a stem onto which different extensions can be attached, or a sketch that can be finished in different ways.

---

external goods are a starting point for discussions by Plato in the Republic, by Aristotle, and by Hellenistic philosophers. Each of Socrates' successors has a different view of how much in Socrates' position is plausible, and what aspects of it need to be revised." Irwin, "Socratic Puzzles," 264. For more discussion of the theme, see A. A. Long, "Socrates in Later Greek Philosophy."

15

Socrates and the Stoics

SOCRATES influenced many philosophers and schools in the centuries after his death.[1] This chapter is the first of two that will show how some of those followers developed his ideas—about method, and about how to live—into more elaborate philosophies and more detailed practices. We will begin with the Stoics, then spend some time on the Skeptics. Together the chapters will illustrate the range of results that Socratic thinking can produce.

Stoicism is a philosophical movement that began about a hundred years after the death of Socrates, became very popular in ancient Greece and Rome, and offers ethical ideas that many people still find attractive. (Please disregard, for the sake of this discussion, the modern English meaning of the word "stoicism"; it has little to do with the ancient philosophy.) The Stoics addressed many topics that Socrates never touched.[2] They had an elaborate theory of natural law, for example, that owes nothing to Plato's Socrates, though it may have roots in the Socrates given to us by Xenophon.[3] But at other points in Stoic thought, including their most interesting claims about how to think and live, the Socratic influence is great and obvious. As A. A. Long has put it, "Socrates is the philosopher whom the Stoics took as their primary inspiration and model."[4]

Stoicism is regarded by many readers as a set of specific teachings about living well. That is indeed how the philosophy ends. But it starts with a certain posture of mind and approach to thinking about

---

1. For discussion of the range of his influence, see A. A. Long, "Socratic Legacy."

2. For an overview that does better justice to the breadth of the philosophy, see A. A. Long, *Hellenistic Philosophy*, ch. 4.

3. See DeFilippo and Mitsis, "Socrates and Stoic Natural Law." For additional discussion of the overlap between Socrates and the Stoics and differences between them, see Brickhouse and Smith, *Socratic Moral Psychology*, 232–47.

4. A. A. Long, "Socrates in Later Greek Philosophy," 362; A. A. Long, *Stoic Studies*, 16–32.

the issues that the philosophy means to address. The recommendations that Stoicism provides are a product of that approach. The approach is Socratic. Epictetus in particular sought to carry forward the Socratic stance, and the Socratic style of analysis, and to apply it to the problems brought to him by his students. He shows how the Socratic method can be applied to some questions more practical than the ones in Plato's dialogues. The student of Stoicism who wants a more complete grasp of the philosophy does well by following it back to these roots.

After a brief historical account, each section of this chapter will show how one of Socrates' teachings lived on in the thought of the Stoics or was further developed there.

History. Stoicism got its name because Zeno of Citium (c. 334–c. 262 BC), the founder of the school, did his teaching in a public colonnade or porch ("stoa") overlooking the central meeting place of Athens—the Agora. Stoicism was known on this account as the Philosophy of the Porch, as opposed to the Philosophy of the Academy (that of Plato), or the Philosophy of the Lyceum (that of Aristotle), or the Philosophy of the Garden (that of Epicurus), with each name referring to the place where the teachings of the school were imparted.

Our knowledge of Zeno is sparse, but he is said to have studied early in his life under Polemo, one of the heads of the Academy who succeeded Plato, and also under the Cynic philosopher Crates. Zeno, in turn, was followed as head of the Stoic school by Cleanthes and then Chrysippus. All three were prolific writers, but none of their works have survived. We know their views only through paraphrases or quotations recorded by others. From the "late" period of Stoicism the surviving writings are much more extensive and will serve our purposes here.[5] These are the principal authors whose works we have from that period:

---

5. For readers who want more evidence of what the earliest Stoics said, A. A. Long, *Hellenistic Philosophy*, ch. 4, provides an excellent overview. Long and Sedley, *Hellenistic Philosophers*, and Inwood and Gerson, *Hellenistic Philosophy*, provide English translations of the fragments that remain from that period.

↠ *Epictetus* (pronounced ep-ic-*tee*-tus), who lived from about 55 to 135 AD. He was born in the region we now know as Turkey, and spent most of the first half of his life in Rome. He was born a slave and freed as a young adult; he suffered throughout his life from an injury of some sort to his leg. When philosophers were banished from Rome by the emperor Domitian, Epictetus moved to Greece and established a school there. He left behind no writings of his own. But one of his students, Arrian, published extensive class notes known as the *Discourses* of Epictetus, as well as the *Enchiridion* (i.e., handbook; Arrian wrote in Greek). Professor Long observes that "Socrates' imprint is present on almost every page of the discourses" and that they are "the most creative appropriation of Socrates subsequent to the works of Plato and Xenophon." [6] We will see examples below.

↠ *Seneca the Younger* (Lucius Annaeus Seneca), who lived from about 4 BC to 65 AD. He was born in Spain; his father, who had the same name (and so is remembered as Seneca the Elder), was a teacher of rhetoric. The son—our Seneca—was taken to Rome when he was young. After a period spent in Egypt, an early career as a lawyer and politician, and a banishment to Corsica, he became a tutor and advisor to Nero, an emperor of odious reputation. Seneca also became very wealthy. He was accused in 65 AD of joining the Pisonian conspiracy, which had unsuccessfully plotted Nero's murder. He was ordered by the emperor to commit suicide, which he did; he cut open his veins and sat in a hot bath, though they say it was the steam that finally did him in. (The episode is the subject of a fine allusion in *The Godfather Part II*.) Seneca wrote letters, dialogues, and essays on philosophy, and also a number of plays. His writings are the largest surviving body of work on Stoicism.

↠ *Marcus Aurelius* (in full, Marcus Aurelius Antoninus Augustus) (121–180 AD) was Roman Emperor for nearly twenty years starting in 160. Mostly while on military campaigns during the last decade of

---

6. A. A. Long, *Epictetus*, 94.

his life, he wrote philosophical notes to himself in Greek that we call his *Meditations*. He never described himself as a Stoic in his writings, but he was a devoted student of the philosophy and has long been treated as one of its defining authors. Mill described the writings of Marcus Aurelius as "the highest ethical product of the ancient mind." [7]

Socratic ignorance. The Socratic method starts with an understanding of how little you know. (See chapter 11.) Epictetus viewed this point as the start of Stoicism as well.

Epictetus,
Discourses
2.11.1

The beginning of philosophy—at least for those who take hold of it in the right way, and through the front door—is an awareness of one's own weakness and incapacity when it comes to the most important things.

Epictetus,
Discourses
2.17.1

What is the first business of one who studies philosophy? To part with self-conceit.

Epictetus brought humility to his encounters with the arrogant. The first question on such an occasion should be whether their problems might also be found in oneself.

Epictetus,
Discourses
2.21.8–10

Living as we do among such people, who are so confused, and don't know what they're saying, or what evil they have within them, or where they got it from, or how they can get rid of it, we should constantly be focusing our attention, I think, on the following thoughts: "Could it be, perhaps, that I too am one of these people? What kind of person do I picture myself as being? How do I conduct myself? Is it really as a wise person, as someone who has control of himself? Can I say for my part that I've been educated to face everything that may come? Is it indeed the case, as is fitting for someone who knows nothing, that I'm aware that I know nothing?"

Marcus Aurelius had a similar idea: resistance to false pride should not itself become a source of false pride.

---

7. *On Liberty*, in Robson, *Collected Works of John Stuart Mill*, 18:236.

For a man to be proud and high conceited, that he is not proud and high conceited, is of all kind of pride and presumption, the most intolerable.

Marcus Aurelius, *Meditations* 12.20

But unlike Socrates, as we shall see, the Stoics also thought they could reason their way to important truths on which they did not hedge.

Cross-examination. Dialectic was part of Stoicism from the start. For Zeno, our evidence suggests that this meant proceeding by question and answer; for Chrysippus, dialectic likewise involved devotion to argument and may also have referred to a broader approach to investigating the truth.[8] The evidence becomes more direct when we reach the Romans. Seneca suggested that "the reason dialogue is highly beneficial is that it works its way into the mind bit by bit."[9] And Epictetus was a declared believer in the Socratic question-and-answer procedure for wiping out false conceits of knowledge.

There are two things that must be rooted out from human beings: presumption and lack of confidence. Presumption lies in supposing that there is nothing more that one needs.... As regards presumption, that can be removed by cross-examination, and Socrates was the first to do that.

Epictetus, *Discourses* 2.14.8

Epictetus offered this account of the Socratic method as he understood it:

How did Socrates act, then? He forced his interlocutor to bear witness for him and had no need of any other witness. He was thus able to say, "I can do without everyone else; it is always enough for me to have my interlocutor as witness; as for the rest, I don't seek their vote, but that of my interlocutor alone." For he would bring the consequences of our preconceptions so clearly to light that everyone, no matter who, recognized the contradiction involved and so abandoned it. "Does an envious man take pleasure in his envy?" "Not at all, but quite the reverse,

Epictetus, *Discourses* 2.12.5–7

---

8. See A. A. Long, *Stoic Studies*, ch. 4, and especially 93–97.
9. Seneca, *Epistles* 38.1 in Graver and Long, *Seneca: Letters on Ethics*, 118.

he is pained by it." Through the contradiction he has shaken his partner. "Well then, does envy seem to you to be a feeling of pain provoked by the sight of bad things?" And so he has made him say that envy is a feeling of pain provoked by the sight of good things.[10]

Epictetus adapts the question-and-answer approach to his own classroom. He uses a variation on the Socratic style. Stoicism often amounts to the practice of pushing through the surfaces of impressions that seem natural. Socratic questioning is a way to carry out that process. Consider this passage, where his student is a father who was too upset by his daughter's medical condition to stay at her side:

Epictetus, Discourses 1.11.4–7

Well then, do you think you were right to have acted in that way? "I was behaving naturally," he said. But that is the very thing that you must convince me of, replied Epictetus, that you were behaving in accordance with nature, and I will then convince you that whatever is done in accordance with nature is rightly done. "That's how all fathers feel," said the man, "or least most do." I don't dispute that, said Epictetus, but the point at issue between us is whether it's right to feel like that. For in that case, one would have to say that tumors develop for the good of the body just because they do in fact develop, and, in a word, that to fall into error is natural just because almost all of us, or at least most of us, do fall into error.

Or this example, in which Epictetus questions his way toward the Stoic idea that we are truly free in the use of our minds but not otherwise:

Epictetus, Discourses 4.1.66–71

When you want your body to remain sound and whole, is that within your power or isn't it?—"No, that isn't within my

---

10. The first part of the paragraph from Epictetus evidently is drawn from *Gorgias* 472bc, which is seen in chapter 10 of this book. The origin of what he says about envy is less clear; it might be *Philebus* 48be, or maybe the lines from Xenophon quoted in chapter 1 of this book (but that passage doesn't run in the dialogical way that Epictetus shows).

power."—And when you want it to be healthy?—"No, that isn't either."—Or that it should be beautiful?—"That isn't either."—And to live or die?—"No again."—It thus follows that your body is not your own, but is subject to whatever is stronger than itself.—"Indeed." ... Have you nothing at all, then, that is subject to your own authority, or exclusively within your power, or do you have something of that kind?—"I don't know."

Well, look at the question in this way, and think it over. Can anyone make you give your assent to what is false?—"No one can."—In the matter of assent, then, you're free from hindrance and restraint.—"Agreed."—Come now, can anyone force you to direct your impulses towards anything that you don't want?—"Indeed he can. For when he threatens me with death or imprisonment, he can force me to it."—If you were to despise death, however, or chains, would you still pay heed to him?—"No."—Now to despise death, is that your own act, or isn't it?—"It's my own act."

These dialogues are broadly Socratic. Epictetus pursues what the student says to an absurd conclusion or shows that it conflicts with other admissions. But there are differences, too. Epictetus is less likely than Socrates to ask for definitions or abstract claims and then challenge them. He is more likely to go after the ethical assumptions of his students directly or use questions to make a point that he wants them to understand. He doesn't seek aporia; he has views about the right and wrong way to look at a problem and pushes his students toward those results. His topics are usually more specific, his inquiries less complicated, and his results more practical than those of the Socrates shown to us by Plato.[11] (In those respects he more closely resembles the Socrates preserved by Xenophon.) Still, though, the approach of the Stoic teachers tends to resemble that of Socrates in spirit. They don't order a student to believe this or that. They appeal to the experience of the student and then say, "don't you think... ?" or "doesn't it seem that.... ?"

---

11. For more complete discussion, see Brennan, "Socrates and Epictetus," 286–91.

This book argues that the habit of Socratic questioning is largely meant to be internalized. Epictetus also regarded it that way.[12]

Epictetus, *Discourses* 2.1.32

Since [Socrates] couldn't always have someone at his side to subject his judgments to examination, or to be cross-examined by him in turn, he used to subject himself to examination, and test himself out, and was always trying out the practical application of some specific preconception.

Epictetus, *Discourses* 1.30.1–3, 5–7

When you are going into the presence of some man in authority, remember that another is watching what is happening from above, and that it is not the man but the other you must satisfy. So the watcher inquires of you: "Exile, prison, bondage, death, disgrace—what did you call these in the lecture-hall?" "I called them 'indifferent.'" "So now what do you call them? Have those things changed at all?" "No." "Have you changed, then?" "No." … Well then, go in confidently, remembering these things, and you'll see what it means to be a young person who has studied, among those who have not studied.

And Epictetus sometimes takes a sharp tone with his students. It is not an approach welcome in the modern classroom. Like Socratic abruptness, however, it can have definite value when you question your own stupidities.

Epictetus, *Discourses* 2.16.32

"So when will I see Athens again, and the Acropolis?" Wretch, isn't it enough for you, what you look at every day? Could you have anything better or greater to see than the sun, the moon, the stars, the whole world, the sea?

Epictetus, *Discourses* 2.16.11–14

What do we admire? Externals. What do we spend our energies on? Externals. Is it any wonder, then, that we are in fear and distress? How else could it be, when we regard the events that are coming as evil? We can't fail to be afraid, we can't fail to be distressed. Then we say, "Lord God, let me not be distressed." Moron, don't you have hands? Didn't God make them for you? So are you going to sit down and pray that your nose will stop

---

12. As discussed in A. A. Long, "Socrates in Later Greek Philosophy," 373.

running? Better to wipe your nose and stop praying. What, then—has he given you nothing to help with your situation? Hasn't he given you endurance, hasn't he given you greatness of spirit, hasn't he given you courage?

Consistency. As we saw in chapter 7, Socrates treats consistency as a test of truth and of the health of the psyche, or soul. People who say different or inconsistent things about a subject are showing that they don't know their own minds.

> SOCRATES. Your complaint about me is that, in your opinion, I'm constantly saying the same things, whereas I find the opposite fault in you—I think you never say the same things about the same issues.

Gorgias
491b

Statements like that one support the conclusion of Vlastos that Socrates "elevates consistency to a supreme desideratum in his own search for truth." [13] The elevation was continued by the Stoics as a matter of both method and substance. Epictetus followed Socrates in treating internal critique, or finding inconsistencies, as the classic route to success in cross-examination.

> Someone who is skilled in reasoning, and is able both to encourage and to refute, will thus be able to show each person the contradiction that is causing him to go astray, and make him clearly understand that he isn't doing what he wants, and is in fact doing what he doesn't want. For if anyone can make that clear to him, he'll renounce his error of his own accord, but if you fail to show him, don't be surprised if he persists in it, being under the impression that he is acting rightly.... Socrates knew how a rational mind is moved: that being like a balance, it will incline whether one wishes it or not. Make the ruling center aware of a contradiction, and it will renounce it; but if you fail to make it clear, blame yourself rather than the person whom you're unable to convince.

Epictetus,
Discourses
2.26.4–7

---

13. Vlastos, *Socratic Studies*, 27.

The value of consistency as a sign of the truth is also spelled out by Seneca.

Seneca, *Epistles* 20.5

To abandon the old definitions of wisdom and use one that covers the whole range of human life, I can be content with this: What is wisdom? To always want the same things and reject the same things. No need to add that little qualification, "so long as what you want is right"—since one could not always be pleased with the same thing if it were not right.

This sentiment closely resembles the Socratic position shown in chapter 6: anything false that you believe will eventually collide with true things you know. Epictetus seems to have had a similar view. He spoke of an innate moral sense on which people can draw to make judgments. Since truths never collide, the consistency of beliefs after long testing is a sign that they're right.[14] To turn the point around, inconsistency is the sign of a mind whose grasp of the truth is infirm, as suggested in the passage from the *Gorgias* above. That was also how Seneca thought about inconsistency.

Seneca, *Epistles* 95.57–58

Peace of mind depends on securing an unchanging and definite judgment. Other people constantly lose and regain their footing, as they oscillate between letting things go and pursuing them. What is the reason for this instability? It is that nothing is certain for people who reply on popular opinion, the most unreliable of standards.

Virtue and happiness. The Stoics generally shared the ethical views of Socrates developed in chapter 14. In some cases they took them further.[15] In the previous chapter we saw that the Socratic philosopher treats the achievement of eudaimonia—happiness, or the good life—as an ultimate goal. We also saw Socrates say that "wisdom is the only good, and ignorance the only evil."[16] Stoicism is a eudaimonistic

---

14. The parallels between the view of Epictetus and this interpretation of the elenchus (associated with Vlastos) are well discussed in A. A. Long, *Epictetus*, 79–84.

15. See Eric Brown, "Socrates in the Stoa," and Striker, "Plato's Socrates and the Stoics," for discussion.

16. *Euthydemus* 281e.

philosophy, too. The Stoic position on the meaning of the good life closely resembles the Socratic one and may be the same.[17]

> The matter can be imparted quickly and in very few words: "Virtue is the only good; at any rate there is no good without virtue; and virtue itself is situated in our nobler part, that is, the rational part."

Seneca,
Epistles
71.32

Socrates also concluded that wealth and health aren't good in themselves. It depends on how they are used. We have seen some examples of this view already; here is another:

> SOCRATES. Now suppose we consider what are the sorts of things that profit us. Take them in a list. Health, we may say, and strength and good looks, and wealth—these and their like we call advantageous, you agree?
> MENO. Yes.
> SOCRATES. Yet we also speak of these things as sometimes doing harm. Would you object to that statement?
> MENO. No, it is so.
> SOCRATES. Now look here. What is the controlling factor which determines whether each of these is advantageous or harmful? Isn't it right use which makes them advantageous, and lack of it, harmful?
> MENO. Certainly.

Meno
87e–88a

The Stoics carried this idea over entirely and more forcefully; it is therefore more often associated with them than with Socrates. From Epictetus:

> "Is health good, and disease evil?" No, you can do better than that. "What then?" To use health well is good, to use it badly is evil.

Epictetus,
Discourses
3.20.4

Seneca:

> So it is with those things we term "indifferent" or "middle," such as riches, strength, beauty, reputation, sovereignty—or their

Seneca,
Epistles
82.14

---

17. For close analysis of the evidence in the dialogues, see Annas, "Virtue as the Use of Other Goods."

opposites: death, exile, ill-heath, pain, and all the others that we find more or less terrifying. It is wickedness or virtue that gives them the name of good or evil. By itself a lump of metal is neither hot nor cold: thrown into the furnace it gets hot, put back in the water it is cold.

As that passage suggests, health, wealth, and other such externals that aren't good or bad in themselves were called "indifferents" by the Stoics. The ones that are helpful if used wisely became known as preferred indifferents.

Virtue and knowledge. In addition to saying that happiness is insepa-rable from virtue, Socrates held that virtue is a matter of knowledge or understanding (and that vice is ignorance). Compare these similar Stoic claims:

Seneca,
Epistles 31.6

What then is good? The knowledge of things. What is evil? The lack of knowledge of things.

Seneca,
Epistles 88.28

There is but one thing that brings the soul to perfection—the unalterable knowledge of good and evil.

Epictetus,
Discourses
1.11.11

To be ignorant of a criterion of colors, or of smells, or tastes, might perhaps be no very great loss. But do you think that he suffers only a small loss, who is ignorant of what is good and evil, and natural and unnatural to man?

Stoicism makes the practical meaning of the Socratic teachings more clear. The Stoics talk about how to handle various problems of life—vanity, anger, fear, greed. They don't just say, as Socrates did, that those can be considered problems of knowledge. They show *how* those problems might be addressed accordingly. They start by sug-gesting that your apparent problems in the world can often be rein-terpreted as problems in your thinking. The approach Socrates took to his own problem provides an example.

Epictetus,
Enchiridion 5

Men are disturbed not by the things that happen but by their opinions about those things. For example, death is nothing ter-rible; for if it were, it would have seemed so even to Socrates.

Rather, the opinion that death is terrible—that is the terrible thing. So when we are impeded or upset or aggrieved, let us never blame others, but ourselves—that is, our opinions.

Cicero described the Stoic perspective in a similar way:

> Grief, then, is a recent opinion of some present evil, about which it seems right to feel downcast and in low spirits. Joy is a recent opinion of a present good, in response to which it seems right to be elated. Fear is an opinion of an impending evil that seems unbearable. Lust is an opinion about a good to come—that it would be better if it were already here.

Cicero, *Tusculan Disputations* 4.7

Compare the following moment from the *Republic*.

> SOCRATES. Courage is a certain kind of preserving.
> GLAUCON. Just what sort of preserving?
> SOCRATES. The preserving of the opinion produced by law through education about what—and what sort of thing—is terrible.

Republic 429bc

If virtue is a form of knowledge and bad behavior is the result of ignorance, or misguided opinions, what follows from this? One Stoic answer is *forbearance*. When people are annoying or do wrong, it's because they don't know any better. Remembering this makes us kinder. Marcus Aurelius starts this first statement of the point by quoting Socrates:

> "Every soul is deprived of truth against its will"—and is likewise deprived against its will of justice, self-control, kindness, and everything of the kind. It is necessary to keep this in mind always, because it will make you milder toward everyone else.

Marcus Aurelius, *Meditations* 7.63

> Begin the morning by saying to yourself: today I will meet with the busybody, the ungrateful, and the arrogant; with the deceitful, the envious, and the unsocial. All these things result from their not knowing what is good and what is evil.

Marcus Aurelius, *Meditations* 2.1

At other times the Stoics say that people who behave badly should be pitied. They are mistaken or ethically disabled, and either way it's a sad spectacle.

Epictetus,
Discourses
1.28.9

Why, then, are you angry with her, that the unhappy woman is deceived in the most important points, and instead of a human creature, becomes a viper? Why do not you rather, as we pity the blind and lame, so likewise pity those who are blinded and lamed in their superior faculties?

Epictetus sometimes suggested that wrongdoers be seen as victims. We saw earlier the Socratic idea that those who wrong others are worse off themselves, and this is a way to see why: they are deceived. (They may also be their own deceivers.)

Epictetus,
Enchiridion
42

Whenever someone does you a wrong or speaks ill of you, remember that he is doing what he thinks is proper. He can't possibly be guided by what appears right to you, but only by what appears right to him. So if he sees things wrongly, he is the one who is hurt, because he is the one who has been deceived.... Starting from this reasoning, you will be mild toward whoever insults you. Say each time, "So it seemed to him."

Emotion. As noted in chapter 14, Socrates is sometimes criticized for taking too little account of emotion.[18] His model of human functioning seems wholly intellectual. But the approach of the Stoics provides a more complete way to account for emotion while still subscribing to the Socratic equation, or near equation, of happiness, virtue, and knowledge. If you have an emotional reaction to any given thing, it's a response not to the thing itself but to what you think about it—to your *understanding* of the thing. That understanding arises from your knowledge or lack thereof, and is something you might be able to change.

This can all be seen as an elaboration of Socratic teachings. The previous chapter used fear as a Socratic case study in a feeling, or emotion, for which any view of human nature must account. We saw

---

18. A prominent example is in Grote, *Plato and the Other Companions of Sokrates*, 399; Grote attributes to Socrates "the error ... of dwelling exclusively on the intellectual conditions of human conduct, and omitting to give proper attention to the emotional and volitional."

Socrates treat courage as amounting to a kind of knowledge. The Stoics put the same idea more directly.

> Bravery is not thoughtless rashness, or love of danger, or the courting of fear-inspiring objects; it is the knowledge which enables us to distinguish between that which is evil and that which is not.

Seneca, *Epistles* 85.28

One may object to this way of understanding emotion—whether attributed to Socrates or to the Stoics—as failing to account for displays of it by infants or animals. They lack knowledge; they don't have the kind of mental life that allows them to form opinions, right or wrong. Yet they seem quite capable of emotions such as rage. The Stoics deal with this objection by treating the rage of animals as a different sort of thing than emotion.

> Wild beasts have impulses, madness, fierceness, aggressiveness; but they no more have anger than they have luxuriousness.... Dumb animals lack the emotions of man, but they have certain impulses similar to these emotions.

Seneca, *On Anger* 1.3.6

This point, too, had its antecedents in the Socratic dialogues.

> LACHES. Are you claiming that those animals which are universally acknowledged to be courageous are more intelligent than human beings, or would you go so far as to contradict everyone else and say that they aren't even courageous?
> NICIAS. No, Laches, I don't call an animal or anything else courageous if it's too mindless to be afraid of threats; I call it "fearless" and "irrational."

Laches 197a

(Nicias is elaborating an approach that he first attributes to Socrates.) Similarly, the Stoics say that some human reactions look like emotions but are something less.

> The courageous man will frown at sad things; he will be startled by a sudden occurrence; he will feel dizzy if, standing at the brink, he looks down from the precipice. This is not fear, but a natural feeling not to be overcome by reason.

Seneca, *Epistles* 57.4

Some readers find this satisfactory. Others regard it as avoiding a problem by relabeling the hard part of it. But if the Socratic or Stoic view of emotions can't account for animals, that doesn't make the view invalid. It just makes the view incomplete. Treating emotions as reactions to thoughts and knowledge is useful and can explain a great deal, even if less than everything.

Notice here, as in chapter 14, that the Socratic and Stoic way of looking at emotions treats "knowledge" as more than what you claim to think. Some beliefs are held in the forefront of the mind and can be dropped or revised when you hear new evidence or arguments. Some run deeper and are hard to change even when we think we know better. You "know" that there is nothing to fear in some situation but you feel fear anyway; so in fact you don't know it, or rather you have conflicting beliefs about whether there is anything to fear. Some of the beliefs will take time to root out because they are ingrained. You "know" that you don't want something but you still feel desire for it—the same pattern: some of your beliefs haven't caught up with others. A principal goal of philosophy is to bring all those beliefs into a state of consistency.[19] It's work.

Invulnerability. Socrates says that "nothing can harm a good man either in life or death."[20] The Stoics took the same view and, as usual, enlarged on it. They describe this invulnerability as a matter of detaching yourself from externals—that is, from all things that are up to others. Instead you identify with what is up to you: your choices, your will, your understanding. No outside force can injure those things.

Seneca, *On Providence* 6.1

"But why does God sometimes allow evil to befall good men?" Assuredly he does not. Evil of every sort he keeps far from them—shameful acts and crimes, evil counsel and schemes for greed, blind lust and avarice intent on another's goods. The good man himself he protects and delivers. Does anyone require of

---

19. See Eric Brown, "Socrates in the Stoa," 279–81.
20. *Apology* 41c.

God that he should also guard the good man's luggage? No, the good man himself relieves God of this concern; he despises externals.

A similar notion from Epictetus:

> I must be put in chains; must I also be wailing about something? I must be banished; does anyone prevent me from leaving with a smile, cheerful and easy-going? "Reveal your secrets." I don't speak; this much is up to me. "Then I will put you in chains." Man, what are you saying? Me? You can chain my leg, but Zeus himself can't overcome my will. "I'll throw you in prison." My poor body, you mean. "I'll cut your head off." When did I ever tell you that my neck was the only one that could not be severed? These are the things philosophers should think about, should write down daily, should use as exercise.

Epictetus, Discourses 1.1.22

Epictetus drew his inspiration for these teachings directly from Socrates, as shown in his response to a student who raised the topic.

> "How strange, then, that Socrates should have been so treated by the Athenians." Slave, why do you say Socrates? Speak of the thing as it is: how strange that the poor body of Socrates should have been carried off and dragged to prison by stronger men, and that any one should have given hemlock to the poor body of Socrates, and that it should breathe out the life.... Where, then, for him was the nature of good? Whom shall we listen to, you or him? And what does Socrates say? "Anytus and Meletus can kill me, but they cannot hurt me."

Epictetus, Discourses 1.29.16–18

That last reference is to a passage from the *Apology* quoted in the previous chapter. Another example of the same idea from Socrates:

> SOCRATES. Let people despise you and abuse you as an idiot, if they like; yes, let them even strike you ignominiously in the face. Why should that worry you? Nothing terrible will happen to you as long as you really are a good and moral person, training yourself in the exercise of virtue.

Gorgias 527cd

The Stoic position—which we can now see is also a Socratic one—has sometimes seemed extravagant, as it suggests that a sage can be torn apart on the rack and yet still be described as happy enough.[21] But the Stoics more or less conceded that nobody had ever reached such perfection of mind.[22] They just thought that, if such an ideal state *were* reached, it would allow its holder peace of mind under every circumstance. They therefore regarded Socrates as their hero not just for his teachings but for his example. He went to death with his virtue intact, and so went to it with equanimity.

---

21. See Cicero, *De Finibus* 3.13.42.
22. See Farnsworth, *Practicing Stoic*, 250–55.

16

Socrates and the Skeptics

OTHERS besides the Stoics claimed to be the heirs of Socrates. The most prominent such claimants are known to us now as Skeptics. This chapter explains who the Skeptics were, what they thought, and why they considered themselves to be Socratic. We will see that the philosophy of the Skeptics, even more than that of the Stoics, amounts to a direct extension of the *methods* of Socrates.

History. The school that Plato founded was known as the Academy. It continued after his death under a series of other leaders (or "scholarchs") for about 300 years. The ideas associated with the Academy sometimes changed under different leaders. For much of its history it was identified with Skepticism.[1] Two heads of the Academy were especially famous Skeptics: Arcesilaus, who took over in 264 BC, and Carneades, who became scholarch in 167 BC.

The Academy was destroyed during a war in 88 BC, at which point its last head, Philo, decamped to Rome. One of his students there was Cicero, who was then about 20 years old and would go on to become one of Rome's foremost statesmen and orators. The writings of Cicero are now our best source of knowledge about the Academy's teachings. Cicero's own philosophy became eclectic; he found appeal in ideas from different schools. But his attachment to the Academy always stayed with him, along with his belief that Academic Skeptics were the most faithful followers of Socrates.[2]

---

1. At any rate, the Academy became identified with ideas that we would now call Skeptical, and I will refer to them that way here. Whether they were described by that label at the time is not clear. See Brennan, "Socrates and Epictetus."

2. Cicero wrote: "Socrates was the first who brought down philosophy from the heavens, placed it in cities, introduced it into families, and obliged it to examine into life and morals, and good and evil. And his different methods of discussing questions, together with the variety of his topics, and the greatness of his abilities, being immortalized by the memory and writings of Plato, gave rise to many sects of philosophers of different sentiments, of all which I have principally adhered to that one which, in my opinion, Socrates himself followed." *Tusculan Disputations* 5.4.10–11.

The word "Skepticism," like "Stoicism," has a modern English meaning that overlaps only a little with what it originally meant. It is derived from the Greek word *skepsis*, a noun meaning "inquiry." A Skeptic thus is one who inquires (and inquires) without reaching a conclusion. Skeptics in the ancient tradition don't say "no" to every claim, or indeed to any of them. They just keep asking questions. They want the truth, and are always trying to get closer to it, but they never reach a stopping point; they never find certainty. They have a dread of "rash assent," and of thinking that you're done thinking before you really are. Skeptics regard that tendency as the great failing of humanity (probably—they aren't certain, of course).[3]

The Skeptics had as strong a claim to Socratic paternity as the Stoics did. But the Skeptics fastened on to other features of what Socrates taught, and drew different lessons.

Question and answer. For Skeptics, the central lesson of Socrates was that wisdom amounts to appreciation of our ignorance, and that this ignorance is best established through Socratic questioning. Cicero recounts the pattern found in the dialogues as the Skeptics understood it:

Cicero,
Academica
1.4.16

[Socrates] argues in such a manner that he affirms nothing himself, but refutes the assertions of others. He says that he knows nothing, except that one fact, that he is ignorant; and that he is superior to others in this particular, that they believe that they do know what they do not, while he knows this one thing alone, that he knows nothing. And it is on that account that he imagines he was pronounced by Apollo the wisest of all men, because this alone is the whole of wisdom, for a man not to think that he knows what he does not know.

One of Plato's students, Aristotle, left the Academy to found his own school (the Lyceum). Others stayed in the Academy and took Plato's theories in various other directions in the century after his

---

3. For further discussion of the meaning of the word, see Cooper, "Arcesilaus: Socratic and Sceptic," 171–72.

death. But the Skeptics thought these were all cases of going astray from the Socratic vision, which was to stick to questioning and come to rest on no final conclusions. Speaking of the Lyceum and early Academy, Cicero wrote:

> Both these schools, being impregnated with the copiousness of Plato, arranged a certain definite system of doctrine, which was itself copious and luxuriant; but abandoned the Socratic plan of doubting on every subject, and of discussing everything without ever venturing on the assertion of a positive opinion. And thus there arose what Socrates would have been far from approving.

Cicero,
Academica
1.4.17

Arcesilaus was the fifth head of the Academy after Plato. He is considered the founder of the Academy's "Second" or "Middle" period. He wanted to return the Academy to its Socratic roots: a school where the teacher's job is to argue against whatever the students say.[4]

> [Socrates'] own way was to question his interlocutors and by a process of cross-examination to elicit their opinions, so that he might express his own views by way of rejoinder to their answers. This practice was abandoned by his successors, but was afterwards revived by Arcesilaus, who made it a rule that those who wished to hear him should not ask him questions but should state their own opinions; and when they had done so he argued against them.

Cicero,
De Finibus
2.1.2

It would be too strong to say that Arcesilaus *refuted* the claims of others. If a claim were refuted, everyone would agree that it's wrong. In that case Arcesilaus might argue that the claim was right after all. He showed not that everyone was wrong, but that there were always good arguments both ways, so that no such arguments should settle anything.

---

4. In the same vein from Cicero: "[Arcesilaus] is said to have employed an outstandingly attractive style of speaking in rejecting any judgments of the mind or senses, and to have been the first to set up the practice—though this was highly Socratic—of not showing what he thought but of arguing against what anyone else said they thought." *De Oratore* 3.67.

Cicero,
Academica
1.12.45

> [Arcesilaus] used to act consistently with these principles, so as to pass most of his days in arguing against every one's opinion, in order that when equally important reasons were found for both sides of the same question, the judgment might more naturally be suspended, and prevented from giving assent to either.

That result—withholding judgment because you can't decide what to think—is called *epochē* (pronounced *ep*-oh-kay). Arcesilaus's approach to questioning became the standard one in the Academy, though Cicero worried that the Greeks were getting soft by the end.

Cicero,
*De Natura
Deorum*
1.5.11

> The philosophical method in question, the method of meeting every position with criticism, and upon no point delivering a straightforward judgment, which started with Socrates, and was taken up again by Arcesilaus, and placed upon a firm foundation by Carneades, continued to flourish down to our own times, and yet I see that at the present moment in Greece itself it is left almost in the condition of an orphan. This I think has come about not through the fault of the Academy, but as a consequence of men's dullness.

Aporia vs. epochē. Many scholars accept, though some with misgivings, that the Skeptics were reasonable in claiming Socrates as their great ancestor.[5] But others note differences between them, and some suggest that Arcesilaus wasn't really getting his Skepticism from Socrates or Plato—that he only *said* he was a follower of Socrates to give his teachings a respectable pedigree. His ideas actually came from other Skeptical philosophers such as Pyrrho (of whom more later).[6] The precise relationship between the teachings of Socrates and the Skeptics is, like many topics in this book, the subject of a large and subtle literature that can't be adequately summarized here. But we can note a few points of tension and interest.

First, epochē isn't precisely what Socrates sought or produced.

---

5. See Benson, *Socratic Wisdom*, 180–188; Annas, "Plato the Skeptic," 324–25; Shields, "Socrates Among the Skeptics," 344–45.

6. See, e.g., Sedley, "Motivation of Greek Skepticism," 16.

If you suspend judgment in the Skeptical way, you don't say that a claim is right or wrong. You say that you don't know. Socrates did something different. His arguments produced aporia—an impasse—by refuting the efforts of others to show that they had mastered important concepts. In epochē, you don't know what to do because you're suspended between different arguments that could both be right. When encountering aporia, you don't know what to do because all possible answers to a question—or all you can think of—have been shown to be wrong.

The reader can consider how much importance to assign that distinction. On the one hand, the practitioner of Socratic or Skeptical inquiry has a similar immediate experience either way: nothing that you say is good enough. And the usual response, whether from Socrates or Arcesilaus, is the same, too: don't give up; keep at it; try harder, even if you can't know whether the truth will ever be reached. At the same time, however, there is a definite difference between a philosophy that says some claims are true and some (most!) are false, and a philosophy that never quite concludes that anything is true or false. Close students of the Socratic and Skeptical traditions regard the frame of mind produced by the two approaches as quite distinct. As Paul Woodruff puts it: "Aporia leads to a state of epistemic *frustration*. Epochē, on the other hand, is a state of *detachment* from belief."[7]

Knowability. Some readers, too, find related differences between Skeptical and Socratic views of whether anything can be known.

> Arcesilaus said that there is nothing that can be known, not even that residuum of knowledge that Socrates had left himself—the truth of this very dictum: so hidden in obscurity did he believe that everything lies, nor is there anything that can be perceived or understood, and for these reasons, he said, no one must make any positive statement or affirmation or give the approval of his assent to any proposition, and a man must always restrain his

Cicero,
Academica
1.12.45

---

7. Woodruff, "Aporetic Pyrrhonism," 141.

rashness and hold it back from every slip, as it would be glaring rashness to give assent either to a falsehood or to something not certainly known, and nothing is more disgraceful than for assent and approval to outstrip knowledge and perception.

In that passage Cicero (or Arcesilaus) describes Socrates as falling into a Skeptic's paradox. If you're sure that you know nothing, the claim seems self-refuting. Evidently you do know something after all: namely, that you know nothing. Shouldn't someone who is in doubt about whether it's possible to know things also be in doubt about *that*? Arcesilaus thought so. But the Skeptics may have been misreading Socrates. He never quite says that he *knows* that he knows nothing. He just says that he knows nothing. Again, the reader can consider how much more modest his actual claim is, and with what consequences.[8] Yet meanwhile Arcesilaus himself has been criticized for falling into the same trap: when he denies in that last passage that anything can be known, then he is the one who apparently knows something after all: that nothing can be known.[9] Skepticism is a slippery business.

Those paradoxes to one side, Cicero makes clear the Skeptical view that certainty is not to be found, and also the Skeptical view that this was the Socratic view.[10]

Cicero,
De Oratore
3.18.67

[Arcesilaus] seized on the following in particular out of various writings of Plato and from the Socratic conversations: that nothing sure can be apprehended by either the senses or the mind.

These are striking ways to read Plato and Socrates because no such

---

8. Vlastos, *Socrates, Ironist and Moral Philosopher*, 82 n. 4, argues for the importance of the difference. See also A. A. Long, "Socrates in Hellenistic Philosophy," 158; C. C. W. Taylor, "Plato's Epistemology," 165–66; Annas, "Plato the Skeptic," 310.

9. See the fine discussion in Cooper, "Arcesilaus: Socratic and Sceptic."

10. See also this from Cicero, *Academica* 2.23.74: "Parmenides and Xenophanes blame, as if they were angry with them, though in no very poetical verses, the arrogance of those people who, though nothing can be known, venture to say that they know something. And you said that Socrates and Plato were distinct from these men. Why so? Are there any men of whom we can speak more certainly? I indeed seem to myself to have lived with these men; so many of their discourses have been reported, from which one cannot possibly doubt that Socrates thought that nothing could be known. He excepted one thing only, asserting that he did know that he knew nothing; but he made no other exception."

statements appear in the dialogues. Socrates says that he knows nothing important. He doesn't say that nothing *can* be known. Such a conclusion has to be an inference: that if Socrates never managed to know anything significant, the search for certainty about big questions must be futile (though maybe still worthwhile). Whatever Socrates may have said, what he *showed* is that any claim to moral truth can be shot down. It's natural enough, on this account, for the dialogues to leave the reader feeling like a Skeptic even if they don't ask for that conclusion.[11] And perhaps that's a sensible way to produce Skeptics. If Socrates argued directly for Skepticism, good Skeptics would have to argue against him. But if he argues in a way that makes readers throw up their hands and *feel* like Skeptics, that's fine. Skeptics can think this or that. They just can't advance their views as knowledge and say that they are founded on conclusive arguments.[12] There aren't any.

Still, this final and largest point of tension remains: Socrates sometimes does make claims about what's right. We saw examples in chapter 14. What way is that for a Skeptic to talk?[13] One possibility, as we have considered, is that Socrates isn't *sure* about what he says. When he offers views of his own (for example, that virtue is a kind of knowledge), he's not claiming that they have been proven. He has merely found, so far, that nobody can refute them. When he claims to have disproven things, it's on the basis of arguments that are ad hominem in the sense we saw in chapter 10: he shows a definite inconsistency between two things you believe, or thought you did. Notice what an attractive style of argument this is for Skeptics. It doesn't commit the questioner to anything.[14]

These points help us see Socrates and the Skeptics as compatible. It isn't possible to show that Socrates was a Skeptic in just the way that Arcesilaus was. Each of them said things that we can't imagine being said by the other. But the *influence* of Socrates on the Skeptics

---

11. Cooper, "Arcesilaus: Socratic and Sceptic," 178–80, provides helpful discussion of this point.

12. See Annas, "Plato the Skeptic," 322.

13. See discussion in Bett, "Socrates and Skepticism," 305–7.

14. For more discussion of these themes, see Annas, "Plato the Skeptic," and Shields, "Socrates Among the Skeptics."

is obvious, even if they didn't carry forward Socratic practice in a simple and direct way. Skeptics are descendants of Socrates, not clones.

Implications of Skepticism; Pyrrhonism distinguished. Where does Skepticism leave its practitioners? It might sound like a philosophy of despair, since you can never be sure you're right. But that's not how the Greeks regarded it. They developed two varieties of Skepticism. One of them was called Pyrrhonian Skepticism (after its founder, Pyrrho of Elis). Those Skeptics said the result of suspending judgment was *ataraxia*: tranquility and freedom from distress, which was their goal. Academic Skeptics such as Arcesilaus were different. They weren't trying to find tranquility. Their aim was to find the truth. They ended up in a state of suspended judgment because that's where they thought reason left them. Every claim can be undercut by some other; most of what anyone has ever believed has turned out to be wrong; so people who claim to be certain of anything are lazy or kidding themselves.

And yet the Academic Skeptics didn't give up on their search for the truth. Falling short made them more diligent.

Cicero,
Academica
2.3.7

Even though all our cognition is blocked by many obstructions, and even though there is so much obscurity in the things themselves and weakness on the part of our judgments that both the most ancient and the most learned philosophers have rightly distrusted their ability to discover what they desired, still they did not give in, and neither shall we get worn out and abandon our effort to search things out.

This might seem a strange position. Why keep searching for something that you think you will never find? The answer is that you can still get closer.

Cicero,
Academica
2.3.7

Nor have our discussions ever any other object except that of, by arguing on each side, eliciting, and as it were, squeezing out something which may either be the truth itself, or may at least come as near as possible to it.

Greek philosophy was comfortable with aims like these that couldn't be reached. (The goal of the Stoics was to reach sagehood, but only a fool would claim to have made it.) The quest for a sure grasp of the truth is ennobling even if we never find it. Socrates thought so, too.[15] But the danger of despair should be noted. Users of the Socratic method constantly occ arguments fail. This can lead to a sense that arguments are worthless. That wasn't at all what Socrates thought, but he wrestled with the possibility and gave a warning about it (as recounted here by Phaedo; Socrates is speaking first):

> When a simple man who has no skill in dialectics believes an argument to be true which he afterwards imagines to be false, whether really false or not, and then another and another, he has no longer any faith left, and great disputers, as you know, come to think at last that they have grown to be the wisest of mankind; for they alone perceive the utter unsoundness and instability of all arguments, or indeed, of all things, which, like the currents in the Euripus, are going up and down in never-ceasing ebb and flow.
>
> *Phaedo*
> *90b–91*
>
> That is quite true, I said.
>
> Yes, Phaedo, he replied, and how melancholy, if there be such a thing as truth or certainty or possibility of knowledge—that a man should have lighted upon some argument or other which at first seemed true and then turned out to be false, and instead of blaming himself and his own want of wit, because he is annoyed, should at last be too glad to transfer the blame from himself to arguments in general: and for ever afterwards should hate and revile them, and lose truth and the knowledge of realities.
>
> Yes, indeed, I said; that is very melancholy.
>
> Let us then, in the first place, he said, be careful of allowing or of admitting into our souls the notion that there is no health or soundness in any arguments at all. Rather say that we have not yet attained to soundness in ourselves, and that we must struggle

---

15. See *Meno* 86bc (in chapter 12).

manfully and do our best to gain health of mind—you and all other men having regard to the whole of your future life, and I myself in the prospect of death.

If reason hasn't brought us satisfaction, in short, we should blame ourselves rather than reason, which is too fine a thing to disparage just because our minds are weak instruments.

What to do. If there are plausible arguments on both sides of everything, how does a Skeptic make choices? Here we're helped by a philosopher who became head of the Academy a century after Arcesilaus and started its "Late" period: Carneades. He was a sage of legendary powers, said to have had long hair and nails because he was too busy with philosophy to cut them.[16] Carneades reasoned that we can still regard some things as more likely true than others, even if we can't be sure about them. Cicero recounted the point:

Cicero,
Academica
2.31.99

> Whatever happens which is probable in appearance, if nothing offers itself which is contrary to that probability, the wise man will use it; and in this way the whole course of life will be regulated. And, in truth, that wise man whom you are bringing on the stage, is often guided by what is probable, not being comprehended, nor perceived, nor assented to, but only likely; and unless a man acts on such circumstances there is an end to the whole system of life.

Carneades thus is associated with the idea of *probability* as a basis for action (though what he meant by "probable," or its Greek equivalent,

---

16. Plutarch writes that "Carneades the Academic, and Diogenes the Stoic, came as deputies from Athens to Rome, praying for release from a penalty of five hundred talents laid on the Athenians.... All the most studious youth immediately waited on these philosophers, and frequently, with admiration, heard them speak. But the gracefulness of Carneades's oratory, whose ability was really greatest, and his reputation equal to it, gathered large and favorable audiences, and erelong filled, like a wind, all the city with the sound of it. So that it soon began to be told, that a Greek, famous even to admiration, winning and carrying all before him, had impressed so strange a love upon the young men, that quitting all their pleasures and pastimes, they ran mad, as it were, after philosophy." Clough, *Plutarch's Lives of Illustrious Men*, 252. Cato arranged to have the visitors sent back to Greece. For discussion of Carneades's trip, see Powell, "Embassy of the Three Philosophers to Rome."

is a complex question; he didn't have the mathematical idea of it that we do).[17] We can't reach certainty about moral and other questions, but we can arrive at conclusions that are likely enough to be true to make rational action possible on the basis of them. This position resembles what nowadays would be called fallibilism.

This idea from Carneades is valuable to users of the Socratic method; for whether or not Socrates was a Skeptic, his method can, as we've seen, easily make Skeptics out of its students. The mature Skeptic is comfortable going forward on the basis of probabilities, sometimes great and sometimes not. (How different, really, are the sciences now?) This approach allows vigorous action without an offensive attitude. Skeptics aren't stubborn and don't mind losing an argument.

> [Let us] bear patiently to be contradicted and refuted; and although those men may dislike such treatment who are bound and devoted to certain predetermined opinions, and are under such obligations to maintain them that they are forced, for the sake of consistency, to adhere to them even though they do not themselves wholly approve of them; we, on the other hand, who pursue only probabilities, and who cannot go beyond that which seems really likely, can confute others without obstinacy, and are prepared to be confuted ourselves without resentment.

Cicero,
Tusculan Disputations
2.2.5

Reliance on probability made Carneades comfortable expressing himself on some ethical questions despite his Skepticism, as in this excellent example:

> If, says Carneades, you were to know that an asp was lying hidden anywhere, and that some one who did not know it was going to sit upon it, whose death would be a gain to you, you would act wickedly if you did not warn him not to sit down.

Cicero,
De Re Publica
3.26

But of course there were counterarguments.

---

17. Burnyeat's unpublished manuscript on this issue, "Carneades Was No Probabilist," is available from the author or various sources online. For more discussion of Carneades's notions of probability, see A. A. Long, *Hellenistic Philosophy*, 95–106.

Skepticism vs. Stoicism. The Skeptics and Stoics were rivals.[18] Skeptics thought that Stoics were sure of things when they shouldn't be—a point subject to intricate arguments that are challenging to piece together from the fragments left to us, but that is very well treated by Long.[19] Despite this rivalry, however, much in Skepticism and Stoicism is compatible, and many have combined them. The Skeptics, so far as we know from what has survived from them, didn't directly object to Stoic teachings about ethics. They objected to the Stoics' theories of knowledge and to their resulting sense of certainty. It is possible to be attracted to Stoic notions about how to live but to hold them with the loose grip of a Skeptic. Cicero is an example; he saw himself as an Academic Skeptic but also praised many views of the Stoics. And Seneca, a leading Stoic, wrote in one of his more broad-minded moments about the good to be taken from the Skeptics, as well as from others:

Seneca,
*On the
Shortness of
Life* 14.2

By other men's labors we are led to the sight of things most beautiful that have been wrested from darkness and brought into light; from no age are we shut out, we have access to all ages, and if it is our wish, by greatness of mind, to pass beyond the narrow limits of human weakness, there is a great stretch of time through which we may roam. We may argue with Socrates, we may doubt with Carneades, find peace with Epicurus, overcome human nature with the Stoics, exceed it with the Cynics.

Montaigne, the great French essayist and contemporary of Shakespeare's, was also a lover of both traditions. He is most famous for having a Skeptic's distrust of claims to certainty. But he also thought the Stoics offered wise counsel; he quoted them constantly, and during his life he was compared to Seneca.[20] If a writer such as Montaigne seems to evade the conflict between the Skeptical and Stoic positions, the question can be put directly: one of these philosophies holds that virtue is the only real good, and is a matter of knowledge. The other

---

18. See Bett, "Socrates and Skepticism," 304–5.
19. See A. A. Long, *Hellenistic Philosophy*, ch. 3.
20. See Frame, *Complete Essays of Montaigne*, vi.

holds that we have no *certain* knowledge, and that the best response to any claim of certainty is always more argument. What sort of person could hold views in such tension at the same time? Perhaps Socrates.

17

Finding Principles

THIS chapter and the next one offer some practical suggestions to help you devise Socratic questions of your own. Assume that you're trying to put Socratic pressure on your partners in a classroom or anywhere else, or that you're putting pressure on yourself. You want to refute a claim or force it to be refined into something stronger (these are friendly things to do). You want to show that the claims are inconsistent with other things believed by whoever is making them. That means coming up with good questions on short notice. Here we will see some ways to do it. The process isn't reducible to a formula; Socrates doesn't paint by numbers. But it's at least possible to talk about some patterns and techniques that can help the practitioner, and to show how they might apply in everyday situations.

These chapters take a flexible approach to their subject. They show how the aims of the Socratic method can be applied to topics beyond the ones Socrates addressed. And they will sometimes suggest the use of questions a little different from the kind he asked. The original Socratic project was noble but narrow: putting questions to those who claimed to have knowledge of difficult and general concepts, and showing by this process that they lacked the expertise they had imagined. That project is just as valuable now, and previous chapters show how Socrates carried it out. But the Socratic method wouldn't have stayed interesting for so long if that were its only use. In fact the structure of it can be applied to all sorts of other topics, major or minor. And when it is applied to other kinds of topics, the types of questions that are most productive for creating an elenchus can change, too, as we shall see.

Understanding how the Socratic method might work in common cases also makes it easier to use in more demanding ones. Socrates liked to show that we might talk about philosophy in the same way we talk about cobbling and cooking. He had the right idea. It's best to make a point with simple and familiar topics, then let it be generalized to others that are less familiar. But instead of cobblers and cooks I'd rather use politics and movies and law. Everyone knows what it is like to argue about those things. Seeing the Socratic approach used there will help show how it can be used anywhere else.

Creating an elenchus. Socratic questions usually build toward a result: an elenchus. Since our topic is the making of such questions, let's recall how an elenchus generally works. You make a claim. Socrates solicits your agreement to a second claim. Then he shows that the second claim is inconsistent with your first one. To put it more concretely, he gets your agreement to some deeper idea or counter-example, and then says, "... but doesn't that create trouble for what you were saying earlier?" He's talked you into contradicting yourself. People often imagine that Socrates pokes holes in what his partners say, but this account shows that his actual approach is a little different. He causes his partners to see for themselves that what they've said doesn't square with other things they believe.

Devising Socratic questions might seem to mostly involve the second half of that process. Your partner takes a position (that's the first half); then you think of questions that show the position to be unsatisfactory by your partner's own lights. That is indeed a large part of the method. But it is the subject of the next chapter, because another important part comes earlier and needs to be discussed here. The *front* half of the elenchus—the claim that will be tested— has to be established first, and this process involves questioning, too.

Establishing the first claim doesn't sound, on its face, like a job for Socrates. It's easy to imagine that he has to work with whatever his partner says. But his craft is not so simple. We've seen that in the *Laches*, Socrates conducts a dialogue on the meaning of courage. But that isn't the question that his partners originally bring to him. They approach Socrates to ask whether their sons need to learn how to fight in armor. Socrates takes them through some initial questions before settling on the one—what is courage?—that serves as the main subject of all that follows. This is typical. Socrates uses preliminary questions to clarify his partner's thinking. Then he proceeds with all the other questions that everyone remembers better.

Good preliminary questions tee up the claims that the parties go on to pursue. That's part of the secret of Socratic dialogue: getting a claim on the table that lends itself to productive questioning. Such claims don't usually spring up right away or on their own. Sometimes they are developed by listening for a while; often they are developed by friendly questioning. The questions aren't testing anything. They just draw out the views of your partner and steer them into a position that will support a good dialogue.

This chapter is about that process of helping your partner produce the first half of an elenchus—that is, a claim you can test. The next chapter is about how to do the testing. "Strategy" is sometimes defined in general as decisions about when and where to fight. On that view, this chapter is about the strategic side of the Socratic method—not because it involves fighting (it doesn't) but because it involves finding or arranging a good topic of inquiry: the *where* of the method. The next chapter is about the tactical side—i.e., *how* the inquiry gets carried out. Good choices about strategy at the start make the tactical part of the method easier later on.

Find the principle. Imagine arguing with someone about whether a movie is good. This goes on for a while, with both of you quarreling over details. Then it occurs to you to ask: What *is* a good movie, anyway? What makes one better than another? You realize that you've been arguing about a particular movie—the question in the foreground—because you have different opinions about those larger questions in the background. The background questions are what you should be arguing about. Now replace the word "movie" with the word "act" or the word "life" and you have the usual Socratic inquiry.

Or make it a matter of law rather than cinema and then we have this famous observation from Oliver Wendell Holmes, Jr., about the reasons given by judges for their decisions:

Behind the logical form lies a judgment as to the relative worth and importance of competing legislative grounds, often an inarticulate and unconscious judgment, it is true, and yet the very root and nerve of the whole proceeding.[1]

Holmes had in mind not just conceptual claims of the kind Socrates rooted out, but other preferences, attitudes, and beliefs about the world. Regardless, that is generally the first order of business in Socratic questioning: find the unconscious judgment that is the "root and nerve" of whatever claim is set forth. You want to get to the bottom of what the argument is really about. Socrates doesn't usually enter a debate on the terms where it is being fought. He moves it to the level of principle, then goes to work there.

The point can be restated more formally. A classic deductive argument contains a major premise and a minor one. The stock example of a major premise, first used in these words by Mill, is *All men are mortal.* The stock example of a minor premise is *Socrates is a man.* Those two premises, taken together, lead to the conclusion that *Socrates is mortal.* The major premise is a general principle. The minor premise is a statement about a particular case. Why is this useful to understand? Because the general principle at stake in an argument often goes unstated and unexamined—the "inarticulate major premise," as it's sometimes called. The first thing Socrates does is smoke it out.

And there usually isn't just one major premise behind a claim. There are layers of them. The first layer might be a reason for whatever has been said in the foreground. Then there's the reason behind that reason—a more general principle. When you're engaged in Socratic questioning, you have to decide when to keep pressing for more general principles and when you've gone far enough. Suppose a dialogue about law starts this way: "I don't think the First Amendment applies to pornography." (That's the claim in the foreground.) Why not? "Because the First Amendment just protects political speech." Good: now we have a major premise—a principle to talk about that

---

1. Holmes, "Path of the Law," 457.

was in the background. This brings us to a fork in the road—or rather to three ways you might proceed.

a. *Use the new principle to test the original claim.* The newly announced principle might serve as the second half of an elenchus; it might be shown inconsistent with the original claim. That possibility could be pursued here with a question like: are you sure that pornography can't ever be political? You have to decide if that question—or smaller questions and examples that lead to it—will be a productive route to pursue. If not, you might choose instead to....

b. *Test the new principle.* The newly announced principle can itself become the first half of an elenchus. In other words, you can make it the target of testing. They've said that the First Amendment only protects political speech; so you develop examples of nonpolitical speech that they might also want to protect. Or you use other questions of the general kind shown in the next chapter. (This approach means putting the original question—here, the treatment of pornography—to one side at least for the moment, just as Socrates put aside the question of fighting in armor while they all talked about courage generally.)

c. *Push for another principle.* Or the questioner can push further, seeking the principle behind the principle just offered: You say that only political speech is protected, but what *is* political speech? (Let's have a definition.) Why does the First Amendment protect it? (Let's have a rationale.) Either of those questions would lead you to other principles that are more general than the one on the table.

Suppose you do push further and ask why only political speech should be protected. The reply comes back: "Because the point of free speech is just to secure self-government." Now you have the same three choices just shown. You can use that new claim to undermine others that were made already. (If you want to secure self-government, are you sure that only *political* speech needs to be protected?) Or you can treat this new principle itself as the subject of scrutiny. (Are you sure the only purpose of free speech is securing self-government?) Or you can push for yet another principle. (What *is* self-government?)

And so it goes. At any point you can choose: take the principle that's been offered and use it to challenge an earlier claim; or make the new claim itself the subject of challenge and testing; or push to find another principle—probably one that's more general. Which of these approaches is best? Here are three ways to think about it.

First, as a matter of Socratic craft, the typical goal is to climb until you've found a claim that you can refute or put into tension with something that has already been said. When a claim can't survive shallower scrutiny, there's no point in going deeper; it already needs work. And practically speaking you need a claim that will lend itself to good questions from you and answers from your partner. If the principle in front of you isn't well suited for those operations, you climb another rung. It's like a musician trying to find a key in which a song can be played, given the vocal range of the singer. You might move up a little at a time until you find a key about which you think: we can work here.

Second, you want to find an angle that does justice to your partner's thinking. The goal isn't to lead people where they don't want to go so that they can be questioned on uncomfortable territory. It's to figure out the true reasons for their views, even if (especially if) they themselves might not be sure what those reasons are. You are probing for the "root and nerve" of the matter under discussion, not trying to avoid it. You want to get to where the action really is. To shift the medical simile a bit, you might imagine a doctor seeking to draw blood and looking for a rich vein.

Third, in some contexts you might climb another rung for a different reason: to find a proposition on which you can agree—in earnest, and not just for the sake of discussion. Most people do care about the same things when you reach a high enough level of generality. Establishing that point of departure early can have great value in efforts to persuade later. It allows you and your partner to reason together from a common understanding.

By whatever of these criteria it may be guided, Socratic discussion starts with a hunt for the right level of generality at which to talk.

Concepts. Let's consider more specifically how to find the major premise that lurks behind a claim in an argument. A major premise will generally take one of two forms. It will be a concept that needs to be defined or a proposition that needs to be defended. To begin with concepts: the major premise might, for example, be a view about the meaning of *good* in one setting or another, or the meaning of *unjust*, or the meaning of *political speech*, etc. If so, you can get to a higher level of principle by asking for definitions of those words: you're using a label; what does it mean? But asking this kind of Socratic question can be challenging for two reasons.

First, it might not be obvious what concept needs defining. If everyone is arguing about whether a label applies to a movie or a person or a law, then yes, it's easy to ask what the label means. But sometimes there's no clear label to talk about. Somebody is saying "down with X" for various reasons but isn't tying the reasons to any principle. You have to start with questions like: Why do you hate X so much? (Or, as the case may be, why do you love it?) What is your objection? As the answer is explained, a concept will eventually come into view. Something will be described as good or bad or unjust or ridiculous, or a word ending with *-ism* will be applied to it. Good: now you can ask about the meaning of that concept.

But this leads to a second issue. Asking what a concept means can sound like a fuss about nothing. You seem to be bickering about the meaning of a *word*, and people don't care about words; they care about real things. The point to stress in reply is that you aren't just talking about a word. You're talking about a judgment. The word under discussion is a placeholder for that judgment. If the word seems unimportant, no problem: we can use another one. Indeed, it's sometimes useful to change out the word at issue for a different word or phrase from time to time, just to make clear that the discussion isn't about semantics. It's about a judgment.

So suppose somebody says that one movie is great and another isn't. You ask about the meaning of the word "great." After a while the response comes back: "Well, who cares? 'Great' is only a word." To which the right reply is, in effect: *you're* the one who is drawing a distinction and using that word to explain it. If you don't want to talk about the word "great," we can talk about "the property—whatever it's called—that you think separates movies from each other." If you don't think such a property exists, then what was your original claim again? If you do think it exists, then let's find a way to talk about it. Any way you like.

If you phrase the point as just shown, maybe no one will want to talk with you about movies; but that is the substance of it. The difficulty is an ancient one.[2] People think they don't care about concepts when in fact they fight and live and die by them. But they often haven't taken the time to understand the concepts very well. They hate something because of property X, but they haven't thought much about *why* property X makes a thing hateworthy. Socratic questions force those beliefs to be brought into the light, or sometimes to be pieced together then and there. If they survive questioning, they end up better understood. If they don't survive, you might see some deserved crumbling of confidence in whatever idea they had supported in the foreground.

Propositions. Sometimes the major premise behind an opinion isn't a concept that needs to be defined. It's a proposition that needs to be defended: a belief about what is so, for example, or about the reason for something. (Mill's major premise—"all men are mortal"—is a proposition.) Instead of asking what the concept means, you'll be asking whether the proposition is true. But first, as before, the proposition simply has to be *identified*. It may again be half-conscious even in the person who holds it. Arguments can go on for a long time with the major premises on each side taken for granted and invisible to everyone.

How do you find the proposition in the background of a claim? A good route is often provided by a persistent use of the question *why*. The question is asked, and then asked again in a nearly childlike spirit—or if not in that simple form, then in the more complex shapes

---

2. See, e.g., Epictetus, *Discourses* 2.17.12–13.

it can take: What is the purpose of the thing we are talking about? What is the reason for it? How do you know? What makes you so sure? And what is the reason for the reason? These kinds of questions can push through layers of principle that usually get more general at each step. They work because the major premise of an argument usually amounts, in conversation, to a reason why the conclusion is true. So asking about the reason for a conclusion takes you back to the premises behind it.

Imagine, then, that a court gives a prison sentence to a criminal defendant in a controversial case—maybe to a convicted terrorist, or a student in a case of date rape, or an officer in a case of police brutality. You are talking with someone who has an opinion about whether the sentence was right. (Or *you* have an opinion.) The Socratic impulse usually isn't to test that opinion on its face. It is to start by identifying the principle behind the opinion. The opinion in the foreground is *the sentence was barbaric* or *the punishment was too light*. You don't say "no it wasn't." You push toward the principle by asking a question like this: what is the purpose of criminal punishment? The answer, whatever it might be, is likely the major premise behind the opinion in the foreground, or at least a clue to the premise. And if the answer is, say, "retribution," then we are at the usual three-way fork in the road. You can accept the premise and ask whether it's consistent with the claim in the foreground. (Assuming retribution is the point of punishment, why does or doesn't this punishment make sense?) Or you can test the premise. (Aren't there other reasons for punishment?) Or the question can be renewed and the pressure to generalize can be continued. (*Why* retribution?)

Another example of the same idea: should universities let students decide for themselves what classes to take, or should there be a required curriculum? Put that question in front of students, or parents, or professors, and you will get an earful of conflicting opinions that probably go past each other. Eventually you can push the discussion down a more Socratic and constructive path by asking the same kind of question as in the criminal case: what is the purpose of a university education? The answers to that question will amount to the major premises behind the views on offer. Suppose the purpose is said to be X. Now you have the same three choices as usual. You can say: if the purpose is X, why is it advanced by your view about letting students decide what courses to take? Or you can say: are you sure the purpose is X? What about these other possible purposes? Or you can say: what does X mean? Or why is X important? Then the answers can be tested with other questions of the kind we'll discuss in a moment.

The questions just shown can, if you prefer, usually be turned into problems of definition. You might be asking for the definition of a just punishment in the first case (or for the meaning of "retribution"), and for the definition of a good education in the second. That is how Socrates would usually do it. But framing these as problems of *why*, or of purpose, is often a more intuitive way to cut to the principle at stake. Those questions call for assertions that may have more complexity in them than a definition does, that are falsifiable in different ways, and that open up a wider range of questions in reply. Propositions sprout implications, and those implications are what the questions go on to test.

18

Testing Principles

THE previous chapter showed how certain types of questions can draw out the principle at stake in an argument. This chapter shows how other types of questions can test such a principle once it's found. In effect we will be talking about how to complete an elenchus. To review the sequence: Your partner has made a claim. Your goal is to test it. But you don't want to do this in a confrontational way. You want to get your partner's agreement to some *other* claim that can be brought into tension with the first one. That is our topic now: how to devise questions that can produce agreement and then put pressure on whatever claim has already been made. In this chapter as in the previous one, we will be looking at some kinds of questions that aren't quite the ones Socrates used, because he was pursuing different issues.

Sometimes thinking up questions for that purpose is easy. The principle on the table is a strong and simple claim. You consider whether it's always true, and can think of counterexamples that make trouble for it right away. Fine; ask about those. But in many cases the first principle is a more complex claim about the way things ought to be. In that case it might be hard to falsify outright (it might not be false!), and your goal becomes a little different. You're trying to show that the claim is inadequate, that it's too simple, that the problem needs more analysis.

So you want to ask questions that have those effects. How do you come up with them on the spot? Below are some classic techniques for that purpose. All of them are versatile, though some are more useful for one kind of subject than for another. The questions don't refute anything. They merely open lines of inquiry—but that's the point. Socratic questions aren't meant to settle things, though they may lead to settlement in due course. In themselves they tend to expose complexity.

The examples to follow have to be offered in a spirit of apology, because they show only a modest number of techniques for questioning. The universe of possibilities is large, within the original dialogues and beyond them. And each technique is illustrated only a couple of times here in a simple way. But this should nevertheless be enough to suggest how one can get started. Without further ado, then, here are some strategies for testing a claim.

Literalism. First, you can put pressure on a principle by taking it literally. Think about cases that might be covered by the wording of the principle but that are outside its intent or that just don't fit. Sometimes a principle is based on a mental picture of a core case but is expressed in words that also cover cases far afield. The need for narrower wording can be made obvious, and then saying something more specific may turn out to be hard. That is where the real action lies.

Laches says, for example, that courage is persistence. So you think: is that always true, taken literally? You might offer a hypothetical case where it isn't; perhaps someone is persistent in trying to find a drug dealer (Socrates uses examples more appropriate to his time). Everyone knows that's not the type of persistence that Laches meant, so the example will seem obtuse. But it's useful to be obtuse, because it forces more clarity: of course we know you didn't mean that, but what *did* you mean? "I meant that courage is a certain *kind* of persistence." Great. Which kind?

This pattern arises easily in legal arguments. Should the government be allowed to issue vouchers that people can use to pay for education in religious schools? Someone will say no and will invoke a metaphor to explain why; you can respond by taking the metaphor literally.

"Vouchers paid to parochial schools are unconstitutional."
Why?
"Because the Constitution puts a wall of separation between church and state."

I know what you're talking about. But is it at least all right for the government to put out fires in churches?

"Sure, that's fine. That's not what I mean."

Is it all right for the government to pick up trash at a church?

"That's okay, too."

The wall between church and state doesn't seem like much of a wall, then.

"Well, it's not *literally* a wall. It's a principle."

Great. What's the principle?

Exchanges of roughly this kind are common enough in legal settings because courts and lawyers often use metaphors to talk about hard questions. There are many other famous ones in the law—the "marketplace of ideas," for example, or rights with "penumbras" (the edges of a shadow, in which other rights can then be found). And notice that the questions above would be about the same if the notion of a "wall" were dropped and the claim just depended on "separation" of church and state—for "separation" can also be viewed as a metaphor. It treats the legal concepts as if they were physical things. Subtle metaphors are often embedded in words of that kind. The metaphors are attractive because they make abstract ideas easier to picture and understand. But metaphors are also a common way to hide analysis or avoid it. Taking a metaphor literally tends to make it dissolve. The conversation can then turn to the details where the work has to be done.

Extremes. Think about extreme cases—that is, the outer limits of what the principle might cover. The model of an extreme case, for this purpose, is one most likely to be objectionable by every criteria other than the one covered by the principle. Sometimes such cases can be pulled from historical and literary sources.

"That judicial decision was terrible."

Why?

"Because decisions should be based on the original understanding of the Constitution, not on vague notions of good policy."

I see the appeal of that. You're worried about judges who smuggle their own policy preferences into their decisions.

"Exactly."

But here's what I wonder about. Suppose a state started punishing criminals by branding them with hot irons. Would you be all right with a court stopping *that*?

"Probably, in a case that extreme. But I don't think branding was still common when the Constitution was ratified."

Well, it was common enough when people punished slaves. But if you don't think that's a fair example, never mind. How about flogging, though? That was still common in 1789.

"I could imagine those things being unconstitutional now. But those are very extreme cases. They aren't the kind that ever come up."

Does your principle only apply in cases that aren't extreme?

"I think it applies all the time. I'd just keep the exceptions as rare as possible."

But you would recognize some exceptions?

"Rarely."

All right. When?

If historical or other real-life examples don't come to mind, it may be easier to use hypothetical examples. Socrates likes this approach. In the *Gorgias* he thinks out loud about showing up in the Agora with a knife and bragging about the great power he has over the lives of everyone there. (See chapter 8.) He's just making a point; but the fantasy does it more vividly than a historical case might. True, a rule will sometimes work well in practice even if it doesn't handle hypothetical cases well. Maybe those cases never actually arise. But if a claim of *principle* can't bear that sort of testing, the principle needs work. It has been exposed as infirm by the strategy more formally known as *reductio ad absurdum*. To go back to an earlier example:

"I don't think the First Amendment applies to pornography."

Why not?

"Because the First Amendment just protects political speech."

No question, political speech is important. But imagine that the government appoints a board of censors, and then puts people in prison when they write fiction that a majority of the board thinks is in bad taste.

"That's ridiculous. It would never happen."

Of course not. But just to be clear, would it violate the First Amendment?

"It probably would."

But you can easily imagine cases where the judgment about bad taste didn't involve politics, right?

"Sure."

So in that case the First Amendment seems to protect more than political speech.

"In some cases, maybe."

Which ones are those?

Change the politics. People often announce principles that sound good to them but are unconsciously supported by politics in their examples of how the principle works. The support can fairly be described as unconscious because the holders don't think that politics are relevant, but then they react differently when the politics are reversed. Or they react differently when the people in an example are made sympathetic or unsympathetic, or are members of their own group or members of a different group, etc. It's good Socratic discipline, when thinking about what your friends do, to imagine it being done by your enemies, and to imagine what your enemies do as if it were done by your friends. Questioning can pull on those same threads.

"The problem with that movie was the politics. Movies shouldn't be political."

I know the feeling. But do you remember that western we saw last year and liked so well?

"Sure."

And remember that moment where the hero gives a speech for the ages as the stagecoach rides off?

"Great moment."

I don't know about you, but I thought that speech was good partly because it was what the world needs to hear. Do you know what I mean?

"Absolutely."

But I guess there must have been people who thought *that* was political.

"Probably."

And you can see what they meant, because the speech was making a point that they probably hated for political reasons.

"No doubt—what idiots!"

Granted. But still, that might be an example of a movie that was political in a sense, but worked well anyway—yes?

"Yeah, that one was all right."

So maybe it's too much to say that politics can't have a place in a good movie. There must be more to it than that.

"I guess there is."

Or suppose it's a legal argument about jury nullification—the practice that occurs when jurors think a criminal defendant is guilty but refuse to vote that way because they view the law as unjust.

"I favor jury nullification."

What do you mean by that?

"I mean that a juror has a duty not to cooperate with unjust laws, and to acquit people who are prosecuted under them."

I'm sympathetic. But a century ago, Southern juries sometimes used that principle to avoid convicting defendants who had lynched Black people. Does that seem all right?

"No, of course that's atrocious."

But didn't those jurors have the same rights and duties that you're supporting now?

"That's obviously not what I meant."

Okay, sorry. What did you mean?

Naturally the process can be reversed.

"I'm totally opposed to jury nullification."

What do you mean by that?

"I mean that jurors should carry out the law no matter what they think of it. They can't acquit people because they don't agree with the law that's being used to prosecute them."

I'm sympathetic. But two centuries ago, jurors in the North used nullification to avoid convicting people who helped slaves escape the South. Does that seem all right?

"I can't condemn that. Nobody would—in retrospect. But that's obviously not the kind of thing I'm talking about now."

Okay, sorry. What kind of thing *are* you talking about, and how do we know it's different?

Change the perspective. A principle can be challenged by asking how it would look to someone in a different position. This is especially useful in conversations about ethics. When talking about what to do and how to live, it is tempting to take positions that are self-serving or short-sighted. Those tendencies can sometimes be overcome by looking at a case through the eyes of someone else or from a different point in time.

For example: A lawyer represents a client in a dispute. The client's adversary seeks to hire the lawyer to help with an unrelated issue. The lawyer stands to make a lot of money, and has to decide whether to take the case.

"I don't think I have a conflict of interest."

Why not?

"My client is trusting me to be loyal. I'm being loyal. The two cases have zero to do with each other. Nothing."

Understood. But put yourself in the shoes of your client. Would you be surprised if you found out that your lawyer were also working for your adversary?

"Well, I might be."

And would you expect to at least be told about it?

"Yeah, I guess I would."

Then are you sure you don't have a conflict of interest?

Or to return to Socratic themes, here is a little line of questioning adapted from Plutarch, who considered himself a follower of Plato and Socrates:[1]

> "I think the best life is the most pleasurable one."
>
> If you knew that you only had an hour or two left to live, and you had the choice, would you rather spend it having fun or doing something that was really valuable for other people you care about?
>
> "I'd probably find it more satisfying to do the valuable thing for others."
>
> Then why isn't that your answer the rest of the time?

These kinds of questions can be productive when examining yourself. In effect they ask for the usual Socratic consistency. But it's not consistency between two different things you believe. It's consistency between your answers to the same question when put to you from different points of view. You're comparing how a problem looks through the eyes of your current self to how it might look to future versions of yourself, to how it might look to others you admire and can imagine as onlookers, to how it might look to your skeptical enemies, or to how it might look if declared publicly, and so forth. If the answers aren't consistent, they might need adjustment.

If that were true, what else would we see? Good questions about a claim can start by assuming the claim is true, taking it for all it's worth, and asking where it leads. A previous section showed one way that can be done: follow the application of the principle into extreme territory. But you can also go in a different direction by asking: If the claim were true, what else would we expect to see? What more would follow, practically or conceptually?

An example paraphrased from the dialogues: Protagoras says that virtue can be taught. But if *that* were true, those who have spent the most time studying and learning about virtue would have the largest share of it, wouldn't they? "They might." But then wouldn't we

---

1. Plutarch, *That Epicurus Actually Makes a Pleasant Life Impossible* 1099ab.

expect those people to be experts on virtue, and to be consulted about it? "We might." Yet we don't see that, do we? Naturally there are comebacks to this (see chapter 15), as there are to all the questions in this chapter. The point is to see the structure of the question. A more modern example:

"Violent video games should be banned or at least regulated. We've got to get them under control."

Why?

"They're a big reason for the real-world violence that we see every day."

Maybe so. But figuring out what causes what seems hard to me. How do you think it works here?

"It's obvious. If kids spend all their time pretending to kill people, it desensitizes them. Eventually you have to see it in their behavior."

I gather it's not an issue particular to American kids, then— you'd expect it to be a problem anywhere?

"Anywhere they spend so much time playing those games. It's human nature."

Then the more those games get played in a country, the more real-world violence you'd expect?

"Up to a point. But holding other things constant, yes."

It'd be interesting to see a study of whether countries where people play more of those games have more problems with violence.

"It would."

Hey, here's one—it seems that the countries where the most money is spent on those games *don't* see a greater increase in violent crime than countries where less is spent on them, doesn't it?

"Interesting. Well, that's elsewhere. There must be something different about how it works in this country."

What would that be?

Notice that this example has an empirical piece to it—that is, a claim about facts in the world (crime rates) that we would expect to see if an argument were right. Socratic questioning typically avoids arguments about external facts. It tries to contradict a claim by using the beliefs of whoever holds it. That's often wise; confronting people with facts is a surprisingly ineffective way to change their minds about anything. But drawing on worldly facts is sometimes important to move a discussion forward and is always fine in a Socratic setting so long as you can get agreement on them; the point is to create each step of the case with your partner's consent. And if you're thinking through an issue for *yourself*, the Socratic approach is to make assumptions that cause trouble for you; you want to make things hard for yourself, not imagine that the facts are convenient.

And meanwhile this same type of inquiry can be used in ways that *don't* depend on facts in the world. If a principle is true, implications might follow from it that are conceptual rather than empirical.

"I think we should be trying to create a society with the largest amount of total happiness in it."

I'm all in favor of happiness. But to me that idea you've described seems more complicated than it looks.

"What's complicated about it? The execution is hard, but the concept isn't."

Well, let me ask you this. Do you think that poor people are better off alive or dead?

"Alive, of course—what a question!"

So if you add one or two more people to the world, but they're poor, is the society better off?

"I'd say it is. But it would be even more better off if they *weren't* poor."

Understood. Yet even if they *are* poor, the society is better off with them?

"Yes."

In that case, it sounds like we have an *obligation* to increase the population as fast as we can, even with people in poverty. The more we add, the more happiness there is.

"I wouldn't go *that* far."

Okay. Why not?

Ask what happens next. This is a question outside the traditional Socratic box but useful now in discussions of many sorts of topics. It's
a favorite of the economist. If you're talking about questions that
bear on how the world should run, it can help to ask how different
answers might change the way people act. It is a common error to
imagine that a situation is static—in other words, that it keeps working the same way no matter what you say about it. Sometimes a rule
that makes sense in the world as it is will cause the world to become
something different. Judging those consequences can become its own
project. The consequences only matter for Socratic purposes if they
matter to your interlocutor, but they might. You can usually find such
questions by thinking about the incentives that a rule would create
for those who appear later.

"I think the defendant's psychiatrist should be forced to
testify."

What if the therapist had promised confidentiality to the defendant when he was her client?

"That's unfortunate. But now the therapist is the one who
knows whether the defendant committed the murder. It's too
bad about his expectations, but getting at the truth should be
our highest priority."

I hear you. But imagine being a patient in the future. If you've
heard that a psychiatrist can testify against you in court, that
might make you less likely to tell the psychiatrist the truth,
no?

"True, it might."

And if you don't tell the truth to the psychiatrist, then I don't
suppose there would be any benefit in court. The psychiatrist
wouldn't know anything.

"Obviously not in *that* case, no."

But then the patient also wouldn't get treated, right?

"To the extent the patient doesn't tell the shrink what happened, no."

If that were the usual result, would you still like the rule that
makes the psychiatrist testify?

"Maybe not, but I'm not sure how often all those things *would* happen."

So maybe the answer depends on that?

"It might."

The last part of that example shows a step that can be valuable generally: asking, in effect, what others would be willing to accept as evidence that they're wrong, or what (if anything) might cause them to change their minds. Here is a similar example that is obvious at least in its beginnings, but that also ends up showing some variations on our themes.

"I think the government should pay the ransom to the hijackers."

Why?

"Because life is more valuable than money, that's why."

I hear you. But imagine being a pirate or a hijacker later on. If you know that the ransom got paid in this case, that might make you more likely to take hostages, no?

"Yes, that's a fair worry. In theory it might be a problem."

Why do you say "in theory"?

Because if that were true in fact, there are other things we would expect to see, wouldn't we? Terrorists would take more hostages from countries that pay ransom than from those that never do, wouldn't they?

Yes, that's the idea.

Well, Spain generally does pay ransom demands, but it doesn't suffer more kidnappings than countries that don't pay—does it?

I'm not sure.

That example illustrates how one kind of question can lead to another. It begins by considering what incentives a rule might create (our current pattern); but that line gets countered by a question of the kind shown in the previous section: if the suggestion about incentives were right, what else would we expect to see—and do we see it? The illustration also shows how the flow of a dialogue can usefully be reversed. The party being questioned turns a Socratic question back at the questioner. The Socratic function can be alive and active on both sides of the conversation.

In both of the examples just shown, the questioning might set the stage for empirical inquiry. The Socratic process has isolated facts that matter and need to be determined. That is a valuable result. Both examples also show how questioning can turn a tension between two values into a tension *within* a value. A dispute starts by appearing to involve life vs. money; but it turns out that both sides of it involve the value of life, just viewed from different perspectives. Or the dispute starts by appearing to involve a tension between truth vs. confidentiality; but it turns out that both positions involve the value of the truth, just seen differently. This is a common pattern in Socratic inquiry. It clarifies trade-offs.

The elenchus as cooperative reasoning. The types of arguments that this chapter describes can be presented in a range of ways rhetorically. They don't have to appear in an elenchus. But they lend themselves well to that device, and the elenchus has powerful advantages over more direct forms of debate. You *could* simply say, "here's a counterexample—X—that shows you're wrong." But instead you say, "can we agree that X once happened?" (Yes.) "Well, X has certain features, doesn't it?" (It does.) "Okay, but then I'm worried that X is an exception to what you said earlier, isn't it?" (I suppose it is.) You've arrived at the same result by a more circuitous route. But the route is valuable because it is cooperative rather than adversarial.

That is how Socrates operates. He avoids contradicting you; he doesn't say "you're wrong." He causes you to contradict yourself. That is a useful approach to argument and dialogue now, too. If you want to persuade people, contradicting them doesn't usually help. They dig in harder. You're better off standing *next* to them rather than opposite them, so to speak. You position yourself as a partner looking for the same answers that they are. You seek their agreement as you go along, and try to put questions in a way that makes them easy to answer with a "yes." Then you share in their puzzlement about the implications. You always say first, in effect, "can we agree on this much?" If the answer is "no," you keep pushing with "why" questions or other questions until arriving at a sturdy point of departure—that is, a point to which your partner will comfortably agree. It is a point to which you will probably agree as well, at least for the sake of the discussion. Then when a problem follows from the principle, it's a problem that you both have. Maybe you can slowly pull the disputed point toward the common ground on which you have agreed to stand.

Many arguments that don't look like an elenchus can be turned into one. You take the exception or whatever other point you're making and start it as a request for agreement. If you want to make the elenchus more interesting and less threatening, you can stretch out the distance between the request for agreement and the payoff. The steps between the start and end provide chances to reinforce your partners' agreement with you and your understanding of them. That last point is important. Real persuasion, in a Socratic setting or any other, isn't a matter of beating other people into submission or confronting them with embarrassing facts. It's about getting them to see things your way. To do that, you have to start by listening and by seeing things *their* way. When you understand what they think, you can start looking for a route from that point to somewhere else.

To test whether you understand the views of your partners, it helps to explain their positions back in a way that is completely satisfactory to them. Socrates does this a lot; he recounts what his partners think in his own words and asks whether they like his way of putting it.[2] You want them happy with the substance and the tone. Then you are in a position to build your case on a promising foundation. Once your partners know that you have listened and "get" their point of view, they won't be so full of suspicion or afraid of losing face when you ask them to agree to something more. That is how an elenchus begins.

These nice features of the elenchus aren't always evident on the face of the dialogues. Socrates has some partners like Callicles who are too clearly his opponents to be convinced otherwise by any way

---

2. See, e.g., *Gorgias* 490a, 492d; *Charmides* 172a; *Meno* 78bc.

the questions are put. Those are the sharp exchanges that many readers remember best. But in other cases the elenchus does let Socrates take apart the views of others while still keeping the exchange good-natured. That is an especially great advantage of the elenchus in our times. It's a way to challenge someone's thinking without being adversarial about it. To be sure, an adversarial approach to your *own* prejudices is very useful, as discussed in chapter 4. It just doesn't work when you're trying to move someone else. Persuasion is a cooperative enterprise, and that is why the elenchus is so useful. Done right, it is cooperative reasoning.

Socratic Rules of Engagement

THIS book has discussed the Socratic method as a set of tools that can be used to aid understanding and wisdom. The book has also discussed a Socratic *ethic* that treats those tools as practical ways of giving effect to larger principles. This epilogue talks about how Socratic principles can be used in arguments and conversations that don't amount to dialogues in the classic sense. A flexible use of those principles can, for example, produce healthier political discourse, a theme noted in the preface and touched on from time to time as the book went along. For the most part I've preferred to keep this discussion separate, because Socrates has ideas to offer that are larger than politics. But his teachings are perfectly relevant to how we think and talk about that subject, as they are to how we think and talk about anything else that is important. The ideas shown below can have use in every sort of contentious conversation.

Rules of engagement. Suppose, then, that you do want to adapt Socratic principles to settings that don't lend themselves to Socratic dialogue as such. It is then useful to think of Socrates as providing not just rules for dialogue but more general rules of engagement. His teachings can be converted into any number of such practical dos and don'ts. The organization of them under a certain number of headings will always be a little arbitrary, but for convenience I would offer these twelve:

1. *The open table.* Everything is open for inquiry; no view is immune from questioning if someone wants to offer it.

2. *The purpose of inquiry.* The purpose of inquiry is to reach the truth or get closer to it. The purpose is not to say or prove whatever will advance a goal in the background, or to make the partners to the inquiry feel good, or to win an argument.

3. *Challenges wanted.* Questioning is the natural and welcome

response to any position one might take. Attempts at refutation are the acts of a friend and are presumptively offered and received in that spirit, even if—especially if—the challenge is made to a strongly held view. You might be wrong, or (if not) there might still be a little something right in what your challenger says. Being shown that you've erred or been imprecise is a favor. Comfort in confessing error is a sign of health.

4. *Arguments met with arguments.* The Socratic approach doesn't say that certain arguments don't deserve a reply because they're contemptible and shouldn't have been made in the first place. If someone thinks something is so and is wrong, the appropriate response is to explain why it isn't so.

5. *The priority of reason.* Arguments are judged on their merits—that is, on the quality of the evidence or reasoning that supports them, not on the identities of their makers. Claims that anyone's perspective is entitled to deference (or skepticism) are themselves judged on evidence and reasons—for example, reasons to believe that one person has access to evidence or experience that others don't, and that the answer to a question depends on it.

6. *Elenctic reasoning.* Inquiry is made, wherever possible, by finding common ground of agreement from which to begin. Then each side does the favor of trying to help the other see inconsistencies between that point of agreement and their position on whatever else is under discussion. Consistency is treated as an important test of a set of claims.

7. *Self-skepticism.* One's own partisanship is distrusted. "Partisanship," for these purposes, means a strongly felt commitment to a certain set of beliefs that makes one want and expect inquiry to come out a certain way, and that makes people who challenge those beliefs seem to be enemies. It's easy to bend reasoning and find it convincing when it leads to results that you like, and it's hard to see this happening when you're the one who is doing it. Everyone stays conscious of this risk, and it's another reason why contradiction is welcome.

8. *Group skepticism.* Popular opinion and easy consensus are likewise distrusted. A room full of people who all agree about something

regarded as controversial outside the room, and especially a group feeling congratulatory about its agreement, is uncomfortable. It is too much like the Athenian jury with its hemlock. A group needs a gadfly.

9. *Manners*. Inquiry is expected to be rigorous, fierce, possibly relentless, but always courteous. Sarcasm and other forms of irony are principally directed at oneself and otherwise reserved for people who claim to have all the answers. There is no name-calling or denunciation. Nobody is shouted down. If someone insists on being wrong, their punishment is being wrong and perhaps having this understood by others. All parties observe the principle of charity in interpreting what others say, and prefer to take on objections in their strongest rather than their weakest form.

10. *Candor*. Partners in inquiry say what they really think. They are not punished for it. Saying something unpopular is, to the contrary, considered admirable; even if it's wrong, it is a service to the cause of getting closer to the truth. If someone is willing to incur a personal cost to put forward a perspective, that perspective is probably shared by others who do not want to bear the cost. It needs to be said so that it can be tested and determined to be true or false.

11. *Offense*. Everyone tries to make claims in ways that do not give personal offense to their partners. Everyone tries to receive claims in ways that do not take offense from their partners. The giving or taking of offense is understood to be a serious threat to the process of getting anywhere in inquiry.

12. *Humility*. Conclusions are provisional. They may seem very probable, so much so that they are well worth fighting for. But there is always a reserve of doubt, an awareness of one's own ignorance and blind spots, and a recollection that others have been equally sure and have been wrong, over and over again. The result of all this is an attitude of humility at all times about how much you know and how sure you should be about it.

These rules are all derived from earlier chapters in the book. If they aren't persuasive, the book isn't persuasive, and at this late date I can only apologize. Or the rules might, to the contrary, seem so obviously sound as not to require endorsement or even naming.

Unfortunately they need both. I don't suggest that they should be immune from challenge, of course. Such immunity would be contrary to their terms, and anyway they stand up to challenge quite well when the challenge is direct and reasoned. But they also can be blown aside by other forces. Some of those forces are famous competitors such as demagoguery, outrage, and the smear. Others are more insidious: orthodoxy, ostracism, and the snub. These are old stories. Just ask Socrates. There is no Socratic age for which nostalgia is in order; the Socratic ethic has never been the dominant force in the world, or in the academy, just as and just because it is never the dominant force in the psyche. It's always the resistance. So these rules are often challenging to observe, but they are worthy aspirations for the Socratically inclined.

That reference to resistance raises natural questions about how to deal with people who *don't* subscribe to those rules of engagement. The presumptive and simple answer is that you use the Socratic approach to decide whether to use the Socratic approach. To put it more concretely, you can ask (and ask again) what purpose you're trying to accomplish and whether Socratic rules of engagement are suited for it. I regard those rules as the right ones, for example, in most conversations about legal issues, whether or not those on the other side are playing by all those rules themselves (often enough they aren't). But then suppose two lawyers are arguing in court. Now some of the Socratic rules are a bad fit because the lawyers aren't trying to find the truth directly; they're each arguing one side of the case so that someone *else* can find the truth—a judge or jury. Socrates offers a particular goal (seeking the truth for oneself) pursued by particular means (his method). Litigation is simply a different game. It has aims and rules that overlap with the Socratic ones only in part.

That example is particular to law, but the principle is general. The Socratic rules are well suited for some ends but not others. They probably aren't the right rules if you're arguing with a child, or trying to get a hostile audience to calm down, or being beaten with a pipe. But let's take an intermediate case: a family gathering where you're seated next to an uncle who has political views that seem crazy, and who doesn't play by Socratic rules. I can only offer friendly advice (he's *your* uncle), but a Socratic approach might be just the thing for that occasion. The gentle use of the elenchus described in chapter 18 involves finding some common ground and, from there, asking good-natured questions about how that point of agreement relates to your points of disagreement. This may or may not help you or him toward persuasion or a better understanding of whatever might be the issue. Still, though, isn't a broadly Socratic approach more likely to have those good effects than other possibilities—even if those rules aren't followed by your crazy uncle? How is breaking them yourself going to help?

But of course the real question is what you want out of this conversation. What is the purpose of it? Perhaps you are better off changing the subject or deferring the discussion to a time when your uncle is not arguing in front of an audience, or has had fewer drinks, or otherwise is more likely to be reasonable. And the same roughly goes for friends, or co-workers, or people you encounter online. You can only control what you do, not what they do. So you have decisions to make about your ends and your means. Socrates has suggestions about both. They are great when everyone else will buy into them. They are often great even when everyone else won't—but not necessarily. You have to think clearly about your goals and how you are trying to reach them. The general point: whether Socratic testing is suitable is a topic suitable for Socratic testing.

Socratic schooling. The worldly conditions for Socratic discourse aren't always the same. I made reference above to some competitors to Socratic rules of engagement: demagoguery, fury, ostracism, etc. Those competitors, too, grow better in some conditions than others. In our times, advances in technology have made conditions unusually severe for the Socratic approach and favorable for its rivals. The advances allow those competing forces to be set loose on a large scale by anyone with a computer, or indeed a smartphone. Socratic habits require patience to develop and use. They don't benefit in the same way from technologies that encourage quick reactions in short bursts.

The result has been a cultural shift away from the values that are the subject of this book; the rules of engagement for discourse online are often the opposite of the Socratic ones on every count. True, things said online get tested, or in any event get attacked. But little about this is Socratic, and the bad persistently drives out the good. Social media in particular amounts to a campus on which atrocious habits of discourse are taught by the pervasive method. The consequences for our political and cultural life have been sad and sometimes calamitous. Nobody doubts this. People only disagree about examples, usually because they don't mind irrationality—they barely recognize it—when it cuts the way they like politically. So some think *this* is an example of the calamity and some say *that* is an example of it. My view is that they are all correct.

These problems cannot be solved. They are embedded in human nature; social media is merely an accelerant, though a powerful one. As suggested earlier, the best we can hope for is a committed resistance. And the most natural and valuable setting for that resistance is the classroom. Different games have different rules, as we've seen, and are suited for different occasions. But if there is one place where Socratic aims and rules of engagement ought to be expected, it's the university. Universities exist in the first instance to advance knowledge of the truth and to teach students to seek it. The classroom in particular—in a university or elsewhere—is a small, temporary, and controlled community in which standards of discourse can be set deliberately. If students don't learn Socratic habits there, they can't be expected to pick them up in worse conditions when they're older and involved in public life. So if you (the Socratic type) see a political discussion spoiled by someone who views Socratic rules of engagement as unimportant, or as outmoded, or as a joke, it is reasonable to think: here is someone our schools let down.

In which classrooms does the Socratic ethic matter? In all of them, whether or not a class is taught Socratically in any strict sense. For whatever else any course claims to teach, it always teaches lessons about standards of discourse, humility or arrogance, and other variables that can be Socratic or not. At a time when the Socratic ethic is in such cultural distress, those lessons need to be taught by their friends deliberately and well. This is more than a matter of technique. It is a project for the heart. Think back to Mill's comment in chapter 3 about how deeply affected he was by the *Gorgias*—not by its precise arguments, but by the commitment that it conveys. In his notes on that dialogue, Mill put it this way: "the love of virtue, and every other noble feeling, is not communicated by reasoning, but caught by inspiration or sympathy from those who already have it." [1] What most affected Mill, in other words, is what most affects any student: time spent with someone who cares enough about an idea to make the feeling infectious.

That is what a teacher of the Socratic school needs to cultivate: knowledge and skill, by all means, but also a Socratic intensity of feeling. You have to care feverishly yourself if you mean to inspire your students to care half that much. This becomes the subtext of every lesson taught, whatever the stated topic might be and whether or not it lends itself to questioning. Let the Socratic rules of engagement be felt as important. Let students see how the hemlock is administered in our times and regard it with contempt and disgust. Let them speak fearlessly and receive refutation the same way; let them listen fearlessly and without offense; let them prefer truth to all else. Let them see, above all, what it is for Socratic values to be not only understood and practiced but also loved.

And if you are Socratically inclined but *not* in the teaching business? Then you might do all those things just the same; for the players in the classroom all have analogues in the self. We are each of us professor and student, just as we all have an internalized Socrates, a Callicles, and an Athenian jury. And the interior versions of all those figures are more consequential in the end. Paid teachers deliver a small measure of our schooling compared to the schooling of ourselves that we carry out well or badly. In the self as in the classroom, the healthiest ethic is a Socratic one.

---

1. Robson, *Collected Works of John Stuart Mill*, 11:150.

Translations & Bibliography

Translations

In the excerpts from classical writings presented in this book, I have generally sought to stick with single translations of each work. It sometimes happens, however, that one translation is suitable most of the time, while another is clearer or felicitous at another point. These notes clarify which translations are used for which excerpts.

1. *Plato.*

Translations of Plato's *Apology* are by Benjamin Jowett, except for 30a (W. K. C. Guthrie), 30cd (Hugh Tredennick), and 31a (John Stuart Mill). Apology 21bd includes a small emendation at the start by Gregory Vlastos.

Translations of the *Charmides* are by Robin Waterfield, except for 166bc (Jowett).

Translations of the *Cratylus* are by Jowett.

Translations of the *Crito* are by Jowett, except for 48b (Vlastos).

Translations of the *Euthydemus* are by Jowett.

Translations of the *Euthyphro* are by Lane Cooper.

Translations of *First Alcibiades* are by Jowett.

Translations of the *Gorgias* are by Waterfield, except for 447d, 449d, and 526de (Jowett).

Translations of *Hippias Major* are by Paul Woodruff.

Translations of the *Laches* are by Waterfield, except for 187e (Jowett).

Translations of the *Laws* are by Jowett.

Translations of the *Meno* are by Waterfield, except for 71b, 79e–80b, 80c, and 87e–88a (Guthrie).

Translations of the *Phaedo* are by Jowett, except for 81b (Tredennick).

Translations of the *Phaedrus* are by Jowett, except for 277c (Waterfield).

Translations of the *Philebus* are by Jowett.

Translations of the *Protagoras* are by Jowett, except for 331bc (Mill) and 360bd (Guthrie).

Translations of the *Republic* are by Jowett, except for 348ab, 514a–517, and 586ab (Waterfield).

Translations of the *Seventh Letter* are by Jowett.

Translations of the *Symposium* are by Jowett (204a), Vlastos (205a), and Nehamas and Woodruff (221d–222a).

Translations of the *Theaetetus* are by Waterfield, except 146a and 155cd (Jowett).

2. *Later sources.*

Translations of Stoic sources are most often taken from my book *The Practicing Stoic*. The following sections of the *Discourses* of Epictetus are from the translation by Robin Hard: 1.11.4–7, 1.29.64, 2.1.32, 2.12.5–7, 2.14.8, 2.16.32, 2.21.8–10, 2.26.4–7, 4.1.65–71. These sections of the *Discourses* are from the translation by Thomas Higginson: 1.11.11, 2.17.1, and 1.28.9. These sections are from the translation by George Long: 2.12.5–7, 1.29.16–18.

The following sections of the *Epistles* of Seneca the Younger are from the translation by Richard Gummere: 95.57, 71.32, 85.28, 31.6, 88.28. The translation of 95.57–58 is by Margaret Graver and A. A. Long. The excerpts from Seneca, *On Anger* 1.3.6, and from Seneca, *On the Shortness of Life* 14.2, are from the translations by John Basore.

The translation of Marcus Aurelius, *Meditations* 12.20 is by Meric Casaubon.

The translation of Plutarch is by T. G. Tucker.

The translations of Cicero are usually by Charles Yonge. The translations of *Academica* 1.12.45 and *De Finibus* 2.1.2 are by Harris Rackham. The translations of *Academica* 2.3.7 and *De Oratore* 3.18.67 are by Julia Annas. The translation of *De Natura Deorum* 1.5.11 is by Francis Brooks.

Bibliography

AHBEL-RAPPE, Sara, and Rachana KAMTEKAR. *A Companion to Socrates.* Oxford: Wiley-Blackwell, 2006.

ANNAS, Julia. "Classical Greek Philosophy." In Boardman et al., *The Oxford History of Greece and the Hellenistic World,* 277–305.

———. "Plato's Ethics." In Fine, *The Oxford Handbook of Plato,* 267–85.

———. "Plato the Skeptic." In Vander Waerdt, *The Socratic Movement,* 309–40.

———. "Scepticism, Old and New." In *Rationality in Greek Thought,* edited by Michael Frede and Gisela Striker, 239–54. Oxford: Clarendon, 1996.

———. "Virtue as the Use of Other Goods." In Irwin and Nussbaum, *Virtue Love & Form,* 97–112.

———. "What Are Plato's 'Middle' Dialogues in the Middle Of?" In Annas and Rowe, *New Perspectives on Plato,* 1–23.

———, and Christopher ROWE, eds. *New Perspectives on Plato, Ancient and Modern.* Cambridge, Mass.: Harvard University Press, 2002.

BENSON, Hugh H. *Socratic Wisdom.* Oxford: Oxford University Press, 2000.

BETT, Richard. "Socrates and Skepticism." In Ahbel-Rappe and Kamtekar, *A Companion to Socrates,* 298–311.

———. "Socratic Ignorance." In Morrison, *The Cambridge Companion to Socrates,* 215–36.

BEVERSLUIS, John. "Does Socrates Commit the Socratic Fallacy?" *American Philosophical Quarterly* 24, no. 3 (1987): 211–23.

BLÖSSNER, Norbert. "The City-Soul Analogy." In *The Cambridge Companion to Plato's Republic,* edited by G. R. F. Ferrari, 345–85. Cambridge: Cambridge University Press, 2007.

BOARDMAN, John, Jasper GRIFFIN, and Oswyn MURRAY, eds. *The Oxford History of Greece and the Hellenistic World.* Oxford: Oxford University Press, 2002.

BOGHOSIAN, Peter, and James LINDSAY. *How to Have Impossible Conversations: A Very Practical Guide.* New York: Hachette, 2019.

BRENNAN, Tad. "Socrates and Epictetus." In Ahbel-Rappe and Kamtekar, *A Companion to Socrates,* 285–97.

234   BIBLIOGRAPHY

BRICKHOUSE, Thomas C., and Nicholas D. SMITH. *Plato's Socrates*. New York: Oxford University Press, 1994.

———. "Socrates and the Unity of Virtues." *Journal of Ethics* 1, no. 4 (1977): 311–24.

———. "Socrates' Elenctic Mission." *Oxford Studies in Ancient Philosophy* 1 (1991): 75–121; reprinted in Prior, *Socrates: Critical Assessments*, 3:119–44.

———. "Socrates on Goods, Virtue, and Happiness," *Oxford Studies in Ancient Philosophy* 5 (1987): 1–27; reprinted in Prior, *Socrates: Critical Assessments*, 4:202–25.

———. *Socrates on Trial*. Princeton: Princeton University Press, 1989.

———. *Socratic Moral Psychology*. Cambridge: Cambridge University Press, 2010.

BROWN, Eric. "Socrates in the Stoa." In Ahbel-Rappe and Kamtekar, *A Companion to Socrates*, 275–84.

BROWN, Lesley. "Division and Definition in the *Sophist*." In Charles, *Definition in Greek Philosophy*, 151–71.

BRUMBAUGH, Robert S. "Dialogue and Digression: The Seventh Letter and Plato's Literary Form." In Griswold, *Platonic Writings / Platonic Readings*, 84–92.

BURNET, J. *Greek Philosophy, Thales to Plato*. London: Macmillan & Co, 1924.

BURNYEAT, Myles F. "Carneades Was No Probabilist." Unpublished manuscript, n.d.

———, ed. *The Skeptical Tradition*. Berkeley: University of California Press, 1983.

———. "Socratic Midwifery, Platonic Inspiration," *Bulletin of the Institute of Classical Studies* 24 (1977): 7–16.

BUSSANICH, John, and Nicholas B. SMITH, eds. *The Bloomsbury Companion to Socrates*. London: Bloomsbury, 2013.

CAIRNS, William B., ed. *Benjamin Franklin's Autobiography* [1793]. New York: Longman, Green & Co., 1905.

CHARLES, David, ed. *Definition in Greek Philosophy*. Oxford: Oxford University Press, 2010.

CLOUGH, A. H. *Plutarch's Lives of Illustrious Men*. Boston: Little, Brown, 1889.

COHEN, Maurice H. "The Aporias in Plato's Early Dialogues." *Journal of the History of Ideas* 23, no. 2 (1962): 163–74.

COOPER, John M. "Arcesilaus: Socratic and Sceptic." In *Remembering Socrates: Philosophical Essays*, 169–87, edited by Lindsay Judson and Vassilis Karasmanis. Oxford: Clarendon Press, 2006.

———. "Plato's Theory of Human Motivation." *History of Philosophy Quarterly* 1 (1984): 3–21.

———. *Reason and Emotion: Essays in Ancient Moral Philosophy and Ethical Theory*. Princeton: Princeton University Press, 1999.

DAKYNS, H. G. (trans.). *The Works of Xenophon*. 4 vols. London: Macmillan, 1897.

DEFILIPPO, Joseph G., and Phillip T. MITSIS. "Socrates and Stoic Natural Law." In Vander Waerdt, *The Socratic Movement*, 253–71.

DEMETRIOU, Kyriakos, and Antis LOIZIDES, eds. *John Stuart Mill: A British Socrates*. New York: Palgrave Macmillan, 2013.

DESJARDINS, Rosemary. "Why Dialogues? Plato's Serious Play." In Griswold, *Platonic Writings/Platonic Readings*, 110–26.

DEVEREUX, Daniel. "Socratic Ethics and Moral Psychology." In Fine, *The Oxford Handbook of Plato*, 139–64.

———. "The Unity of the Virtues in Plato's Protagoras and Laches," *Philosophical Review*, 101 (1992): 765–89.

DORION, Louis-André. "The Rise and Fall of the Socratic Problem." In Morrison, *The Cambridge Companion to Socrates*, 1–23.

DOVER, Kenneth J. "Socrates in the Clouds." In Vlastos, *The Philosophy of Socrates*, 50–77.

DUNNING, David, and Justin KRUGER. "Unskilled and Unaware of It: How Difficulties in Recognizing One's Own Incompetence Lead to Inflated Self-Assessments." *Journal of Personality and Social Psychology* 77, no. 6 (1999): 1121–34.

EMERSON, Ralph W. *Representative Men*. Boston: Phillips, Sampson & Co., 1850.

EVERSON, Stephen, ed. *Epistemology*. Cambridge: Cambridge University Press, 1990.

FARNSWORTH, Ward. *The Practicing Stoic*. Boston: Godine, 2018.

FINE, Gail, ed. *The Oxford Handbook of Plato*. Oxford: Oxford University Press, 2008.

FINK, Jakob L., ed. *The Development of Dialectic from Plato to Aristotle.* Cambridge: Cambridge University Press, 2012.

FISH, Stanley. *Self-Consuming Artifacts: The Experience of Seventeenth-Century Literature*, 5–21. Berkeley: University of California Press, 1972.

FLEW, Antony, ed. *A Dictionary of Philosophy*, rev. 2d ed. New York: St. Martin's, 1984.

FORD, Paul L., ed. *The Writings of Thomas Jefferson.* 12 vols. New York: G. P. Putnam's Sons, 1899.

FRAME, Donald M. *The Complete Essays of Montaigne.* Palo Alto: Stanford University Press, 1958.

FREUD, Sigmund. *A General Introduction to Psychoanalysis.* New York: Boni and Liveright, 1920.

FRIEDLANDER, Paul. *Plato.* New York: Bollingen, 1958.

GEACH, Peter T. "Plato's *Euthyphro*: An Analysis and Commentary." *Monist* 50 (1996): 369–82.

GILL, Christopher. "Dialectic and the Dialogue Form." In Annas and Rowe, *New Perspectives on Plato*, 145–72.

GOLDSTEIN, Rebecca N. *Plato at the Googleplex.* New York: Pantheon, 2014.

GRAHAM, Daniel W. "Socrates and Plato." *Phronesis* 37, no. 2 (1992): 145–65.

GRAVER, Margaret, and A. A. LONG, trans. *Seneca: Letters on Ethics.* Chicago: University of Chicago Press, 2015.

GRISWOLD, Charles L., Jr., ed. *Platonic Writings / Platonic Readings.* University Park, Pa.: Penn State University Press, 1988.

———. "Plato's Metaphilosophy: Why Plato Wrote Dialogues." In Griswold, *Platonic Writings / Platonic Readings*, 143–70.

GROTE, George. *Plato and the Other Companions of Sokrates.* 3 vols. London: John Murray, 1865.

GULLEY, Norman. "The Interpretation of 'No One Does Wrong Willingly' in Plato's Dialogues." *Phronesis* 10 (1965): 82–96.

———. *The Philosophy of Socrates.* New York: Macmillan, 1968.

GUTHRIE, W. K. C. *A History of Greek Philosophy.* Vol. 3, *The Fifth-Century Enlightenment.* Cambridge: Cambridge University Press, 1971.

———. *A History of Greek Philosophy*. Vol. 4, *Plato—The Man and His Dialogues*. Cambridge: Cambridge University Press, 1975.

———. *A History of Greek Philosophy*. Vol. 5, *The Later Plato and the Academy*. Cambridge: Cambridge University Press, 1978.

HARD, Robin, trans. *Epictetus: Discourses, Fragments, Handbook*. Oxford: Oxford University Press, 2014.

HAZLITT, William C., ed. *Essays of Montaigne*. Translated by Charles Cotton. London: Reeves & Turner, 1877.

HOBLAND, Fiona, and Christopher TUPLIN, eds. *Xenophon: Ethical Principles and Historical Enquiry*. Leiden: Brill, 2012.

HOLMES, Oliver Wendell, Jr. "The Path of the Law." *Harvard Law Review* 10, no. 8 (1897): 457–78.

HOWLAND, Jacob. "Xenophon's Philosophic Odyssey: On the *Anabasis* and Plato's *Republic*." *American Political Science Review* 94, no. 4 (2000): 875–89.

INWOOD, Brad, and Lloyd P. GERSON. *Hellenistic Philosophy*. Indianapolis: Hackett, 1997.

IRWIN, Terence H. *Plato's Moral Theory*. Oxford: Oxford University Press, 1977.

———. "Review: Socrates and Athenian Democracy." *Philosophy & Public Affairs* 18 (1989): 184–205.

———. "Say What You Believe." In Irwin and Nussbaum, *Virtue Love & Form*, 1–16.

———. "Socrates the Epicurean?" *Illinois Classical Studies* 11 (1986): 85–112; reprinted in Prior, *Socrates: Critical Assessments*, 4: 226–51.

———. "Socratic Puzzles." *Oxford Studies in Ancient Philosophy* 10 (1992): 241–66.

———, and Martha C. NUSSBAUM, eds. *Virtue Love & Form: Essays in Memory of Gregory Vlastos*. Apeiron 26, nos. 3–4 (1993).

JANSSENS, Emile. "The Concept of Dialectic in the Ancient World." *Philosophy & Rhetoric* 1, no. 3 (1968): 174–81.

KAHN, Charles H. "The Beautiful and the Genuine: A Discussion of Paul Woodruff, Plato, *Hippias Major*." *Oxford Studies in Ancient Philosophy* 3 (1985): 261–88.

KAHN, Charles H. "Drama and Dialectic in Plato's *Gorgias*." *Oxford Studies in Ancient Philosophy* 1 (1983): 75–121; reprinted in Prior, *Socrates: Critical Assessments*, 3: 60–96.

———. *Plato and the Socratic Dialogue*. Cambridge: Cambridge University Press, 1996.

———. "Vlastos's Socrates." *Phronesis* 37 (1992): 233–58; reprinted in Prior, *Socrates: Critical Assessments*, 1:156–78.

KIERKEGAARD, Søren. *The Sickness Unto Death*. Translated by Walter Lowrie. Princeton: Princeton University Press, 1849.

KRAUT, Richard, ed. *The Cambridge Companion to Plato*. Cambridge: Cambridge University Press, 1992.

———. "Comments on Gregory Vlastos, 'The Socratic Elenchus.'" *Oxford Studies in Ancient Philosophy* 1 (1983): 59–70.

———. "The Examined Life." In Ahbel-Rappe and Kamtekar, *A Companion to Socrates*, 228–42.

KREMMYDAS, Christos, and Kathryn TEMPEST, eds. *Hellenistic Oratory: Continuity and Change*. Oxford: Oxford University Press, 2013.

LACEY, A. R. "Our Knowledge of Socrates." In Vlastos, *The Philosophy of Socrates*, 22–49.

LESHER, James. "Socrates' Disavowal of Knowledge." *Journal of the History of Philosophy* 25 (1987): 275–88.

LEVY, Oscar, ed. *Friedrich Nietzsche: Human, All Too Human*. New York: Macmillan, 1913.

LONG, A. A. *Epictetus: A Stoic and Socratic Guide to Life*. Oxford: Clarendon Press, 2002.

———. *Hellenistic Philosophy*, 2d ed. Los Angeles: University of California Press, 1986.

———. "Socrates in Hellenistic Philosophy," *Classical Quarterly* 38 (1988): 150–71.

———. "Socrates in Later Greek Philosophy." In Morrison, *The Cambridge Companion to Socrates*, 355–79.

———. "The Socratic Legacy." In *The Cambridge History of Hellenistic Philosophy*, 617–41, edited by Keimpe Algra et al. Cambridge: Cambridge University Press, 1999.

———. *Stoic Studies*. Cambridge: Cambridge University Press, 1996.

————, and David SEDLEY. *The Hellenistic Philosophers*, Vol. 1: *Translations of the Principal Sources, with Philosophical Commentary*. Cambridge: Cambridge University Press, 1987.

LONG, A. G. *Conversation and Self-Sufficiency in Plato*. Oxford: Oxford University Press, 2013.

MCPARTLAND, Keith. "Socratic Ignorance." In Bussanich and Smith, *The Bloomsbury Companion to Socrates*, 94–135.

MILL, John Stuart. *Autobiography*. London: Longmans, 1873.

————. "The Early Draft of John Stuart Mill's Autobiography." In Robson, *Collected Works of John Stuart Mill*, 1:4–290.

————. "Grote's Plato." In Robson, *Collected Works of John Stuart Mill*, 11:375–440.

————. "Whately's Elements of Logic." In Robson, *Collected Works of John Stuart Mill*, 11:3–35.

MORRISON, Donald R., ed. *The Cambridge Companion to Socrates*. Cambridge: Cambridge University Press, 2011.

————. "On Professor Vlastos's Xenophon." *Ancient Philosophy* 7 (1987): 9–22.

NAILS, Debra. *Agora, Academy, and the Conduct of Philosophy*. Dordrecht: Springer, 1995.

NEHAMAS, Alexander. *The Art of Living: Socratic Reflections from Plato to Foucault*. Los Angeles: University of California Press, 1998.

————. "Voices of Silence: On Gregory Vlastos's Socrates." *Arion*, 3rd ser., 2 (1992): 156–86.

————. *Virtues of Authenticity*. Princeton: Princeton University Press, 1999.

————. "What Did Socrates Teach and to Whom Did He Teach It?" *Review of Metaphysics* 46, no. 2 (1992): 279–306.

NETTLESHIP, Richard L. *Philosophical Lectures and Remains*, Vol. 2. London: Macmillan, 1897.

NOVAES, Catarina D. "Reductio Ad Absurdum from a Dialogical Perspective." *Philosophical Studies* 173 (2016): 2605–28.

NUSSBAUM, Martha C. "Aristophanes and Socrates on Learning Practical Wisdom." *Yale Classical Studies* 26 (1980): 43–97.

————. "The Chill of Virtue." *New Republic*, September 16 & 23, 1991, 34–40.

PENNER, Terry. "The Unity of Virtue." *Philosophical Review* 82 (1973): 35–68.

POPPER, Karl. *The Open Society and Its Enemies*. London: Routledge, 1945.

POWELL, J. F. G. "The Embassy of the Three Philosophers to Rome in 155 BC." In Kremmydas and Tempest, *Hellenistic Oratory*, 219–47.

PRIOR, William J., ed. *Socrates: Critical Assessments*. London: Routledge, 1996.

——. *Socrates*. Medford, Mass.: Polity Press, 2019.

ROBINSON, Richard. "Forms and Error in Plato's *Theaetetus*," *Philosophical Review* 59, no. 1 (January 1950): 3–30.

——. *Plato's Earlier Dialectic*, 2d ed. Oxford: Clarendon Press, 1953.

ROBSON, John M., gen. ed. *The Collected Works of John Stuart Mill*. 33 vols. Toronto: Routledge & Kegan Paul, 1963–91.

RORTY, Richard. *Philosophy as Cultural Politics*. Cambridge: Cambridge University Press, 2007.

ROSS, W. D. *Plato's Theory of Ideas*. Oxford: Oxford University Press, 1951.

ROWE, Christopher. "Socrates in Plato's Dialogues." In Ahbel-Rappe and Kamtekar, *A Companion to Socrates*, 159–70.

RUSSELL, Bertrand. *A History of Western Philosophy*. New York: Simon & Schuster, 1945.

SANTAS, Gerasimos X. *Socrates*. London: Routledge & Kegan Paul, 1979.

——. "Socratic Goods and Socratic Happiness." In Irwin and Nussbaum, *Virtue Love & Form*, 81–96.

——. "The Socratic Fallacy." *Journal of the History of Philosophy* 10, no. 2 (1972): 127–41.

——. "The Socratic Paradoxes." *Philosophical Review* 73, no. 2 (April 1964): 147–64.

SAYRE, Kenneth M. "Plato's Dialogues in Light of the Seventh Letter." In *Platonic Writings, Platonic Readings*, 93–109, edited by Charles L. Griswold, Jr. London: Routledge.

SCHAUER, Frederick. *Profiles, Probabilities and Stereotypes*. Cambridge, Mass.: Belknap, 2003.

SEDLEY, David. "The Motivation of Greek Skepticism." In Burnyeat, *The Skeptical Tradition*, 9–30.

———. *Plato's* Cratylus. Cambridge: Cambridge University Press, 2003.

SEESKIN, Kenneth. *Dialogue and Discovery: A Study in Socratic Method.* Albany, N.Y.: SUNY Press, 1987.

SEGVIC, Heda. "No One Errs Willingly: The Meaning of Socratic Intellectualism." In Ahbel-Rappe and Kamtekar, *A Companion to Socrates,* 171–85.

SHIELDS, Christopher J. "Socrates Among the Skeptics." In Vander Waerdt, *The Socratic Movement,* 341–66.

SHOREY, Paul. *The Unity of Plato's Thought.* Chicago: University of Chicago Press, 1903.

———. *What Plato Said.* Chicago: University of Chicago Press, 1933.

SIDGWICK, Henry. *The Methods of Ethics,* 7th ed. New York: Macmillan, 1907.

SPRAGUE, Rosamond Kent. "Platonic Unitarianism, or What Shorey Said." *Classical Philology* 71, no. 1 (1976): 109–12.

———. *Plato's Use of Fallacy.* London: Routledge, 1962.

STRIKER, Gisela. "Plato's Socrates and the Stoics." In Vander Waerdt, *The Socratic Movement,* 241–51.

SZAIF, Jan. "Socrates and the Benefits of Puzzlement." In *The Aporetic Tradition in Ancient Philosophy,* 29–47, edited by George Karamanolis and Vasilis Politis. Cambridge: Cambridge University Press, 2018.

TALISSE, Robert B. "Misunderstanding Socrates." *Arion* 9, no. 3 (2002): 46–56.

TARRANT, Harold. "Socratic Method and Socratic Truth." In Ahbel-Rappe and Kamtekar, *A Companion to Socrates,* 254–72.

TAYLOR, A. E. *Socrates.* London: Peter Davies, 1932.

TAYLOR, C. C. W. "Plato's Epistemology." In Fine, *The Oxford Handbook of Plato,* 165–90.

———. *Socrates: A Very Short Introduction.* Oxford: Oxford University Press, 1998.

THESLEFF, Holger. *Studies in Platonic Chronology.* Helsinki: Societas Scientiarum Fennica, 1982.

TRIVIGNO, Franco V., and Pierre DESTRÉE, eds. *Laughter, Humor, and Comedy in Ancient Philosophy.* New York: Oxford University Press, 2019.

TROTTER, W. F., trans. *Blaise Pascal: Thoughts*. New York: Collier & Son, 1910.

VANDER WAERDT, Paul, ed. *The Socratic Movement*. Ithaca, N.Y.: Cornell University Press, 1994.

VLASTOS, Gregory, ed. *The Philosophy of Socrates*. New York: Doubleday, 1971.

———. "The Paradox of Socrates." In Vlastos, *The Philosophy of Socrates*, 1–49.

———. *Socrates, Ironist and Moral Philosopher*. Ithaca, N.Y.: Cornell University Press, 1991.

———. *Socratic Studies*. Cambridge: Cambridge University Press, 1994.

———. "The Unity of Virtues in the 'Protagoras.'" *Review of Metaphysics* 25, no. 3 (1972): 415–58.

WALSH, James J. "The Socratic Denial of Akrasia." In Vlastos, *The Philosophy of Socrates*, 235–63.

WATERFIELD, Robin. "The Quest for the Historical Socrates." In Bussanich and Smith, *The Bloomsbury Companion to Socrates*, 1–19.

———. "Xenophon on Socrates' Trial and Death." In Hobland and Tuplin, *Xenophon*, 269–305.

WHITE, James Boyd. "Plato's *Gorgias* and the Ethics of Legal Argument." *University of Chicago Law Review* 50, no. 2 (1983): 849–91.

WHITEHEAD, Alfred North. *Process and Reality*. New York: Macmillan, 1929.

WIGMORE, John H. *Evidence in Trials at Common Law*, 3d ed. Boston: Little, Brown, 1940.

WOLFSDORF, David. "Socrates' Avowals of Knowledge." *Phronesis* 49 (2004): 75–142.

———. "Socratic Philosophizing." In Bussanich and Smith, *The Bloomsbury Companion to Socrates*, 34–67.

WOODRUFF, Paul B. "Aporetic Pyrrhonism." *Oxford Studies in Ancient Philosophy* 6 (1988): 139–68.

———. "Expert Knowledge in the *Apology* and *Laches*: What a General Needs to Know." *Proceedings of the Boston Area Colloquium in Ancient Philosophy* 3 (1987): 79–115.

———. "Plato's Early Theory of Knowledge." In Everson, *Epistemology*, 60–84.

———. "Self-Ridicule: Socratic Wisdom." In Trivigno and Destrée, *Laughter, Humor, and Comedy in Ancient Philosophy*, 165–81.

———. "The Skeptical Side of Plato's Method." *Revue Internationale de Philosophie* 40, no. 1/2 (1986): 22–37.

———. "Socrates Among the Sophists." In Ahbel-Rappe and Kamtekar, *A Companion to Socrates*, 36–47.

———. "Socrates and the Irrational." In *Reason and Religion in Socratic Philosophy*, 130–150, edited by Nicholas D. Smith and Paul B. Woodruff. New York: Oxford University Press, 2000.

———. "Socrates on the Parts of Virtue." *Canadian Journal of Philosophy*, supp. v. 2 (1976): 101–16.

———. "Socrates's Mission." In *Readings of Plato's* Apology of Socrates: *Defending the Philosophical Life*, 179–83, edited by Vivil Valvik Haraldsen, Olof Pettersson, and Oda E. W. Tvedt. Lanham, Md.: Lexington Books, 2018.

YONGE, C. D., trans. *Diogenes Laertius: The Lives and Opinions of Eminent Philosophers*. London: G. Bell & Sons, 1915.

A NOTE ON THE TYPE

This book is set in a digital version of Monotype Fournier (series 185), cut by the Monotype Corporation of Britain in 1925 under the direction of its typographical advisor, Stanley Morison. It follows a particular face found in Fournier's masterwork, *Manuel typographique* (1764; 1766).

Pierre-Simon Fournier (1712–1768) not only cut an astonishing series of roman, italic, script, exotic, and music types, but introduced a standardization of type sizes that developed into the modern system of typographic points. Into the bargain, he created a veritable garden of typographical flowers that defined the Rococo style in French printing that blossomed throughout Europe and beyond. Fournier was called *le jeune* to distinguish him from his father, Jean-Claude, and brother, Jean-Pierre, who, in succession, managed and owned the Le Bé foundry, which included the work of the Parisian masters Claude Garamond and Robert Granjon.

*

DESIGNED AND COMPOSED BY

MARK ARGETSINGER

Library of Congress Cataloging-in-Publication Data

Names: Farnsworth, Ward, 1967– author.
Title: The Socratic method : a practitioner's handbook / Ward Farnsworth.
Description: Boston : Godine, 2021. | Includes bibliographical references.
Identifiers: LCCN 2021010784 (print) | LCCN 2021010785 (ebook) | ISBN
    9781567926859 (hardback) | ISBN 9781567926866 (ebook)
Subjects: LCSH: Socrates. | Questioning. | Methodology. | Thought and
    thinking. | Plato. Dialogues.
Classification: LCC B317 .F37 2021 (print) | LCC B317 (ebook) | DDC
    183/.2–dc23
LC record available at https://lccn.loc.gov/2021010784

LC ebook record available at https://lccn.loc.gov/2021010785